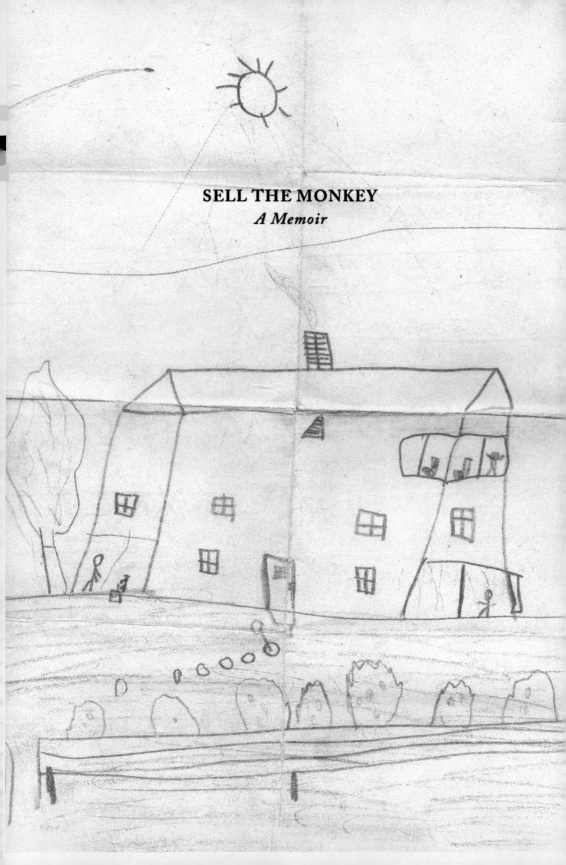

SELL THE MONKEY
A Memoir

This is for Ida, my mother,
and her mother, MaUdi,
and all the what-ifs
in between.

ISBN: 978-0-692-08463-2

Acknowledgements

I'd like to thank my first-grade teacher, Mrs. Johnson, for teaching me which way the letters go, Mrs. Jenkins, my third-grade teacher, for combing my hair before my class photo, and my brother, Bernard Garwood, for his exhaustive and dedicated research about our family and its history. His efforts have been inestimable in determining what happened to whom, when, where, and sometimes why.

Further gratitude goes to many others who have commented on, and assisted in the delicate and minutial process of proofing my endeavors; also those who have encouraged me: Kathleen Moles, Joanna Maclean, Alvin Neely, William O'Daly, Stewart Simpson, Nirupa Umapathy, Peter Weltner, Lennie Kesl, and Merch Pease.

Poems:
p. 171: 'Don't Trip' © James Broughton, *Graffti for the Johns of Heaven*, Syzygy Press, 1982
p. 185: 'The Measure' ©Sam Hamill, from *Passport*, Broken Moon Press, 1989
p. 206 'Three Turns' © Galen Garwood, 1992
p. 217: 'King Selinus' from *The One-Winged Body*, ©Peter Weltner, 2012, Marrowstone Press
p. 230: 'Stain' © Galen Garwood, 2003
p. 249: 'In Winter' © Ed Cain, 1983
p. 251: 'Afterlife' ©William O'Daly, 2017
p. 258: 'The Fisherman' Galen Garwood, 2012

All paintings, monotypes, and photographic artwork © Galen Garwood.

SELL THE MONKEY
A Memoir

GALEN GARWOOD

with much love and affection

Galen

Marrowstone Press, Seattle

CONTENTS

When I was five, my brother dared me to jump from the highest diving board at the New Casino swimming pool, built just beyond the dunes on the beaches of St. Simons Island, close to the lighthouse.

"No, it's too high. I don't want to," I cried.

He kept yelling, "Go on up there. Go on. Do it. Jump."

I finally gave in and climbed the ladder, turning just once to look down at my brother's grinning face. Children were huddled together at the shallow end, watching me, waiting to see if I'd do it.

Trembling and crouching low, I crept toward the end of the board, too afraid to look down, my skinny legs shaking, my arms tight against my body, hands clasped in prayer, my eyes fluttering to the heavens. I could feel the wind coming in from the sea, breathing on my back. I could smell the sweet scent of oleander and seagrasses billowing up around me. I could hear the sound of seagulls cawing over the crashing tide.

The children were laughing, taking up my brother's dare.

"Jump! Jump! Jump!" they sang.

I was scared, but I wasn't going to chicken out and give my brother ammunition for a summer of teasing. I took a deep breath, filled my lungs with sky, spread my arms like wings, and jumped.

L‍ord Buddha said, "Jump into the middle."
So I shall.

The year was 1980, and I was thirty-six, living in Seattle. I'd been exhibiting my art at Foster/White Gallery for a decade. I'd just moved into my new studio on 12th and Pike in April, and a month later, I stood on the roof of the building and watched Mount St. Helens erupt into the heavens. Jimmy Carter would soon end his only term as President, Jean-Paul Sartre died in June, John Lennon was assassinated in September, and Shelly's Leg closed its doors that winter. I was delighted to leave my dismally small studio downtown at First and Pike Street, and happy to have just ended a fractured relationship with someone far too fond of alcohol.

Time for a change.

With renewed energy, a better working space, upcoming exhibitions, and my single life back, I was ready to make art. When I wasn't painting, I'd head across the street to the gym, have a workout, and chat with the regulars. In fact, it was here where I bumped into Jimmy, someone I'd known since 1973. Back then, I was bartending at the Mocombo Lounge, and Jimmy was not quite eighteen. He'd hang out in the adjoining café then sneak into the bar when no one was watching. A few years later, we shared a biology class at the University of Washington. Jimmy, a charming and intelligent young man, was precocious, confident, and sexy.

When I walked into the work-out room, Jimmy was pumping iron. He spotted me right away, smiled, and strolled over, holding two thirty-pound dumbbells, sweat pooling down his bare shoulders.

"Hey, Galen, I haven't seen you in a long time. Where've you been?"

"Hey, Jimmy. I'm just there, across the street, upstairs," I said, pointing through the windows. Jimmy stood in front of me, looking out across the street while I discreetly inspected his sweaty body.

"And you? What have you been up to?"

"Skydiving!" he beamed. "So cool, man. You'd love it."

"I've thought about it, Jimmy. Whenever I go swimming at Lake

1

Sammamish, I watch those guys sail through the sky, thinking, yeah...I should do this one day."

"Alright," he said. "Let's do it. We'll go tomorrow. It's a trip, man. You'll love it. I promise. You will."

In fact, I had considered it, but never seriously, not enough to act on it. I stepped back a few feet, sat on a bench, and muttered out excuses why I couldn't go.

"I'd like to, you know...but I don't, um, I don't have the money right now. And I don't know what's on my plate for tomorrow. Maybe another time, Jimmy."

He put the two weights on the floor and sat next to me. "I want you to come with me."

I hesitated, feeling a bit foolish.

"Aw, come on, man," he said, leaning into my shoulder.

How could I say no to such an enchanting face?

"OK, Jimmy, why not?"

"Super," he said, slapping me on the back, grabbing his weights, bending back into his routine. "Eight a.m. sharp."

"Alright," I said, second thoughts already crawling in.

Next morning, we met at the gym, then drove from the city, across Mercer Island out about twenty miles on Highway 90, toward a small airfield on the edge of Lake Sammamish.

The skydiving school was in a building on the airstrip. There were only three of us for the six-hour training course, a class Jimmy had already taken, but, for my benefit, he signed up again to make me feel more at ease. Our instructor went through every adverse scenario imaginable, dozens of times.

I learned all about the chutes, where and how to pull your ripcord, what could happen if you accidentally deployed your emergency chute inside the aircraft, how to count down after jumping, how to steer, how to land, and what to do if your parachute malfunctions. After processing all of these negative possibilities, the idea of being back in the studio, pushing paint around, became more and more appealing.

Too late. We were suited up, marching onto the field toward a single-engine aircraft. We greeted the pilot and boarded. There were no seats, just an empty floor on which we scooted our butts across; we leaned against the curved wall, ever mindful of our equipment, especially the emergency chutes located on our chests. If anyone of us accidentally deployed one during flight, it would eject so forcefully, it would shoot

2

through the open door, and within a second, destroy the aircraft and everyone on board.

We were airborne in no time at all, rising above three thousand feet, circling toward our target position at a severely steep angle. My stomach was churning. I began to question my sanity. Why am I here? What are my options? I knew I could back out, cancel at any point in the process; many did. No, I wasn't going back out now. Besides, what would Jimmy think?

I sang a silent mantra, "OK, OK, OK, Jump, Jump, Jump."

The first student dropped into the blue abyss, and the plane quickly veered up and to the left, circling back. Jimmy's turn came. He grinned and waved as he sat in the open door. Then he was gone.

I sat alone, bundled and strapped, waiting, and terrified.

"Get on up here," yelled the pilot.

I slowly and carefully crabbed across the floor, holding both arms across my chest, praying I wouldn't accidentally deploy my emergency chute. I squatted near the open door and looked out. The view was spectacular. I could see the Pacific Ocean in the far distance and the Cascade Range on the left side of me, with Mt. Rainier piercing the clouds. The Olympic Range was in front of the aircraft. I wanted to sit and meditate on the beauty of it all, the sea below and the sky's intensity, but it was impossible; the plane's engine reverberated through my body with too much clamor. "Holy Shit! Are you doing this? Really?" I asked myself.

"Knees in the breeze," yelled the jump master.

I scooted further out, both legs dangling in the wind.

He bellowed over the noise, "Get on out there!"

I grabbed hold of the bar at the back of the wing, then placed my right foot on a small peg attached to the lower strut. The noise from the propeller, just in front of me, was deafening. The wind was fierce. I curved my left leg back behind my body, waiting for the command.

"GO!"

I released my grip and tumbled backward into the sky. Everything went dark. I learned only later that during one's first jump, the rush of adrenalin is so forceful that one often passes out. Two or three seconds later, I regained consciousness. I could see the plane rise upward, veering to my left.

My first jump, captured on film by the instructor, was perfect. Of course, with my static line connected to the aircraft, all I had to do was let go. As soon as my chute opened, I looked up and shouted out loud, "Big, round, and symmetrical." If it weren't: trouble.

Away from the noise and turbulence of the aircraft, I descended slowly through the sky, enjoying every spectacular moment of it. The sensation was profound. But it didn't last; the ground was coming up too soon. The eight hours of training kicked in: "Pay attention, make sure you guide the chute's steering lines, pull left or right to land near the target."

The closer to the ground I got, the faster I fell, or so it seemed. Here was not the place to daydream. Nor was it a place to gaze at the ground through my feet. I could easily break both ankles on impact. To make sure they stayed together, I was told to imagine holding a hundred-dollar bill between my heels. At thirty meters above the ground, I heard a voice, "Don't look down. Don't look between your feet. Look at the horizon." As soon as I hit the ground with my feet, I collapsed and rolled like a rag-doll ten yards from the target area, just like in the movies.

I stood and gathered my chute and lines, grinning like a monkey.

The next three were static line jumps, followed by three in which I'd have to pull the ripcord, deploying the chute myself. On my seventh, however, because I didn't bring both arms up at the same time, I went into a barrel roll. I panicked, thrashed about in the air until I managed to pull out of it, deployed successfully, and landed.

"I've got to get it right, Jimmy. I'm going back up."

Back out on the wing, foot on the peg, I waited for the "GO!"

I jumped. I began my countdown, saying it out loud: "1/1000, 2/1000, 3/1000." At 10/1000, I reached to pull my cord, but, yet again, my timing was screwed. My body spun. I desperately clawed at the air trying to get at my ripcord. I was spinning like a top. Finally, I grabbed and pulled, and the parachute opened. Next protocol: I looked up, but I didn't like what I saw. My words stuttered out, "Big...kind of round...oh shit...oh, no...not symmetrical at all."

I was hanging lopsided in my harness, disconnected on one side, the strap fluttering above me in the wind. I tried to reach up, grab it, and pull it back, thinking I could reconnect it. Not even remotely possible. Nothing but a sliver of Velcro held me in the sky.

I was falling fast, and without control of my descent, I knew what might happen: I could plummet into the lake, the parachute dragging me to the bottom. Or I could land on the freeway and get crushed by an eighteen-wheeler on its way to or from Seattle. There was also the possibility of getting entangled then being fried by the power lines that snaked below me. Pure panic. A voice inside screamed, "Galen, what are you supposed to do!"

"Get rid of my main chute," I shouted.

"Then do it! Now!" I screamed.

Since the emergency parachute is attached to the main chute, my only hope was to reach up and undo the strap that held me in the sky. I had to get rid of my main chute. I shut my eyes, gritted my teeth, reached up and pulled the Velcro strap, immediately disconnecting myself; the main chute quickly buffeted upward, collapsing into the winds. I started falling all over again. I dropped at least two hundred feet before hearing the sweetest sound I'd ever heard: 'fwoof-fwoof-fwoof.' My emergency chute unfurled, slapping the air, kissing my face like an angel, quickly slowing my fall, then bouncing me gently upward as it fully opened, four hundred yards above the ground.

I fell considerably faster, and steering the emergency chute was like operating a toy. Still, my heart calmed. I could breathe again. I wasn't going to splatter and become fertilizer. People far below me were running from every direction toward where they expected me to land. When I hit the ground, it was with a jolt, but I wasn't hurt, just slightly embarrassed, grateful for the hours of negative training. I would later think about those few seconds determining my fate. I'd read about such events when death seems right there, standing on the threshold, and one's entire life spools out in a nanosecond, from first memory until that final darkness explodes across the cerebral cortex.

I suspect those who feel with absolute certainty that death is inevitable experience this. I didn't. My brain was too busy trying to remember then follow instructions; my past never had a chance to participate.

On the drive back to Seattle, we had a great laugh about the day's events. We talked about doing more skydiving. Jimmy did. He'd go on to do much higher jumps with longer free falls. I never did. I rarely had the money when I had the time, and when I had both, there was no Jimmy to entice me.

I was born in Blakely, Georgia, a small farming town in Early County, the lower southwest corner of the state, bordering the Chattahoochee River, just east of Alabama and north of Florida. I might have been conceived in Blakely, but I'm not sure. I was born in July, 1944. As to the exact date, I can't be sure of that either. When I was twelve, living with my mother in Charleston, South Carolina, I saw my birth certificate for the first time. My birthday was recorded, not as the 7th, as I'd always thought and had celebrated, but the 13th. I pestered my mother one afternoon. "Why?" I demanded. I followed her around the house until she finally stopped with whatever she was doing, sat down and began to lay out the peculiar circumstances of my birth.

"We were living on Folly Beach," she began, "and in April, I went to the doctor for a checkup. I was pregnant with you. The doctor told me he couldn't find your heartbeat. And after further testing, he said that most likely you were stillborn, and unless he terminated the pregnancy, my life would be in danger. You had to come out and soon."

"You mean I was dead?" I asked with befuddled concern.

"Uh-huh. That Monday afternoon I wrote a letter to Mama and told her what was happening, that I was scheduled to have the operation on Friday. It arrived in Blakely on Thursday, but your grandfather apparently didn't think it all that important. He tossed my letter on the mantel in the living room without telling Mama. She found it that afternoon, by pure accident. She wasn't happy, at all, and as soon as she could pack a few clothes, she jumped in her car and drove all night. She didn't get to Folly Beach until midnight and had plenty to say when she got there.

"'Eleanor, I'm not going to let you have that operation up here in South Carolina. I'm taking you home first thing in the morning.'"

"We had breakfast then drove straight over to Blakely. The following day we went to see Doc McConnell. He poked around a bit with his stethoscope. '"There's nothing wrong with this baby, Eleanor. It's healthy as a damn colt, got a strong heartbeat.'"

"You were born several months later, on July 7th. I should know."

"Then why does my birth certificate have it different, a whole week

7

later? And why does everybody else say a different day? Somebody in the family wrote the date down as being July 10th. Not the 7th, not the 13th, but the 10th. Aunt Cena was sure it was the 12th. Why?" I asked, my voice rising to a pubescent crack.

"Honey, Blakely's a little town. Not much of a hospital. Doc loved his whiskey. Everybody in Blakely knew he kept bad records. I doubt he even recorded your birth until weeks later."

I nodded, but I wasn't all that convinced.

"I'll tell you how I know for sure," she said, smiling at my worry.

"Tell me then," I said, folding my arms, looking up at her face, waiting for that familiar tell-tale sign of a tease.

"July 6 was the day all the Blakely gals went picking blackberries for pies and cobblers. It was a tradition back then, every summer, always on July 6th. I was determined not to miss it. But the girls said, "No, Eleanor, your baby's late, and you're too big. You might drop it in the blackberry bushes."' I went anyway, of course. You know me.

"Honey, you showed up the very next day. That's how I know, how I remember for sure. It was the 7th."

I came into the world, two weeks late, weighed 12.5 pounds and stretched out to twenty-six inches. I had blue eyes and a good start on a mop of blonde curly hair. I was the fourth child from a failing marriage; I slipped into the world through the last surge of passion my parents shared.

My mother, Eleanor Lillian Loback, was born in 1919 in Brunswick, Georgia, to Lucile and Chester Loback. She was the older of two daughters. In school, her friends called her Fritzi, but I never heard her called anything but Eleanor by her family. Later in her life, as an entertainer, she assumed the professional name of Ida Lane, taken from her maternal grandmother. To my brothers and me, she was always 'Mama.'

She was a beautiful, wild, and unruly child, somewhat of a tomboy, always getting into mischief. She was the polar opposite of her younger sister, Cena. In those days, playing the piano was considered necessary for a young girl's proper study, and my grandmother insisted both her daughters take lessons. While my aunt studied with fervent discipline, preferring classical music and religious hymnals, my mother had to be locked inside the parlor until she'd finished her piano exercises. She practiced, but was easily distracted. Ida had a natural gift, and while she played the classics well enough, it was popular music she loved most, songs like 'Sophisticated Lady,' 'Jealousy,' and 'Runnin Wild.' She knew

Lucile (MaUdi) with daughters Eleanor(in back) and Cena, ca. 1930

them all by heart. With natural rhythm and near-perfect pitch, she could hear a song once on the radio, go home and play it, note for note. It was this talent, along with her good looks and outgoing personality that helped shape her future as an entertainer.

My great-grandfather, Charles Middleton, was a doctor, but he was also involved in other businesses, mostly farm-related. Papa Charlie was a well-educated, generous man, who traveled by horse and buggy

Eleanor (Ida) Lillian Loback, ca. 1934

to check on his patients, always willing to accept a few hens, a bushel of corn, or a mess of catfish for payment.

In those days, on Saturdays, the town square was crowded with a few cars and trucks, lots of mules and wagons, and plenty of farmers who came to town for shopping, to go to church, or just to watch a movie. Banks and such places had sawdust spread over the wooden floors to soak up tobacco spit. They had spittoons in the corners, of course, but most old-timers would just spit across the room, usually missing the mark.

Black citizens also ventured into town, and while they shared the same streets, the blacks lived quite a different reality than white citizens. Harsh experience had taught them well: Never look directly into the eyes of white folks, don't speak unless spoken to, and always keep your head down. If a black man or woman happened to be on the sidewalk and saw a white person approaching, they knew they'd better move into the street, no matter how inclement the weather.

I'm sure Papa Charlie held me in his arms at some point, but I have no recollection of it. What I knew of him came later through stories told to me. He died in 1946 when I was less than two years old. Still, I recall—perhaps my earliest memory—riding the bus with my mother from Brunswick, Georgia to Blakely. She brought us home for his funeral. I vividly recall a large house, full of people, silence, shadows, and sadness.

Most everything I know about my mother's early life came from stories my grandmother told me. Ida loved to flirt and tease, captivating a procession of older boys and young men, most of whom her parents disapproved. Her father was adamant about who she could and couldn't see, and, invariably, those forbidden, she sought. One such teenager on the 'not-to-see' list was a boy by the name of Will Dalman. "Eleanor, I don't want to ever—I mean ever—catch you or even hear about you being with that Dalman boy. You understand?"

"Yes, Daddy."

Of course, her father's edicts never penetrated; when she found excitement, she took it. It was just such a temptation that nearly ended her life before she had a chance to live one.

One spring afternoon, after school, her girlfriend picked her up in her friend's father's car, and they headed into the countryside. Along the way, they spotted two boys hiking along of the road, one with a gun. As the girls drove by, my mother looked out and yelled, "Stop the car. That's Will Dalman and his friend. Maybe they need a ride." The teenage girls pulled over, and the boys clambered into the back seat.

"Where y'all going?"

"Huntin' squirrel,' replied Will.

The four of them took off down the country roads, deciding to slip away and do a little target practice. They headed out of town on Highway 62 onto Chancery Mill Road toward the Chattahoochee River to a secluded field of pine trees, a get-away place for the local school kids. Will, sitting directly behind my mother, had the rifle across his lap. Halfway

Lucile (MaUdi), Middleton, far left, with parents and siblings, ca. 1910

there, whether from a sudden twitch of a leg, or a jolt from a pothole, the gun went off so unexpectedly, with such noise, it took a while before the teenagers realized what happened. Her girlfriend looked over and screamed. Blood was spurting out of my mother's back, soaking through the fabric of the seat. Ida wasn't even aware she'd been shot. Not at first. Not until she felt the blood against her skin. She told me years later she thought someone had jabbed her with a needle, nothing more.

The kids panicked, turned the car around and sped back toward Blakely, parking in front of Hall's Drug Store on the town square. Why there and not the hospital? Perhaps my mother thought she could repair herself with Mercurochrome and a little bandaging. What was mostly on her mind was her father. She'd disobeyed him, and she didn't want to get caught.

A few people walking by the car realized something was wrong. They saw the blood. More people came running until just about everyone in town stood in front of Hall's. Eleanor, by this time, was going into shock, slumped over on the dashboard. She lifted her head and looked out of the window down the sidewalk. Beyond the craning faces, she saw her father rushing toward the hullabaloo. She bolted upright, jumped out of the car, skirted through the onlookers like a football quarterback, and rushed into the drugstore. The crowd followed the bleeding girl inside, her father closing in quickly.

12

Ida ricocheted down one aisle, over and through another, until she found the back exit. She bolted through the door into the parking lot, pirouetting a few times, then collapsed to the ground.

The local ambulance arrived and rushed my mother thirty-five miles over to Dothan, Alabama, the closest hospital large enough to perform life-threatening surgery. The emergency surgeon was afraid to remove the bullet without further risking her life. He left it there, only a millimeter from that vital organ that was her life.

When I was ten, she told me about it, how it happened, and that the slug was still there, hugged up against her heart. I'd watch her move about the house or play the piano, wondering how it was possible my mother could live with a bullet inside her. It never seemed to bother her, though; it remained with her until she died. Decades later, when she did pass away, I thought about asking the funeral director to remove the bullet before they cremated her, something I'd keep as a souvenir, a badge of her childhood disobedience. She'd have loved the idea. I suspect the place being Alaska, and that she was the legendary Ida Lane of the famed Malamute Saloon, he probably would have. But I didn't ask.

Sam Garwood, ca. 1946

I n 1942, my father went to work at the naval shipyards in Charleston, South Carolina, a few months after the Japanese bombed Pearl Harbor. A year later, my mother joined him, bringing her youngest son, Glenn, leaving their two older boys in Blakely, with her parents. She was more than ready to explore new environments, to escape parental scrutiny and the weight of small-town gossip. At twenty-three, she desperately wanted out of that girdle of Christian conservatism.

The couple rented a small cottage on Folly Beach, the main settlement on Folly Island, a narrow stretch of land, seven square miles of mostly sand, palmettos, oaks, and horseflies, ten miles from Charleston.

Folly Beach proved advantageous to the Union Army as it prepared to assault the Confederates at Charleston's Fort Sumter. By the time Sam and Ida arrived in the early 1940s, the island had become a place for winter tourists and a handful of laid-back full-time residents, many of whom worked in or around Charleston. The Naval Shipyard, accessed by the Cooper River, employed nearly twenty-six thousand people during the war years.

My father was an alcoholic and had been since his teenage years. When they married, he was only eighteen, Ida sixteen, so the odds of their staying together were not favorable. In those days, in that culture, marriage counseling was non-existent, and there was no such thing as Alcoholics Anonymous. Help came mostly from family or church, and Ida and Sam were bound to neither.

I'm sure their marriage was over long before I squeaked in.

Sam was born in 1918, in Donalsonville, only thirty miles from Blakely. His father, Glover Bernhard Garwood, founded and ran the town's newspaper, and, upon retirement, became the local Justice of the Peace. Sam was his youngest child from Glover's second marriage, and only five years old when his mother died. His father immediately remarried, and neither he nor his new wife paid much attention to the child, still emotionally traumatized by his loss.

My father, naturally gifted in mechanics and electronics, had no formal education and by the time he was eighteen, he was working as a projectionist for the Blakely movie theater.

Sam and Ida met during the early 1930s in high school. When my mother was sixteen, she made a list of eight potential husbands, all young men she'd dated, or wanted to. My father was near the top, and, as she later explained to me, she ultimately chose him not because he was her favorite, but because her girlfriends dared her to. He was handsome, older, from a different town, already drinking and smoking—attractive qualities to a rebellious young girl of sixteen. I'm sure this played a role in her choice.

Just as I'm sure, my grandmother had big plans for her first-born's wedding—elegant gown, a church filled with flowers, and half the town in attendance. It didn't work out that way. Sam and Ida slipped over to Donaldsonville and eloped. There's speculation the two teenagers had to marry because of an unplanned pregnancy and that Sam's father conveniently backdated the young couple's marriage certificate so that the date of birth fell within proper decorum.

My mother already had plenty of experience with her father's drinking, but still, at sixteen, and with the severity of her husband's disease, it was an unsustainable marriage. Once Sam started on the alcohol, he couldn't stop, not until he collapsed. It was on such a day that led to their final breakup some months before I was born.

That Saturday afternoon, Sam left to play pool and have a few beers at a bar in the village. Instead of returning home for dinner, he stayed and drank long into Sunday morning. He probably passed out on the beach for a few hours, recovered, then had a few more before returning the cottage.

Between the village and our house, as he staggered up the sandy road, he heard sounds of an organ, a choir singing. He followed the music until he found the church. Barefoot, wearing only his bathing suit, he climbed the pine stairs to the double doors, pushed through, and made his way down the aisle. The singing slowed, then stopped. Everyone just stared.

My father stood and looked around the room with all the drunken swagger of someone incapable of embarrassment. He sputtered out a jumble of incoherence to no one in particular, then he stumbled his way up the aisle, back to the front doors, taking a deep bow to the room. As he turned to leave, he tripped and tumbled all the way down the stairs, rolling into the middle of the street, unconscious and covered in sand.

The service ended abruptly, the congregation quickly spilled out of the church and gathered around my father passed out in the street.

One woman, who knew my mother, jumped in her car, drove down Center Street, over to East Arctic, stopping in front of my parent's rented beach house. She rolled her window down and yelled, "Eleanor, your husband's gone and passed out in the middle of the road, right in front of the church. He's drunk. You better do something, honey, before somebody runs over him."

Eleanor (Ida Lane) Loback Garwood, Blakely, ca. 1944

"Somebody should," my mother probably wanted to say, as she came out of the house, her son, Glenn, in her arms. She was angry enough. Only weeks before, he'd showed up in the wee hours of the morning, drunker than a coot, stumbling around the house, breaking things. He wandered into the bathroom at the end of the hall, opposite their bedroom, and switched on the light, and stood, staring at his reflection in the mirror for several minutes.

My mother was in bed in the room at the end of the hall. She could see him wobbling beneath the light above the sink. She watched as he picked up a straight razor, hold it to his face, then, in slow motion, move the blade up and down his neck. Then he turned and came toward the bedroom. He stood in the doorway, looking at my mother, turning the razor over and over in slow circles as if he were leaving a message. He didn't know my mother was awake and watching. She could hear his breathing and smell the alcohol. She was terrified.

Finally, after a few minutes, he turned, staggered into the living room, and passed out on the sofa.

"What did you do?" I asked when she told me the story years later.

"I don't remember. I guess I prayed. Your daddy was a troubled soul."

Most of the congregation had already gone home for lunch when my mother arrived. A few curious souls milled about, hoping to witness the final act of this bizarre drama.

Six months pregnant with me, my mother stood over her husband, prodding him with her foot.

"Sam! Get up!"

He tried but couldn't.

"Can Y'all help?" she asked several women standing near the church. They looked at each other, nodded, walked over, and together they rolled my father from the middle of the road, beyond the shoulder into a swath of seagrass and sand spurs.

"He'll get up directly, I reckon," my mother said through tears of anger and embarrassment.

"I'll take you home, honey," said the woman, putting her arm around Ida's shoulder.

"No thanks, Margie. I'll manage on my own." Then she turned and marched up the street, back to the house with her third son in tow.

A few weeks later, my grandmother showed up and drove us home to Blakely, me still inside my mother's womb, very much alive.

My father stayed on the island, but not for long. Because of his drinking, he soon lost his job. Alone and not knowing what to do, he joined the army. He disappeared from our lives until after the war ended. My first recollection of knowing I had a father wouldn't come until 1947 when I was three years old.

By then, Ida and Sam had permanently separated.

I was only two years old when my mother moved us to the coastal city of Brunswick, Georgia to live with our grandfather's mother, Lilla Belle Loback, or Nanny, everyone called her.

The large, two-story Victorian house on George Street that William and Lilla Belle built in 1913, like many sizable houses in those days, doubled as a boarding house. Back then, nearly half of urban populations either offered rooms for tenants or were tenants themselves. Brunswick had grown significantly during the American Civil War and both World Wars. Boarding houses were common.

Nanny's late husband, William Loback, a Finnish immigrant, spent most of his life at sea. He began as a cabin boy and eventually, after immigrating to the United States in the 1880s, became one of many harbor pilots, navigating ships through the treacherous shoals of one of the busiest port cities in the country. He died in 1938, but Nanny continued to keep a few boarders. By 1946, other than her granddaughter and great-grandchildren, Nanny had only one tenant, Miss Prentice, an older woman who kept a room upstairs, across from ours. She was a stern-faced spinster who worked as a nurse at Brunswick General Hospital.

I don't know, but suspect Nanny also received some money from her sons, especially from my grandfather, to compensate for the five of us. My mother was only making $35.00 a month as a receptionist and pianist at the local radio station, and most of that went for food

With my father in the army, my mother wasn't about to remain in Blakely under parental scrutiny, in a place where everyone seemed to know everything about everyone.

In 1946, at the end of WWII, a surge of optimism was flooding the country. Jobs were plentiful. The country's dark mood had lifted, and anxieties were easing. My mother was twenty-seven years old, and even though she was single with four boys to raise, she was excited to begin her career as a professional musician.

Memories of my great-grandmother are few, and I have only the dimmest recollections, but I don't think she ever held me, or even spoke to me,

1302 George Street, built in the early 1900s, photograph taken in 2015

for that matter. I suppose she would have, but I only remember her as part of a house full of dark rooms, heavy furniture, and thick shades. I remember her black dress, her legs sheathed in tan, opaque stockings that barely reached her knees, before wrinkling back to her ankles. She traipsed about with little conversation. She was always in the kitchen, puttering about, drinking coffee. She loved her caffeine and suffered incontinence. A strong odor of urine followed her around the house like summer gnats.

One afternoon, while my brothers played, I slipped out of the big house. I vaguely recall that I followed someone down the street. It may have been the cleaning woman who came once in every few weeks. She didn't know I was behind her, and I tried to keep up, but not yet three, I couldn't keep up. She soon disappeared around the corner. I wasn't worried. My attention shifted to a man heading into a building at the corner of an intersection. I changed directions, crossed the street, and followed him inside. A man stood behind a counter pouring golden liquid into tall glasses, then setting them in front of several men. They looked over and smiled, expecting my father to follow. When they realized I was alone, they started chattering, cooing, and coaxing me for my name. One of the customers picked me up and sat me on a stool at the bar, next to his dog he'd also perched on a stool. The man offered me a stick of gum which I happily accepted and shared with the dog. The animal took it and tried its damnedest to chew it. But it couldn't; the gooey mess just kept getting stuck in its teeth, causing the dog a great deal of anxiety, its short snout distorting in strange, comical expressions, it's long tongue trying to escape the wad of gum. I giggled wildly, and the men at the counter followed suit.

"What's your name?" asked the bartender, becoming more concerned.

"Galen," I said.

"Where's your Daddy?"

"I don't know."

"Where do you live? Where are your folks? Where is your Mama?

"I don't know."

"You want a Coca-Cola?"

I nodded for the coke, but I had no idea, none at all, where I was or where I was supposed to be. The bartender made a phone call, and a few moments later a policeman strode into the bar. He picked me up and carried me to his car, and we drove away. With my mother working two jobs and my great-grandmother seldom venturing beyond her kitchen or bedroom, I suppose my older brothers were expected to take care of me, even though they were young children themselves. To this day, I don't think anyone knew I was missing. No one ever spoke about it. My mother never scolded me, never queried me, or cautioned me to stay in the yard. More than likely, the police officer drove me around the neighborhood asking me where I lived until I recognized 1302 George Street. In those days, he would have been comfortable dropping me off in front, waiting until I scampered onto the porch, running through the screened door, and down the hallway. More than likely he knew my great-grandmother. Most of Brunswick did.

My three older brothers and I shared the bedroom upstairs across the hall from the spinster, Miss Prentice, who didn't approve of my mother's lifestyle of being gone most nights until midnight.

One such evening, my brothers and I were playing in our room. All three were jumping up and down on the bed, tossing me between them like a ball. They were making quite a racket when the old nurse rushed into the room, picked me up and spirited me back to hers, my brothers immediately trooping behind her, pleading for my release. She slammed and locked her door. "Stop that noise, children. Go to bed," she hissed.

I was petrified.

When my mother returned that evening and discovered the old crone had kidnapped me, she marched upstairs and pounded on her door. "Give me my child, right this minute." The woman refused. I had to sleep next to

21

her all night; terrified she'd never let me see my mother again. Not until morning, when the old nurse left for the hospital, would I gain my freedom. After that, I stayed as far away from her as I could and so did my brothers.

Animosity between the young and glamorous granddaughter and the old nurse was seriously ratcheting up, in part because Miss Prentice loved to snoop through my mother's mail, rifling the mailbox when no one was watching. Ida was sure the woman was opening and reading her letters. Nanny, oblivious to this infraction and, frankly, to most everything else going on at 1302 George Street, was unconcerned. When my mother cornered her in the kitchen and complained, Nanny merely shook her head, "Ain't no business of mine, Eleanor."

Nanny wasn't about to lose a paying tenant.

Still, Ida wanted justice, but how? My seven-year-old brother, Gray, had the perfect solution. One, I'm sure, our mother would have put in motion had she thought about it first. He set a trap. Literally. He waited until the right moment, just after the postman delivered the mail. Timing was critical. He scurried outside and into the back of the mailbox, on top of a stack of letters, he slipped a mousetrap with its copper mechanism cocked and ready to kill or maim. Then he scampered back inside the house, never saying a word to anyone. Later that afternoon, we heard the scream, then the muffled swearing as the old snoop slammed the front door behind her. She stormed down the hall, up the stairs and disappeared into her room.

Ida was pleased, and Gray was delighted he could shine a bit brighter in her eyes. He felt his older brother, Bernard, got most of the attention, especially from MaUdi. My grandmother always wanted a son, and now she had one. She doted on Bernard, and he'd spend most of his childhood with her. Gray would spend most of his trying to understand and resolve the hurt of perceived neglect.

In 1962, while finishing his degree, he wrote to our mother: "Somehow, on a subconscious level, I saw Bernard as someone I wasn't. To me, he seemed to be getting all the attention from everyone, so I set out to better him. But in doing so, I had to isolate myself from people and not let them help me, not depend on them, for they might let me down, which would mean, to me, that I wasn't any good. And above all, not to show to anyone that I felt or cared about anything; what I wanted most was your love, but because of the way I defended myself, it was the last thing I could ask for."

When my father joined the Army in January 1945, he was part of the 511 Airborne Division. He ended a year of duty in Japan, then later joined the Air Force. He would occasionally attempt to visit us when on leave, usually when drunk, and mostly without success; our mother wouldn't let him inside or any of us outside. Once, he slipped through the window late at

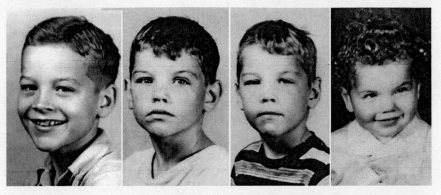

The Lineup: left to right, Bernard, Gray, Glenn, Galen, ca. 1946

night, and crawled into bed with his older boys, slept for a few hours, then quietly left through the same screened opening before Ida woke.

When I was three, my mother moved us out of Nanny's big house to a small apartment not far away. I remember our father showing up one early evening, beating on the front door with his fist, yelling to be let in.

"I want to see my boys!" he bellowed.

"Go away, Sam, or I'll call the police. I mean it. Go away!"

My brothers were hiding somewhere in the back, terrified. I was holding onto my mother's skirt in the living room. My father was roaring like a wounded bear. Suddenly, one of the glass panes above the lock exploded. I watched his right arm push through and reached down for the bolt. He twisted it open, then stumbled into the room, blood dripping across the floor.

My mother stood in front of me, but he pushed her away and grabbed my arm trying to pull me into a hug. But Ida grabbed my other. They began tugging me back and forth like a rope in a tug-of-war. I howled, and they hurled curses at one another. Finally, the neighbors called the police.

After a few minutes, two officers appeared in the doorway and contained my father. Immediately his rage calmed. My mother stood, and stared, and fumed. My three brothers tip-toed out of wherever they'd been hiding, rushed over to hug him, and as the police escorted our father outside, we all followed, including Ida.

Just as they were about to load him up in the paddy wagon, Sam said something to the policemen. They nodded then escorted him across the street, into a little store. In a few minutes, he came out holding a small paper bag. He reached in and pulled out a gift of candy for each if his boys. Mine was a roll of Neccos, those thin, candy wafers thick as a quarter, a different flavor for each pastel color. Brown was chocolate, my favorite. One

23

package cost a nickel. These became my candy of choice until I was old enough to tackle a Sugar Daddy, those leather-like slugs of melted sugar designed to destroy the teeth.

Sam turned and climbed into the police van. "Y'all be good boys, you hear," he said, looking through the bars, trying to smile. He told us he loved us and waved goodbye. We stood, huddled together, watching our father disappear down the street. Then our mother herded us back inside the house.

I don't recall seeing him again until I was six.

Chapter Five **THE HOUSE IN THE WOODS**

A necklace of islands protects the coast of Georgia, the 13th American colony, established by James Oglethorpe in 1733 and named after England's King George II. It became a state in 1788. The largest of its barrier islands is nine miles from Brunswick, separated by an enormous expanse of marshland. Earlier in history, it was known as Guadalquini, used primarily for hunting and fishing by the Guale Indians, but the arrival of the Spanish in the 16th century eradicated the Indians and their customs, renaming the island after an obscure Christian apostle, St. Simon, known for his zealotry.

In the early 18th Century, St. Simons Island (colloquially spelled without an apostrophe) moved from Spanish possession to the English, and by the end of the century, at the height of the plantation and slave era, the island was one of the largest cotton suppliers in the south.

When the Civil War brought an end to slavery and the plantation era, a few of the surrounding islands, such as Jekyll and Cumberland, became private property for the wealthy. They built lavish estates, but during World War II, fearing an invasion by the Germans, the homes were abandoned to the elements. Eventually, thirty years later, most of them were restored when the islands became part of the Georgia State Parks system.

By the 1930s, St. Simons was a favorite tourist spot for the general public. Its main attraction, The King & Prince, was built in 1935 as a dance club, and by 1941, it became the island's first hotel resort. During the war years, however, when German U-2 boats were occasionally sighted cruising the island's coastal waters, the hotel closed and became a military facility until 1947.

After the war, optimism flooded the country. A rise in economic productivity brought more and better-paying jobs. People relaxed and enjoyed life more. With its sunny climate and wide sandy beaches, shallow saltwater creeks teeming with seafood, its lowland forests filled with wildlife, the island was ideal for a fast-growing tourist industry.

Both my parents and grandparents divorced that winter, alcoholism the primary cause. My paternal grandfather had recently died, and this only added more fuel to my father's troubled spirit. Sam disappeared from all of us, appearing only intermittently every few years.

My mother decided to leave Brunswick and head across the marshes for St. Simons. She rented a small beach house, halfway between the main village and the King & Prince, where she landed her first job as a musician. Life was tough with four boys to feed and clothe. Our mother worked nights, late into the evenings, for low wages. It was virtually impossible for her to keep all four of us, so my oldest brother, Bernard, was sent to live with MaUdi, who was thrilled with this arrangement. Gray was sent to live with our grandfather and his new wife, Sarah. Glenn and I remained with our mother on the island. Glenn was seven, and I was four. We had to fend for ourselves most of the time, especially with meals. Catsup sandwiches and pancakes were high on our menu.

Out of the blue, our grandmother would show up with Bernard. We never knew when. She'd stay a few weeks and, as suddenly, she'd depart. I was never privy to any calendar of events of who was coming and who was leaving. I seldom asked.

Glenn and I roamed around the island like wild goats, each going our separate ways with a good bit of freedom. By the age of five, I was swimming in the Atlantic Ocean, often alone, and learned how to move confidently in the strong tides and currents. Sometimes I'd try to follow Glenn, but more often he wouldn't let me. It wasn't uncommon that I'd spend all afternoon alone, playing on the beaches, swimming in the surf or the public swimming pool. I'd hang around the village, or climb on the long pier that jutted into the ocean at the end of Mallery Street.

I was between five and six when my mother got Abie. Where she got the monkey and why she got it, she never said. It was a small South American Squirrel Monkey, always fearful, anxious, and agitated. I liked it but was afraid if it, especially its sharp teeth and unpredictable moods. Abie preferred sitting on Glenn's shoulder, where it seemed most secure until a sudden move or noise startled it; the monkey would then sink its tiny fangs into Glenn's ear hard enough to draw blood.

My mother took Abie with her to work most nights, where it sat perched on her shoulder, while she played piano and jazz organ, songs like 'Caravan,' 'Slowpoke,' or 'Chattanoogie Shoeshine Boy.'

Ida usually went to work in her fancy dresses, lots of makeup and fake jewelry, but sometimes, for pure devilment, she'd show up in one of her grandmother's old baggy dresses, barefoot, wearing a large rhinestone ring on her big toe, smoking a corn-cob pipe.

Glenn and I would take the animal on forays, around the village or at the New Casino, sometimes the beach. The monkey was usually allowed to roam freely in and out of the house, getting into everything, traipsing about the neighborhood, no doubt looking for other monkeys. There weren't any, of course, so Abie made do with the neighborhood cat, dragging it home, then up to the top of the ladder in the garage. It would cradle the cat on its lap and groom it, feasting on fleas and sand ticks. The cat adored it.

Abie eventually disappeared. One day it was there, the next day, gone. My mother later said the monkey died from a bad cold. Maybe it did. Or perhaps it just took off for the woods and freedom.

We moved frequently. I suspect this was because of Ida not having the rent money when it was due. After living on the beach, we moved to a place not far from the village Post Office, close to the Trophy Room, where she worked.

It was here, on a lovely sunny afternoon, I had my first erotic experience at the ripe old age of five. My mother had gone shopping. I was alone, outside. Suddenly, I had this irresistible urge to undress. I stripped off my clothes, and sat on the edge of the road in the hot sand, rolling about in sensual delight, the body naked.

I was pulled out of my reverie, however, when I saw my mother's old Ford turn the corner, heading back home. I was suddenly aware that what I was doing might not be such a good idea, exposing myself to the neighborhood. I'd never been told not to do what I was doing, but I guess part of me knew my mother wouldn't be too happy about it. I jumped up and scurried into the house. I didn't even have time get back into my clothes before my mother came storming inside. I got a good whipping for my first dance with Eros.

I never understood why. Adults were confusing.

Ida had lovers, of course, briefly appearing at the beach house every now and again, men whose names I never knew. After about a year, she decided to marry one. I suspect my mother hid the fact that she had a passel of sons. It was somewhat easy to do because my two older brothers had been farmed out to our grandparents, and Glenn and I were often traipsing around the island for most of the day.

I never asked her why she married Lou Fincher, my first step-father. I suspect she was tired of the financial burden of feeding and clothing of four boys. She needed a plan and set one in motion on a summer day in 1950.

She called me into the house. "Go find your brother, tell him to get ready. "

"Where're we going, Mama?"

"My friend Mittie and I are taking you boys to a picnic. Hurry up, now."

"A picnic?"

"Yeah, there's gonna be fried chicken, coleslaw, chocolate cake, ice cream, other children. You boys will have lots of fun. Now go on and get your brother. We gotta leave soon."

When Mittie arrived, they loaded up her car, called Glenn and me from the house, and took off for Brunswick.

We drove across the causeway, toward the city, and after a few miles, turned down a long, straight road, toward a mustard-colored, two-story Victorian house, nearly invisible behind the live oaks that grew on both sides of the sandy street, their limbs heavy with Spanish moss.

When we drove up, I could hear children in the backyard. Everything seemed harmless enough. But suddenly—I don't remember why—I grew suspicious. Something was wrong. I could feel a shift in the tide of my young life about to happen; I knew I wouldn't like it. I froze. I plowed my feet into the sand. My mother grabbed one arm and Mittie the other and dragged me toward the backyard, coaxing me with promises of balloons and gifts. Glenn, three years older, followed. We knew our mother had tricked us.

I bellowed and cried like a branded calf.

An older woman, along with her middle-aged, over-weight daughter, met us at the back gate and escorted us into a yard full of children, laughing, playing games. There were balloons tied in the trees, a cake, a table laden with food, the whole shebang.

I relaxed. I must have been wrong. Just as I was beginning to calm down and enjoy myself, my mother came up, kneeled beside me, and dropped the news. "Honey, Mittie and I have to go now. I want you and your brother to stay here for a while."

"Stay? Here? No. I wanna go home with you."

"Galen, you have to stay."

"How long?"

"I don't know…maybe a week, maybe longer."

I started crying again.

"Honey, I need to go. I've got a job all the way over in Tennessee. But I promise I'll be back soon."

She stood and gave my brother and me a kiss and a hug. She and Mittie scooted out of the yard and left us with this crowd of strangers.

By late afternoon, Glenn and I were taken inside, toward the front of the house into a small bedroom, nicely appointed, with twin beds. I'd always shared a bed with one or more of my brothers, so this wasn't too bad, I thought. They fed us special meals, and we got to sleep in late. But when Monday morning rolled around, this bit of luxury and attention disappeared. Mrs. Blaize moved us to the back of the house into a large room with several swaybacked beds pushed against the walls. Each bed slept as many as five or six children, of all ages. In my bed, I was the youngest; the oldest boy was fifteen.

I didn't know at the time, but the place was an orphanage. Some children were temporarily housed, for weeks or months, and some were permanent. The daughter was the disciplinarian. She was cruel, and punishments were frequent and harsh. Often the older boys were enlisted to hold down a younger boy while she administered whippings with a long, bamboo cane. I was too young and terrified to do anything other than what I was told to do. I stayed by myself.

We dined at a long table in the kitchen, Mrs. Blaize at one end and her daughter at the other. Meals were regimented and the food bland. Every morning, without fail, we had a bowl of oatmeal and two pieces of toast. No one was allowed to talk at the table, except the two women. My brother and I hated the place.

Living on the Island, we'd learned to survive pretty much on our own. We never had parental guidance, there were few restrictions, and usually, we had total freedom to run wild, exploring wherever our curiosity led us. Now we felt incarcerated. And I guess we were. I retreated into hurt and silence, Glenn into anger and stubbornness. At one point, he ran away, climbing over the backyard fence one late afternoon, disappearing into the woods. He got as far as the marshes, stole an old rowboat tied to a pier on the muddy bank and managed to get the skiff into the currents before being caught. He earned himself another painful caning. I hid in the backyard, behind the woodshed, listening to his cries.

Had my nine-year-old brother succeeded in getting the boat out of the marsh and into the ocean, who knows if he'd even have survived, so treacherous were the currents?

I began my first grade in Brunswick, but I have little recollection of it— how I got there, the school, my teacher, classmates: nothing.

Our father showed up, unannounced one day. He was probably on leave, between postings, or maybe even AWOL. We didn't know and didn't care. We were so happy to see him. He took us out for a walk around the city, telling us about his life, his new girlfriend, his work, and asked us how we were doing.

"How do y'all like living with Mrs. Blaize?"

"We hate it."

By late afternoon, our father returned us to the yellow house, leaving us at the front gate. We stood and watched him hike back down the road to catch his bus to wherever he was going.

Before suppertime, I'd always slip out to the backyard and look between the fence boards, down the long sandy road, hoping to see my mother's car turn the corner. It became my daily ritual. After about five or six months, finally, she did. She loaded us up and took us home.

Once we got back to the island, we learned we had a stepfather, and he soon discovered his wife had four children. Neither side was happy.

"I'm not paying one god-damned penny toward these boys, Ida. Not one. These are your kids and your responsibility!"

I don't believe he ever did, and he never paid out much kindness, either. He wasn't physically abusive, but he could injure a young spirit with cruel words. Because I was so happy to be home, I was often over-excited, jumping about like a puppy, hungry for affection. It drove my stepfather crazy. Like a drill sergeant, Lou would order me out to the backyard. "Stand there, in that spot, and jump up and down until I come back and tell you to stop. Move."

I did, but it was humiliating, and I hated him for it.

Fortunately, we didn't see him that often. He worked during the day as manager of SeaPack, a seafood processing plant. At night, while my mother played piano, he'd hang out at Pete's Place, a local bar where he'd spend his evenings drinking whiskey, watching boxers like Rocky Marciano beat the daylights out of Roland LaStarza on the black-and-white TV that sat on the counter behind the bar. He'd usually be drunk by the time he got home. We'd be asleep.

In 1952, we moved again, the fifth time since 1950, into an old house in the middle of the Island in a dense habitat of mostly oak and palmetto. Our house was the last one at the end of the road, between the airport and the site of the Battle of the Bloody Marsh where the British pounded the Spanish in a deciding battle two centuries earlier. It had a low-slung roof over three tiny bedrooms on the west side and a small living room, dining room, and kitchen on the east, with a full-width front and back porch. Our mother seemed excited to have all of her boys at one place, even though the house needed a lot of repairs, and, as she already knew, it would only be temporary. Initially, my two oldest brothers were back living with us, but only intermittently. Here, I began my third grade.

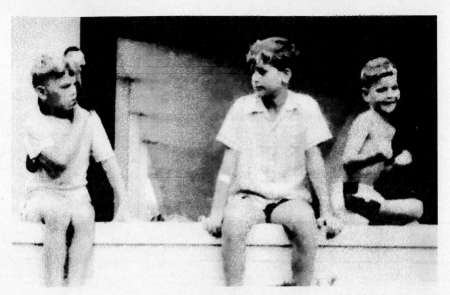

left to right: Glenn with Abie, Bernard, and Galen, ca. 1950

In the first few weeks of moving in, Ida had us all helping make the house habitable—painting walls and floors, fixing windows, hacking back the thick woods that had swallowed most of the backyard. After a few weeks, the place began to look and feel like a home.

Ten meters beyond the back porch, the woods were thick with palmetto, holly, laurel, live oak, pine, and pignut hickory, under which thrived wild grasses, poison oak and ivy, and wild poinsettia. Insects reigned—ants, mosquitoes, gnats, horseflies. Armies of grasshoppers somehow managed to find their way into the house, taking up residence inside the kitchen cupboards. Every morning, before we hiked down the road to catch the school bus, we'd gather in the kitchen for our breakfast cornflakes. As soon we opened the box, clouds of bright green hoppers would explode out into the room like confetti, flying in all directions.

Everywhere outside were tree frogs, bullfrogs, toads, chameleons, green anoles and skinks that whizzed across the dirt, their neon blue tails flashing in the sunlight. Feeding on these were a variety of snakes—Cottonmouth moccasins and Eastern diamondback rattlesnakes, yellow rat snakes, kings, and black racers. Some preferred to bivouac beneath the house, and some liked being inside, slithering their way through cracks and holes in the floor.

One evening, while Ida was getting ready for a trip to Savannah, she discovered an adult black snake beneath her bed, balled up and hibernating in an old suitcase. She looked at it and thought what a grand departing gift. She carefully picked it up and put the snake in her purse, finished packing, then headed over to the Wayside Grill to meet my stepfather and several friends for dinner before driving up the coast.

Halfway through the meal, Ida said, "I've got a little present for you, Lou." She reached into her purse and grabbed the snake, assuming it would still be asleep. It wasn't. It was awake and angry; it sank its fangs deep into one of her fingers. Ida screamed, yanked her arm upward, then popped the snake like a bullwhip, trying to get it off, but it wouldn't release her, coiling around her arm like a bracelet. Terrified, she stood and flung her arm so fiercely, the snake finally broke loose and tumbled onto the table, into a bowl of clam chowder. The terrified snake slithered through the cocktails and across the bread plate toward her Lou, furiously slapping the air with both his hands, pushing away from the table, cursing my mother. The snake skidded off the table, into crazy-eights across the floor, looking for any avenue of escape. So were the customers. They ran in all directions. The waiter finally appeared with a broom and swept the poor reptile into the parking lot.

After a few minutes when things settled down, and most customers returned to their tables, looking at Ida like she was a mad woman, my mother tried to pick up the conversation as if nothing had happened. Lou was livid, embarrassed, and met my mother's attempt to mollify his anger with stony silence. Still, she loved every minute of it, bloody finger and all. She knew, though, it wouldn't be long before he'd find a way to return the gift.

It happened a few weeks later, out in the marshes that bordered the causeway between Brunswick and Saint Simons. My mother was hell-bent that Sunday afternoon on harvesting oysters. She had in mind to steam a mess of them for dinner. She'd build a fire under a sheet of corrugated roofing, lay out the oysters on top, cover them with wet burlap bags until they popped open.

To get a decent mess of oysters, she had to muck around in low tide, wearing only her bathing suit, dig them out of the mud. She stuffed them into an old 'croker' sack she'd brought along. Lou stood on the causeway, leaning against the car, watching and waiting for his opportunity. When Ida was out far enough, he yelled, "I'm leaving. Going to catch a movie in Brunswick. See you later."

Before she could muck her way out of the marsh and get back to the road, he was gone, leaving her stranded, miles from anywhere, without transportation. Fuming, Ida dragged the bag of oysters up to the causeway and stashed them behind a bush, then, covered in mud, she hiked several miles to the closest beer joint. She went inside and asked to use their phone.

"Come get me, Mittie. That son of a bitch left me stranded out here on the causeway."

left to right: Galen and Glenn, ca. 1953

"What the hell are you doing out there?"

"You'll see. Just come and get me."

Mittie drove out, they retrieved the oysters, then headed on into Brunswick, toward the Ritz Theater on Newcastle Street.

"There's the car. Stop. You got a screwdriver, Mittie?"

"There's one in the glovebox."

Ida grabbed it. "I'll be back. Wait for me."

She jumped out, disappeared in front of the old Ford for a minute or two, then reappeared, jumped back into Mittie's car. "Let's get out of here."

The two women made it back to the island in time to cook up the oysters and sip on bourbon.

The movie ended, Lou got into the car, and as soon as he started down the road, a rattling came up from below so deafening he needed to slam on the brakes. When he stopped, the noise stopped. Lou started again, and the racket returned. The car sounded like it coming apart. He crept all the way back to the island at ten miles an hour and found a service station still open. The guy checked under the hood. Nothing. Then he drove the car around the lot, stopped, started, listened, then jumped out and stooped down by the left front tire. He pried loose the hubcap.

"What is it, Bill?"

"Hellfire, your hubcap's full of gravel. That's all it is. Who'd a done a thing like that, Lou?"

By the time my stepfather got home, everybody was in bed, asleep. Ida's score: six to four.

And so, it went, back and forth between the two—everything from her cutting his best suit pants off just below the knees with a pair of pinking shears to his hiding the car keys beneath the oak tree in front of the house in a foot of sand. That one backfired. He was drunk at the time; the next morning, he couldn't remember where he'd buried them. We all stood inside the house and watched him crawling around on all fours, hungover, digging in the sand like a squirrel. He never did find those keys.

These fractious events between my mother and stepfather were ongoing, not unlike like those early TV comedies, but darker and very real.

We had no bathroom inside the house. A room on one end of the back porch had a toilet, a sink, and a claw-foot bathtub below a small window. But we had no water heater. To have a hot bath, we had to fill a two-gallon metal pail with water, put it on the kitchen stove, bring it to a boil, then lug it out across the back porch to the bathroom, then pour it into the tub, which we'd partly filled with cold water. It was a tiresome and awkward chore, especially for me as I was only seven and usually, by bath time, my mother was at work, Lou was at the bar, my brothers elsewhere. Additionally, because it was pitch black outside, I was always scared and tended to hurry so I could get my bath done and into bed, beneath the blankets, where I felt safe.

I heated the pail of water, lugged it out to the bathroom, undressed, and just as I began pouring the boiling water into the tub, the bucket slipped in my hands. The boiling water went cascading down my chest and stomach, sautéing my genitals on its way down. The neighbors heard my screams and called the nightclub where Ida worked. She rushed home right away and then my brothers showed up. They laid me on the bed in the back bedroom and all during the night took turns placing cold, wet towels across my body. After a few hours, I finally fell asleep. For weeks, I could barely stand any clothing against my lobster-red body. The burnt skin shriveled up and eventually sloughed away. I recovered, fortunately, without any scars or permanent damage to my little jiggle stick and dangles.

It wasn't long before Ida showed up with another monkey. Where she got it, I don't know. She and Bernard dragged the crate into the house and pried it open. The monkey exploded out of it like a projectile, leaping from

34

counter to table, to the top of the fridge, onto kitchen shelves, crashing through plates, bowls, and glasses, breaking everything in its path.

Ida chased it around the room until she cornered and grabbed it, and when she did, it bit her hand deep enough to puncture the radial artery. Blood spewed out like a geyser, everywhere across the kitchen She cursed and screamed, and the monkey howled. Eventually, she and Bernard threw towels over the animal and wrestled it back into its crate, dragged the wooden box outside, stuck it in the trunk of the car, and my mother drove it back to wherever she'd gotten it.

Next came a couple of skunks.

"They smell like skunks, Mama," I said.

"They've been de-skunked. That's what the man told me."

To me, the still smelled pretty bad. And they didn't like being in captivity any more than the monkey did. By next morning, no more skunks; overnight they'd chewed their way out of the crate, and disappeared into the woods behind the house.

Still, Ida seemed dead set on having exotic pets, one way or the other, no matter if they weren't all that exotic. Later that winter, she came home with a black and white piglet, less dangerous than skunks and monkeys but a bit strange nonetheless. The little pig Ida called Queenie and, of course, my mother insisted on taking Queenie to work with her, where the baby pig sat by her side on the piano bench, wearing a bright red ribbon around its neck.

Queenie ate only fresh acorns from the trees that grew in the woods near the house. My job was to go out and harvest her food. I didn't mind. I liked the woods and was fond of the pig. She wasn't afraid of me, she didn't bite, and she didn't scream. After a few months, however, as living things tend to do, the pig grew. Queenie doubled in size in no time at all and needed much more than a handful of acorns several times a day to satisfy her hunger. In less than two months, she was too big for the bench. I woke up one morning, and Piggy was gone. Like Abie, my mother never told where or why, but I'm sure Queenie ended up alongside fried eggs and grits on somebody's breakfast table.

All of this was part of my mother's 'Shtick' or, as we might say today, her 'branding.' She knew how to get attention when she wanted it. For example, a group of women who frequented the Trophy Room decided to hold a monthly hat contest. Whoever created the most original hat would win a bottle of champagne.

The first event my mother won. She crafted a hat made of cardboard, bowl-shaped, and lined with tinfoil, then, somehow, managed to secure it to the top of her head. The bowl, Ida filled with cocktail sauce, and all around the outer edge, she hung boiled shrimp, which bobbed and turned as she played the piano. The customers circled her, plucking lose the shrimp, dredging them in spicy cocktail sauce, then greedily devouring every pink decapod.

The second month rolled around and the competition thickened. Ida wasn't worried. She began with a large straw hat, covering the brim with lettuce and ripe tomatoes. My mother fashioned around the crown what appeared to be a nest made from hay. From the backyard, she caught a couple of small pullets and tied them on top. For several hours, as she played the piano, smiling from beneath this ridiculous sombrero, the poor chickens struggled and pecked, but after an hour, the incessant pounding gave her such a terrible headache, she could barely stand it. Ida won again, of course, as she knew she would, but she quickly grew disinterested in any further participation, and the women refused to further compete with such whacky madness. The competition ceased.

My brothers and I were like fragile planets, shifting from one orbit to another. We never knew where we'd wind up, for how long, or with whom. Conflicts between us would break out, from top to bottom. Bernard passed on his emotional pain and anxiety to Gray. Glenn got Gray's, and by the time it dribbled down to me, it had tripled. Out of necessity, I had to develop my own unique set of survival strategies.

Occasionally, though not often, Glenn would be half-way decent to me, or so I thought. He'd lasso me into one of the schemes always percolating inside his head. When I was seven, he taught me how to heist comics and candies from the drugstore on Mallery Street. I tried it once by myself, but, right away, I got caught.

"You do that again, kid, and I'm calling the police. Now get out of here and don't come back." ordered the manager, pointing to the door. I never did, too afraid I'd be hauled off to jail. In fact, for at least a year, no one—not my mother, my brothers, nor friends—could drag me into the place.

Glenn's other scam was sneaking into the movie theater.

He'd hide outside in the bushes by the back exits until the first feature was over. When folks came out, he'd quickly thread through the crowd, slip into the fourth row, scoot down on the floor and wait for the movie to begin. No one noticed. He was already proficient at it when he dragged me along one night. We got caught right away, but before anyone could grab us, we escaped, rushing out the same way we'd snuck in. We took off at a gallop. My brother went one way, and I hightailed it back home. I never tried it again.

Anything of mine he wanted—a new toy, a coin, a comic—he'd take. If I complained or cried, "That's mine," he'd grin, inspect the item top to bottom, turning it over in his hands, then proclaiming, "I don't see your name on it." Whatever was mine, was his, if he wanted it. I had no recourse, other than never showing or bragging about anything I had.

I did, however, once in a while, conjure up ways of revenge.

One afternoon, he asked me if I'd like to go on a hike with him. I usually stayed clear of him, always wary, but part of me was hungry for attention, no matter how it came.

"OK," I said, putting on my shoes. "I'm ready."

We set out from the backyard moving deep into the woods, down one path, onto another, until there was nothing but dense brush. We pushed in further, batting away gnats and horseflies, slapping at mosquitoes. The inland habitat was thick, almost impenetrable, rich in wildlife—whitetail deer, bobcat, fox, raccoons, and opossums. We rarely saw them, but we knew they were there.

Eventually, we came to a clearing of tall grass, with trees all around us. My brother's eyes grew wide and fearful. He pointed his finger at something behind me.

"Watch out!" he yelled.

I twisted around to see what it was, squinting from the sunlight, trying to peer into the shadowy trees. There was nothing there. My brother had tricked me. Again. I turned back to complain, but he was already down the trail, galloping through the trees, his laughter following him like a kite tail.

I should have known his plan all along was to take me out and get me lost. Did he want me to disappear altogether? I doubt it. There'd be no more fun in his life. Still, his deceit upset me more than usual.

But I knew my way around the woods as well as he did. Better. I spent a lot of time there, playing with imaginary friends. I wasn't afraid.

I turned and fumed in the clearing, gathering up ideas for payback. It had to look authentic. A plan quickly took shape. I ripped my shirt in several places, pulled lose some prickly weeds and scrubbed my arms and face, scratching the skin until it was beet-red. I delighted in the pain. When I came out of the woods, into our backyard, covered in dirt, I began limping. As soon as I saw my mother moving inside the house, I turned on full-force the tear spigot. Bingo. She came running out on the back porch to see what the racket was. I blubbered out my sad tale: Glenn had taken me far into the woods and left me there to suffer, to die, to be bitten by bugs, eaten by alligators, and anything else I could conjure up to make sure he paid dearly for his trickery.

37

My mother didn't say anything, but I could tell from her expression that I'd succeeded. I also knew it'd be best if I weren't around when he got his whipping, so I high-tailed it into the village for the rest of the day until it was time for supper.

I never stayed angry at him for long. I knew, even when I was a child, that Glenn suffered more than the rest of us. He seemed to reap the broadest swath of Ida's anger and frustration. I never understood then why my brother got into such mischief. I did later. Pure survival.

The more our mother punished him, the wilder he became. Once, in desperate frustration, she shaved his head. He looked pitiful, like a child from a concentration camp, sulking around the house for weeks, until his hair grew out.

There were times Gray's and Glenn's conflict grew fierce, even dangerous; it seemed a miracle either one survived. On one occasion, they nearly destroyed the house. The argument started, as it often did, over me as Gray was my protector. It began as a dare and a taunt, turning into yelling back forth, a light slap, a tossed punch, then full-bore thrashing, tumbling over, and across the floor. Gray, though two years older, was no match for his twelve-year-old brother's speed and fury.

The battle finally migrated into our mother's bedroom, where Gray was able to shove Glenn into the closet, leveraging his weight against the door, trapping him inside. I could hear Glenn growling like a caged animal from within our mother's dresses and coats while Gray tried to calm his younger brother's temper, offering him treats and other concessionary bribes. Gray knew he couldn't keep the door blocked forever.

After a few minutes, everything went quiet. Gray, thinking he was safe, relaxed and moved away from the door. When he did, his brother exploded out of the closet, holding a WW II Japanese sword in his hands, screaming like a maniac, foaming at the mouth. Gray flew out of the bedroom, through the living room, on into the back bedroom, locking the door behind him. Glenn, only a few yards behind, was slicing the air with the sword, his anger pitched uncontrollably. I froze like a statue in the corner of the living room, trying to be as innocuous as the paint on the floor.

He beat the bedroom door so hard the hinges broke, and the door fell open. He advanced into the room, prepared for what I don't know, but wisely, his older brother had slipped out of the window, disappearing down Broadway to the safety of friends. There was no one but me now. I feared the worst and slumped behind the sofa, scrunching up my eyes and waiting. Nothing happened. Finally, I heard the back door open then slam shut. Glenn was gone, no doubt in a relentless search for his brother or just to cool down.

The house was a wreck. I straightened up what I could before our mother came home, though there wasn't much I could do about the splintered door. I sat the chairs upright and cleaned up a few broken dishes; then I took off.

Life rumbled along at the house in the woods.

Our closest neighbors were Mr. and Mrs. Sutton and their two children, Kenny and his younger sister, Gussie Sue. They lived across the road in a house similar to ours. Gussie Sue was my age and always wanted to hang out with me. I tolerated her, but usually, I'd hide from her, if I could.

In 1952, we didn't have a television, but the Suttons did. They'd let Glenn and me come over and watch a movie on Saturday night. But, for some reason, we weren't allowed inside their house. We had to stand outside on tiptoes, slapping away mosquitoes, peering into the room through the side window. It was here I saw my first horror movie, 'The Son of Frankenstein' with Boris Karloff. I had nightmares for weeks.

Every once in a while, the Suttons would send Kenny and Gussie Sue away for the afternoon. An hour later, from our house, we could hear such a racket of moans, groans, squeals, and screams coming from inside their shuttered house, I thought Mr. Sutton was trying to kill his wife. The first time I heard her cries, I asked one of my brothers, "Shouldn't we go over and help?"

"Nah. They havin' sex."

"That supposed to hurt?"

My brother just laughed.

Only once did all three of my brothers join forces to make my life hell. I was getting ready for bed one evening and, again, as far as I knew, I was alone in the house. I was used to it, sort of, but still, at seven, surrounded by dense woods with nights as black as tar, my imagination would often gallop into terrifying possibilities. Until I got into bed and fell asleep, I was always scared. On this particular late night, I had to get up and go pee. I ran from the kitchen, across the back porch as fast as I could, never looking out into the woods.

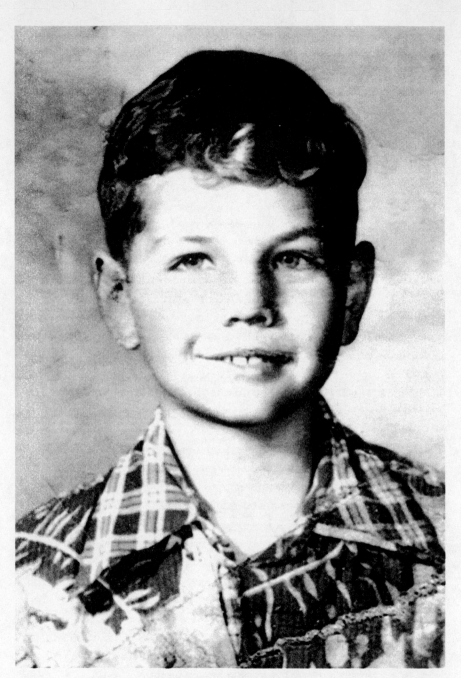

wearing my kaleidoscope of patterned shirts, ca. 1953.

I was standing at the sink, washing my hands, when I heard screams coming from the woods. Horrible sounds. My heart lurched into my throat. I turned, ready to make a run back into the house, into my bedroom, and dive under my covers, but before I could gather the courage, something began scratching at the window above the tub. I looked and saw Frankenstein leering in at me. My lungs seemed to collapse. My heart stopped. I opened my mouth to scream, but before I could make one sound, the door flew open.

A hunch-backed figure wearing a stocking over his face, lurched in, stabbing at the air with a large butcher knife, grunting and growling like a wild beast.

It was all too much. My screams came one after the other, non-stop, except to fill my lungs and start again. I was crying and shaking uncontrollably. All three of my brothers quickly appeared, laughing as children do when they believe they've succeeded with a prank. But they soon realized they'd gone too far. They hovered about me, soothing and cajoling, promising me this and that if I'd stop crying. I finally managed to, but I still couldn't utter a word, only shake my head up and down, squawking out hiccups, trying to catch my breath.

I suppose my brothers were sorry they'd scared me so, but they also knew it was essential to get me back to my usual, happy, malleable self, the Galen they could easily manipulate into keeping his mouth shut. If they didn't, if I squealed on them, and told our mother what they'd done, they knew they'd pay a painful price. Thay sang entreaties. They made offers—stamps from Bernard's so-called rare stamp collection, two weeks relief of kitchen-duty, candies, even a movie. I don't remember exactly, but whatever promises or gifts they offered, it seemed to work. I fell for it. I never said a word to our mother. Anyway, I was too weak to be angry, grateful it was only my brothers and their mischief, and not real monsters ending my young life, slicing me up, tossing me into the woods for the snakes to swallow.

Even though our mother worked at night, she'd usually make dinner for us before she left. She was an avid collector of Gourmet Magazine and had been for years. On her days off, she'd try out new recipes, experimenting with whatever foods we could afford. With little income, she had to buy the most inexpensive cuts of meat, grinding them up in a hand-cranked meat grinder she'd clamp onto the side of the table. She'd make meat loaves, stews, and seafood was always plentiful and not expensive.

Occasionally she'd make her mystery dishes when we'd have to guess what exactly it was she was feeding us.

41

"Do you know what this is?" she asked, one night, setting our plates on the table. It was deep-fried is all we could tell. I took a bite. It tasted good, but I had no idea what it was.

"Chicken?" I guessed.

"It's beef," chimed in brother Gray.

"Nope. Both wrong," she said, going to the fridge and pulling out an uncooked, unsavory looking sample, plopping it down in the middle of the table. We all put our forks down and stared at two alien creatures, floating in blood and water, looking like something out of a sci-fi movie.

"What is it?" we asked in unison.

"Mountain oysters," she said with mock seriousness.

I tried to conjure up that possibility. Oysters? In the mountains?

My mother laughed. "Y'all just ate sheep testicles."

I didn't know what that was and shot my brother my usual "what's that?" look. "Balls," he said, getting up and leaving the table.

Occasionally, for breakfasts, she'd secretly pull out her little bottles of food dyes, then serve up blue toast, purple eggs, and bright green grits. We never knew what to expect.

She boiled, baked and fried, roasted, and barbecued, but she never cleaned. Never. She'd leave a trail of dirty pots and pans, cooking utensils, dishes, glasses, flour, and spilled gravy spread from one side of the kitchen to the other. She didn't have to clean because she had her boys to do it. Each of us had kitchen detail one or two days a week. If the older two were living elsewhere, as was often the case, then Glenn and I got it all.

Sometimes we'd hide the impossibly hard-to-clean pots outside, behind the old stove that sat on the back porch, next to the bathroom and I think, on one occasion, we threw a few into the woods behind the house.

We'd be done eating by 7 pm, and my mother would disappear into her bedroom to get ready for work. She'd reappear looking like a movie star in her tight dress, makeup, and jewelry, wearing lots of perfume. The scent of it would linger about the house until I fell asleep. In the mornings, we'd roll out of bed, dress and feed ourselves, walk up the road to catch the school bus while our mother slept in, usually until about ten. Or even later. We didn't know since we'd be in school.

Because I was the youngest, I wore mostly hand-me-downs. I dressed in an assortment of faded and frayed shirts, of different styles, colors, and patterns that didn't always like each other. My shoes were scruffy, and my hair seldom combed, except when the school did our class portraits. My teacher would brush my curly hair as best she could.

At one point, she became suspicious, wondering perhaps if I even had a mother. She found out where I lived, drove out to our house one Saturday morning, unannounced, to check on me. I saw her car drive up. She walked to the front porch.

"Uh-oh, gotta go," I said to myself, scooting out to the backyard, listening behind the chicken coop

My teacher roused my mother out of her sleep. Ida wasn't happy. And I never knew what they discussed, but my mother never mentioned it, never said a word. She was embarrassed the teacher felt it necessary to drive all the way out and check on us. A week later, Ida showed up at my school—she'd never done that—smiling brightly, carrying a large tray of freshly baked cookies she'd made for my classmates and me. Absolved.

I have few memories of birthday celebrations. When I turned eight, I decided to take matters into my own hands and have a party. I invited all the neighborhood children, most of whom I hardly knew at all. The morning of the 7th, I waited for my mother to say something, hoping she might remember it was my birthday. She didn't. She, of course, knew; she just wasn't aware that that particular day was the seventh of July. Not a word. By lunchtime, I couldn't wait any longer, so I confessed.

"A party? What on earth for?" she asked.

"Um…it's my birthday today, Mama" I mumbled.

She looked at me incredulously. "Today? What time?" she asked.

"All day, I think," I answered her back.

"No, silly, what time is your party?" more panicked than angry.

"Four." I whispered, "I think so. Maybe?" my young voice rising to meet the possibility she'd say no.

She didn't say a word, just shook her head, rushed out, jumped into the car and sped down the road. In two hours, she was back with a cake and candles, ice cream, a birthday gift, and a handful of balloons. She never scolded me. In fact, the following year for my 9th, my mother put together a party for 30 or 40 children, even inviting adults, and planned it in the old village, on the beach, beneath a canopy of live oaks. She made BBQ sandwiches, coleslaw, fried chicken, a big cake with candles, and had lots of soft drinks, balloons, games for the children, and even beer for the adults. Absolved.

So many parts of my mother I never understood. Ida could be self-ish, sometimes eccentric, but still, we knew she loved us. Was she happy? Sometimes, I think. But later in her life, she was often unhappy, I'm sure, regretting many of her decisions, wishing she'd been a better mother, more attentive. Still, in spite of the ups and downs of growing up in Ida's world, she was who she was, and I loved her nonetheless.

By 1954, we saw little of our stepfather. Ida stayed busy at the club, and Bernard was again living with our grandparents. Gray was fifteen, now in high school and taking the school bus over to Brunswick. Glenn was thirteen and becoming more and more difficult for my mother to handle. I was struggling to finish up fifth grade.

On December 25th, Glenn and I rose early. The house was quiet. Our Christmas tree lights were twinkling in the darkness. I rushed to the living room to see what I might have gotten. A bicycle, a bright green beauty with a cane basket, was leaning against the wall by the tree. My first one. I don't remember what Glenn got, but there were other smaller gifts beneath the tree. There were cookies left out on the table in the kitchen. We called out to our mother, but no answer. We checked the backyard. No one. We went to the kitchen, and on the table, near the cookies, she'd left a note: "Boys, I had to go out of town. This afternoon, somebody's coming by the house to get you and take you to their house for Christmas dinner. Be ready by five, and behave yourselves. I'll be back in a few days. Love, Mama."

The winter of 1955 would be our last one at the house in the woods. Changes, once again, were in the winds, but I had no idea what kind and from which direction they'd come until summer.

"Go wash. Change your clothes. I'm driving us over to Brunswick," my mother yelled, searching her purse for the car keys.

"Not again," I mumbled, wondering if she had in mind to leave me with old lady Blaize and her boring oatmeal and toast.

"Where're we going?"

"We're going to see Nanny. She's not well."

I hadn't seen her or heard anything about her since we'd moved to St. Simons in 1948. We drove across the long, narrow causeway, through the marshes onto the mainland, and parked in front of the hospital. We found Nanny's room on the second floor and stood quietly at the end of her bed, sunlight flooding the room from tall windows on either side. I don't recall their conversation, but Nanny smiled at me kindly. I remember looking at her tired, old face sunk into the white pillow, her frail body covered with blankets, her withered hands at her side. When we lived in her house on George Street, I was only three and the rooms were dark. She always seemed vague, in the shadows, and out of reach. Now, at seven, I could look directly into her eyes. I knew who she was, but I didn't know her, not really, and I knew nothing of her family, which of course was my family.

She seemed at peace. At eighty-three, I'm sure she knew her days on earth were coming to an end. Her husband, William, died in 1938. Her mother, brothers, and sisters, aunts and uncles were all buried in Brunswick. The local funeral home had, in fact, gotten so much business over the years from her extended family that in later life when Nanny needed to go somewhere—to visit friends or go shopping—she'd ring up the funeral home and request a ride. They'd send over a long, black hearse. She'd climb in the front seat, next to the driver, and he'd shuttle her about town, then bring her home when she'd finished.

She died soon after our visit. I don't remember if Ida went to the funeral. I'm sure she did, but she didn't take me. Nanny's sons, Charlie, my grandfather, Chester, and Ralph, attended and stayed long enough to finalize her Estate. They sold everything—the Victorian tables and chairs, sideboards and wardrobes, the beds, all the kitchen paraphernalia, and trunks filled with mementos. And, eventually, the house. My great uncle's wife, Martha, inspected all the rooms one last time, making sure everything was cleaned

DEAr DADD♥

I AM GLAD you came to ♥

See us.   ♥

i AM soorr That you ♥

Lost your bAG.   ♥

We hope We can come♥

to stAy with You.   ♥

hoW Are your GirlFiErinD.

I hope You Got A Lob. ♥

A bog can mane Bow. ♥

Think You for the DIrnk in

the Drys stoYre♥ ♥ ♥ ♥

Llve Gavien

A letter to my father written ca. 1950. My spelling has improved, but only measurably so.

Frances Fowler Taylor, ca. 1898   *Lilla Belle (Nanny) Taylor Loback, ca. 1938*

Ida and her boys, left to right: Gray, Glenn, Galen, and Bernard, ca. 1950

properly, that nothing was forgotten, and that no repairs were needed. As she went through the empty rooms one last time, Martha discovered in one of the upstairs bedrooms—perhaps where Nanny's mother, Frances Fowler Taylor, lived during her final years—a bulge behind the wallpaper, in an area long hidden by a chest of drawers. Wondering what it could be, Martha pulled the wallpaper from the plastered surface. With a little prying, she reached behind and gently removed a manuscript, the pages stained, the faded handwriting executed with meticulous precision.

Martha quickly realized she'd uncovered something quite extraordinary, a memoir by Nanny's mother, Frances Fowler Taylor. The narrative, written in a Victorian, expository style, recounts stories about her childhood, her parents, her first love, her failed marriage, and raising her children during and after the Civil War.

I was over forty before I even knew about Frances or her memoir and after I'd read it, what struck me, rather profoundly, were the similarities between my mother and my great-great-grandmother.

Both women had married when they were only sixteen to men severely crippled by alcoholism. Ida to Sam, Frances to Willis Taylor. Both women struggled to raise a family of four children on their own during the uncertain times of war.

In her narrative, Frances soon leaves Willis and travels here and there, eking out the best she can for her four children. In her life's progression, one son is murdered, the other arrested for killing a black man. Her oldest daughter, Georgie, fell to some mysterious affliction, was eventually committed to the Milledgeville insane asylum where she died and was buried without her mother being notified until after Georgie's burial.

In her travels between Georgia and Alabama, Frances met my maternal grandmother's grandfather, J. P. Lane, near Blakely, Georgia. Through this extended friendship, Frances and her clan would spend entire summers with the Lane family in southwest Georgia. Frances's youngest daughter, Lilla Belle (Nanny) became close friends with J.P. Lane's daughter, Miss Ida Lane, mother to Lucile who married Chester and had Eleanor who married Sam.

In closing, she leaves a bit of heartfelt advice:

"Kind reader, my story is nearly ended. I have lived very quietly with my family for the past five years, and if it weren't for the painful recollection of the past, I would be happy. My children are devoted to me and I to them. They are all grown. My last child of that awful night is now a blooming young lady and the pride of my heart. I've had a hard road to travel, but I'm nearing my journey's end. I have given all my children an ordinary education. They are all healthy, able to work for their living, and are honest; that is my great consolation. I have a house and plenty to live on. I've good health, though old before my time. I am yet able to assist my children in making a living. My story is true (except the names) with every word as near as my memory can tell. I can hardly understand that I have as good a mind as I do.

"Young ladies, I can't close my narrative without saying a few words to you. Never marry against the wishes of your parents. If you do: Marry in haste and repent at leisure. Such has been my sad case. When that father objects to your beau, he knows far better than you do. You may be blinded by love as I was and think the man you love incapable of treating you wrong. But I know by sad experience that if I had taken the advice of my dear parents, I might have been spared all this trouble, all the suffering, both mental and physical, but it's too late now. I have reaped well the reward of disobedience to them.

"A few words to parents. Although I don't feel competent of giving you advice, what I say may help you. Don't let your daughters get grown too soon. Keep them in short dresses until they are old enough to be grown in age as well as in size. Never allow them to keep a young man's company till they are of a proper age. Never joke about young men that you would not be willing for them to marry. When they begin to pay their respects to your daughters, if you think they wouldn't be a suitable match, object to them at once. Don't let them keep each other's company, for after young girls fall in love, they certainly love with all the power of their souls, and it is almost impossible to turn them against a young man when they do fall in love as I did. For I certainly did love him in my childish innocence, and if you have read my story, you have seen how it turned out."

Frances Fowler Taylor, 1895

I'm sure Nanny must have told my mother stories about her mother. Frances died in 1914. My mother was born in 1919, at 1302 George Street. It's possible that Ida was born in the same room where Frances stashed her memoir, where she died. My mother never spoke of her, not to me. In fact, she rarely talked about Nanny.

Curiously, sometime after she'd completed her narrative, Frances went back and clumsily changed family names, writing over the original. Who knows why? Embarrassment? Is that why she hid it? Maybe. Still, she didn't burn or bury it. She apparently hoped, one day, someone would find it. She wanted her story told.

I've only seen one photograph of Frances, captured in those typical stern poses of the Victorian era. I don't need to feed my imagination too much to see her sitting on the edge of the bed in her room, beneath the soft glow of gas lamps. Nanny is busy downstairs preparing the evening meal, her husband, William, is on his way home from guiding the ships safely into harbor. Frances holds the manuscript in her frail hands, turning the pages one last time, changing a name here, a place there.

I hear the sound of her laughter, its low pitch, and sweet resonance as she rises and shuffles across the room, pulls back the bureau, then hides her story behind the wallpaper. She wonders how much of her life is left to live as she gathers her shawl and moseys downstairs to the kitchen to help her daughter finish making supper.

My brothers and I knew almost nothing about either our maternal or paternal family history. We'd had little contact with anyone other than my mother's parents. We were like parts of a jigsaw puzzle scattered over a vast ocean. It would be decades before the pieces came together, giving us any sense of our history. As children, few stories of our extended family got passed down. I knew nothing of the Lobacks, the Garwoods, and little of the Middletons and Lanes. In fact, I was fifty before I knew about Frances Taylor and the narrative she'd left us.

I never knew my father's father or anything much about the Garwoods. I learned only late in life that the Garwood clan came to America in the early 17th century from Suffolk, England, married, multiplied, and, over time, drifted in various directions. One line founded Garwood, New Jersey and remained. Another branch went west, and yet another headed south to prosper in the textile industry. I come from the latter. My great-great-grandfather, Barnett Johnson Garwood, migrated down to Georgia in 1844, a century before I was born. We were initially Quakers, but soon after moving, the Georgia line became Southern Baptists. And unlike the remaining Quakers up north, who fought for the abolition of slavery and the rights of Native Americans, my ancestors had no problem owning slaves. In fact, Johnson's second-born son, John Bledsoe Garwood, became a slave profiteer. His youngest son was John Wesley, father to Glover Bernhard Garwood, Justice of the Peace and editor of the local newspaper in Donalsonville, and my grandfather.

May 30, 1955: School was out. Oh, happy day. I threw my books on the shelf, kicked off my shoes, jumped into my swimming suit, and hit the beaches. I spent entire mornings or afternoons on the dunes or climbing about the end of Mallory Street pier fishing for croakers. On other days, I'd go crabbing near the Mackay River, using a long hemp twine with rotten meat tied to one end, thrown out into the salty water. I'd wait for a few minutes, and then slowly pull in the line. When the bait was still a foot or two below, I could see if crabs were feasting on it. If they were, I'd pull it up very slowly, then quickly scoop them up in a wooden-handled net. I'd dump them into a bushel basket and keep at it until I had a good dozen or so, enough to take home for my mother to cook. However, I didn't like to stick around and watch her drop them into the boiling water. I knew a little of how that felt.

By the time my eleventh birthday rolled around, I was as brown as a coconut husk, the bottoms of my feet tough as shoe leather. I came and went as I pleased. I felt comfortable being me, slowly becoming more aware of what life might hold for me.

My mother moved us from the woods into a house a few streets up from the beach. Gone were the grasshoppers, snakes and monkeys, the chickens, the pet pig, and apparently our stepfather. I was mighty happy about the latter.

My brother Glenn was seldom around, so I no longer had to contend, for the most part, with his bully tactics. On some days, I'd head over to the pier and wait for a few tourists to wander out toward the end of the jetty. When they came close, I'd hold up several of the big Blue-Point crabs and ask if they wanted to see my trick. They'd usually say yes, so then I'd carefully pick one up by its back legs, turn it over, and gently rub its underside with my finger. For some reason, this caressing put the crab to sleep. I'd turn it back over and cradle it in my hands, where for a short time, it lay motionless, its claws calmly tucked under its beautiful blue and red armor. The crab didn't mind, and occasionally the tourists liked my trick well enough to tip me a nickel or a dime.

My mother also gave me ten cents a day with which I could either swim all afternoon at the pool or buy a ticket to see a movie. The pool was in the New Casino, a multi-purpose building that also housed a bowling alley on the

Fishing on the Mackay River, St. Simons Island, Summer 1955

second floor and an opened-aired space on the main floor. I'd hang out here in the early evening, listening and watching teenagers dance to songs like Bill Haley's 'Rock Around the Clock,' or 'The Great Pretender' by The Platters.

Across the street, was the Old Casino, built in the 30s. It had a movie theater on one side, the public library on the other, and in between was an open-air courtyard used for public events. If I'd already spent my ten cents on a movie or at the pool, I'd swim in the sea, sometimes joining a few boys from my fifth-grade class.

On one of these summer forays, I experienced my first sexual stirrings. Several boys from school and I spent the day swimming near the King & Prince Hotel. In the afternoon, we headed back to my house, took off our swimsuits, showered, then played around in my bedroom for a while, before getting dressed. I recall becoming transfixed with one of the boys, his naked, brown body, and his small penis. I didn't understand this feeling at all. I had no words for it. While there was no explicit sexual desire, I felt helplessly beguiled. At the same time, however, I intuitively knew not to express these feelings to another soul.

My oldest brother was doing well in Edison, Georgia, living with MaU-di and PaChuddy, now separated from his second wife, back with our grand-mother. Gray would soon be a junior in high school. That summer he'd bleached his hair almost white with hydrogen peroxide, a popular fad at the time with teenagers. He worked part-time at the village drugstore, the same store that busted me when I was seven for my bungled shoplifting attempt. Glenn and I moved into a wary détente. He was now fourteen and seemed less interested in tormenting me, and I was better at staying out of his way.

I still had my metallic-green bike from Christmas before; I went everywhere on it. I'm sure I would have slept with it if I could have. It was my most prized possession, and even brother Glenn knew better than to try any of his 'Don't see your name on it' shenanigans.

One Sunday morning, Gray rushed into the kitchen, "I've got to take your bike. I'm late for work."

"No, you can't take my bike. I need it." I lied. I didn't need it, but I didn't like anyone using it.

"Then, we'll both go," he ordered. "I'll pedal. Sit on the crossbar. I'm late. Come on."

"OK, OK." I relented.

For reasons I can't recall, I was dressed and ready for Sunday School, though I seldom went. Ida didn't go to church, and she never made me go, so I don't recall what prompted me that Sunday, but I was wearing my one good pair of slacks and my Sunday shoes.

After I crawled up on the cross-bar, my long legs dangling off to the side, we were traveling as fast as my brother could pedal when my heel got caught in the spokes of the front wheel. We went from 20 mph to 0 in a quick second. Catapulted into the air, my brother and I flipped over and over like acrobats, landing in a heap on the road. I was knocked out for a few seconds, and when I came to, Gray was picking himself up. We checked ourselves for injuries, but other than a few scratches and torn clothing, we were fine.

I lifted the bike by its handlebars.

"Hurry up, let's go!" my brother bellowed, pulling the bike from my hands. "Wait...wait!" I yelled, tugging at his tug. "Something ain't right."

The bicycle's front wheel had somehow reversed itself, the front of the handlebar pointing backward.

"What happened?" I cried, scratching my head, struggling to push the handlebar back around. I turned to my brother to complain, but he'd taken off, halfway down the block, his yellow hair flashing in the sun.

I pushed my bike back home and leaned it up against the back of the house, where it remained for weeks. As it turned out, it didn't matter all that much. Ida announced one morning that Glenn and I would be living with our father and his new family. I didn't know what to think or how to feel about that. I'd always idolized my father in a distant, mythic way, but, truthfully, in my entire eleven years, I'd spent maybe no more than a full day

Ida Lane, ca. 1955

with him. I hardly knew him, only that he was my father. The year before, he showed up on the Island unexpectedly, called my mother and said he wanted to see me. She didn't want to see him herself, but she told me where to find him.

"Sam wants to see you, wants you to have supper with him at the café up on Mallery Street. You need to be there by five."

I hiked the four streets down to the village, stood on the sidewalk outside the café and peered through the window. I hadn't seen my father in three years, and I was nervous. I pushed opened the door and went inside. Several customers were dining at tables along the wall. A waitress stood at the service window in the back, loading her tray with dishes. The jukebox was blaring. My father was in the middle of the room, drunk, dancing with a broom, laughing as he pirouetted in great clumsy circles. I froze, embarrassed into silence. I wanted to turn and run the other way. But my father spotted me. He stopped, put the broom back in the corner, came over, gave me a big hug, then pulled me over to his table.

I wasn't angry with him because I didn't know why I should be. I did love him, and as little as I'd seen of him, I missed him. We sat for an hour, and he bought me a sandwich and a glass of tea. He ate a little, not much, and drank more beer. I finished my meal, and that was it. We hugged and said goodbye. As I headed down the street toward home, I had no idea when or if I'd ever see him again.

Now, a year later, I learned I'd be living with him for the first time. Ida was moving to South Carolina. I don't think Ida wanted to leave us or even leave St Simons. The island was her home. But she wanted her freedom back. Her marriage to Lou was over, and Ida's way of dealing with her problems was to run from them.

In August, Glenn and I packed and waited in the front yard. Eventually, my father arrived with his new family—my pregnant stepmother, Ruby, and her two children, by a previous marriage, Steven and Clair.

I didn't want to go. I knew I'd miss my mother, the island with its beaches and oleanders, the friends I'd made, even my green bike, but I had no choice.

We loaded our bags in the trunk of our father's car, squeezed in the back seat with our new brother and sister, and drove off threading up Highway 25, onto US 341, over to US 41, north through Atlanta into Marietta.

In those first months, I moped about my new home, missing my vagabond childhood and my freedom. But like most children, I adjusted. I got to know my step-siblings and began to bloom in a more stable environment—meals on time, new clothes, help with homework. I did better in school.

Glenn had a more difficult transition. He'd suffered a lot and bore too many scars. As much as our stepmother tried, she couldn't adjust to his temperament. Still, Sam and Ruby did their best to give us both a good measure of love and security.

Before moving in with my father, I don't think I'd ever seen him sober. But now, for the most part, he was. Though every once in a while, he'd fall off the wagon, and when he did, all hell broke open—pitched battles, hurled dishes, phones ripped out of the wall, screaming, cursing, children crying. But it always quickly calmed, the next day as if nothing had happened.

Ruby was tough as nails, even when she was expressing her love. She grew up during the war years with nine brothers and sisters. Her father grew cotton, and her mother raised children.

Sam and Ruby worked at Lockheed Corporation, my father as an electrical supervisor and Ruby in the blueprint department. When the workers at Lockheed went on strike in 1956, Sam, having five children to feed, decided to cross the picket line. I was sent with my step-siblings to stay with Ruby's brother and his family on a large farm near Snellville, Georgia. I thrived in the landscape, the schedule, and the duties assigned to me. I was up at five, and with my step-cousins, Fred and Terrell, we fed the chickens and collected eggs. They showed me how to milk the cows. We'd bathe, dress for school then gather at the big table for a considerable amount of praying before breakfast. Then we'd feast on fresh scrambled eggs, grits, bacon, biscuits and gravy, and fresh buttermilk. The big meal came in the middle of the day—fried chicken and pork chops, casseroles, beans and peas, tomatoes, cucumbers, potatoes, cornbread, sweet tea, and two or three different desserts. Suppers were leftovers. After homework and evening bible study, we were in bed by nine. For some reason, I took to my new life on the farm. The stable family structure and the shared love nourished me. It only lasted a month or so, the strike was over, and I returned to Marrietta.

I made it through my sixth grade well enough and was looking forward to summer with my new friends when our father informed Glenn and me that our mother wanted us back. He had no choice but to send us.

Soon after Ida moved to Charleston, she met and married her third husband, Charles 'Mac' MacAfoos, captain of a minesweeper at Charleston Naval Base. He was a short man with a meek, almost non-existent personality, the opposite of Lou Fincher. Like Lou, he had no idea whatsoever what he was getting himself into when he agreed to partner up with our unpredictable mother.

After a year of living in a relatively stable environment, Glenn and I were loaded onto a Greyhound bus and shipped back to Ida's World.

When it was time for me to register for my seventh grade, Ida dropped me off in front of the school. "Just go on in and…"

"But, Mama," I protested, wanting her to come in with me. It was a new school, a new city. I was shy and nervous.

"Go on in and tell them who you are, where you live, and what grade you're in." she said, "That's all you need to do. You'll be fine."

I skulked off, went inside the school and moseyed through the halls until I found what looked like the principal's office. I stood at the door waiting. An older woman, looked up from her desk and asked, "Can I help you?"

"I…I'm here to…go to school," I stuttered awkwardly.

"What's your name, son? What grade are you in?"

"My name is Galen. Seventh." I replied, barely above a whisper. She looked at me for a while, tapping her pencil on the dark green desk blotter, then said, sternly but kindly, "Go on down to room 12, son, and tell the teacher I sent you. Go on, then."

I went quietly.

We lived near the Charleston Battery, a defensive seawall on which cannons had been placed in response to the War of 1812, as a last line of defense in case of naval invasion. The area was famous for its antebellum architecture—the Charles Drayton House, Villa Margherita, the Louis DeSaussure House, the James Spear House—with their grand columned porches, plush lawns, and thick hedges of bright pink azaleas. I sometimes wondered what it might feel like to live in such grandiose homes.

Our neighborhood, though close to the battery, was not so grand. My mother rented a shotgun apartment, so called because they were a series of rooms, one in front of the other. We lived on the second floor, and my brother and I shared the bedroom on the backend, though he was seldom there. To get to any other part of the house, I had to go through our mother and stepfather's bedroom. I hated it, especially at night when I had to pee. Once, in the middle of the night, I began to tip-toed through only to discover my mother and Mac in the midst of having sex. I froze. I shut my eyes quickly but had already seen enough to disturb my young brain. I crept back through my room, to the back porch and pissed off the balcony into the dark.

Ida played piano and jazz organ at the Fort Sumter Hotel for a while and later worked at the Carriage House, a local nightclub. On weekends, I'd get up, make my breakfast, then head out and hike around the old city. About four blocks from our apartment, I discovered an area that had once been the Charleston Slave Market, a series of open-air brick stalls selling mostly tourist items instead of people. One area housed a small history museum, with rows of glass cases displaying various artifacts from Charleston's early days—confederate flags, rifles, clothing, faded photographs, and 19th-century newspapers. I stopped at one cabinet displaying editions of the Charleston Courier; one paper spread open to the classified section. I started reading the various items and was shocked when I came to a four-line ad announcing the sale of a black woman and a child. Seeing the words in print made it real. I'd grown up in the deep south. I knew about our history. I knew about racism and bigotry. But this was the first time its impact entered my thinking in such a sadly disturbing way.

I walked everywhere in the city. I loved the old 17th- and 18th- century architecture, the churches with their soaring white steeples, and live oaks, their limbs, covered in Spanish moss, arching over the streets.

On weekends, throughout the old city, were outside art exhibits, featuring local artists painting mostly cityscapes or scenes of the bygone days, and always variations of that iconic southern flower, the magnolia.

On a Saturday afternoon, walking down Meeting Street, near Saint Michaels, I discovered an exhibit in the garden area of a small church. I strolled into the courtyard to look at the paintings, trying to act as if knew more than

I did, remembering things my grandmother had taught me about color and how to make things appear far away.

I was looking at a landscape painting when a man standing just behind me said, "I like your jeans. Where did you get them?"

I turned around. The guy was in his late twenties, perhaps early thirties. I was only thirteen, so he seemed old to me.

"I don't know."

He laughed.

"'You must like art."

"I do," I said. "My grandmother's an artist."

"That's good," he replied, looking around the courtyard, stepping a little closer. "Hey, do you like to swim?" he said.

I nodded yes, thinking it a strange turn in the conversation.

He looked around again, turned to me and said quietly, "Do you like to swim naked?"

I didn't say anything. I let the question seep into my thirteen-year-old brain and simmer. That year I'd had my first experience with masturbating. I didn't learn from an adult, or by reading. No older kids or even kids my age ever talked about it. No one showed me. I was self-taught, probably like most, through miraculous discovery. I was floating in a bath of warm water, slathering soap all over my body. I looked down and realized my penis was poking out of the water like a bamboo fishing cane. Curious at its new size and rigidity, I twanged it, and then again. The more I played, the better it felt and the harder it got. It didn't take too long before my dick shot out a stream of thick, gooey cream, oozing over my hand, down into the tub, floating and spreading across my little sea of soapy water.

It scared me at first. I thought I'd broken something. But there was no pain. In fact, the opposite. What I'd done felt so heavenly, I decided whatever it was, it had to be OK.

Things seemed to always come to me a little late. I recall the day I discovered I was missing one of my testicles. I was sure I had three. When or how I came to this certainty, I've no idea. I suppose there's a chance my brother Glenn had tricked me into believing it, or, more than likely, given my disinterest in anything to do with math, I'd miscounted. Now I had only two. And I had no idea there was any connection between what had just happened in my warm bath, and however many balls were in this pouch of skin between my legs. In any case, though I quickly became proficient at jacking off, I didn't, for yet a few years, fantasize about having sex with another person. Even if I had, for sure, this much older person standing before me wouldn't have much of a role in my imaginary script.

58

"I bet you'd like it, though," he added, smiling, looking around to see if anyone was paying any attention to us.

I just nodded, wondering where he was going with the conversation. "There's a place on the end of Folly Beach. Nobody ever goes there. You'd have a lot of fun playing in the water. You wanna go?"

I shrugged my shoulders, "I guess so."

"I'm Barry. What's your name?"

"Galen."

"How about tomorrow I pick you up...say, on the corner of King and Fulton Street. Alright? OK? We'll have lots of fun."

I had to think it about it. The next day was Sunday, and I needed some excuse for being away all afternoon, though I usually came and went as I pleased. Still, it was good to be prepared, just in case, and this was, after all, a whole new kettle of crabs.

I nodded OK, my heart beginning to race. The idea of being naked took on a shape all its own. I was intrigued, not with Barry, but being naked on the beach, out in the open. When I turned to head home, he said, "Oh, by the way, you'd better not say anything to your folks. I mean, well, you know how parents can be. They might not let you go."

I looked over my shoulder. "OK, I won't tell," I said, leaving the church square, turning toward home. Barry took off in the opposite direction.

I'd walked several blocks, playing this new possible adventure in my mind, already beginning to undress, when my mind's radar caught up with me. Alarm bells pinged. Something wasn't right. I'm sure if Barry hadn't told me not to say anything to my parents, I would have gone with him. I would have sneaked out of the house after lunch the following day and waited, all excited, at the corner. Who knows what might have happened?

Scenario Number One: We swim naked. We play in the surf. Barry takes me to the top of the beach into the bushes and gently brings me into the world of sex, then drives me back to the city better prepared to tack through the turbulence of my life as a gay teenager in the somnolent 50s.

Scenario Number Two: My young body is found, decomposed, floating in shallow tides, ravaged first by Barry, then by crabs and gulls, and what's left of me dries and curls up like snakeskin, then rolled over the dunes by salty winds.

When I got home, the first thing I did was tell my mother. Her jaw dropped, her face grew ashen. She mumbled something about being glad I had enough damned sense to stay away from 'those' kinds of people.

I didn't know what she meant by 'those' kinds of people, and I wouldn't understand until a few years later. Still, I wasn't at all inclined to dwell on her darker 'what-if' scenario. In fact, and not much later, when Eros did take hold of me, and for a long time afterward, I'd often fantasize about that day and having sex on a secluded beach. I carved a myth in my mind and set it free.

Well into the school year, my mother decided she was tired of working, tired of having to entertain night after night, of squeezing into her girdle and the routine of getting glamorous. Mac was making enough. She quit her job and informed us we'd be moving, of all places, to Folly Island. She'd found an old house right on the beach, close to the same one in which in which I was conceived thirteen years earlier. Ironically, here I first met crazy Genevieve and her husband, Doc Watterson, after whom my mother had named me. They still lived in the same cottage as they did when Ida met them in 1943.

Of course, I had to change schools again. There were no schools on Folly Island, so I had to catch a school bus to and from James Island Middle School, the island between Folly and the mainland. I was unhappy and anxious, dealing with new teachers and classmates, registering myself, having to explain who I was and that, yes, I did, in fact, have parents.

It didn't help that my young brain's hypothalamic trigger had begun shooting out hormones like fireballs from a Roman candle. I grew withdrawn and made no friends. I can't, to this day, remember anything about the school and I did terrible in my studies.

There is one thing I do remember. I'd become so painfully shy and bashful I had difficulty going the restroom, even to piss. I'd hold it in until I got home. Sometimes it was painful, but I had a young bladder, so I managed OK. Until that one Friday afternoon, on the bus ride back to Folly Island. I thought I could make it. But I couldn't. I squirmed and grimaced, until finally, the piss just exploded out of me, through my underwear and pants, down my legs, and over my shoes. Bright yellow rivulets of urine rolled beneath the bus seats, across the floor, zigzagging left and right as the bus turned, running all the way to the front, pooling underneath the driver's seat.

I heard the teasing chortles begin, then outright laughter. I kept my head down and my eyes closed. I remember trying not to cry, but I'm sure I did. After an agonizing twenty minutes, the bus stopped. I stood and walked down the aisle between smirking students, holding my books in front of my wet, stained pants all the while staring at my feet.

By this time, no one was laughing; at least I didn't hear them. I think I might have been embarrassed to the point of deafness.

I climbed off the bus and trudged home. I sneaked into the house unobserved, undressed, quickly showered, and scrubbed away the painful episode as best I could. On Monday, I pretended to be sick and played hooky. When school was out, I couldn't have been happier. I never wanted to go back. I moped about the house. I read. I watched TV. I'd spend hours walking on the beaches or just hanging out in town.

It was that summer of 1957 when I experienced my first dead person. Two, in fact. I was bumming around Center Street when I saw a crowd of adults standing around a pickup truck, parked on the side of the street, everyone craning their necks to get a look at whatever was in the back. I got curious. I nosed my way through the crowd until I was right up against the tailgate, craning over the sides but could see only a large canvas tarp. I heard someone say, "There's two of them. Their plane crashed down the beach."

After a few minutes, the sheriff came up and pulled the tarp away, exposing the bodies of two young men, gruesomely mangled. Deep gashes had all but severed their arms and legs, their faces crushed, much of their clothing had been ripped away, exposing bluish-white skin. There was no blood. It now belonged to the sea.

No one seemed at all concerned that I was allowed to stand so close to such carnage. My stomach started churning, and my knees weakened. I turned and headed home, wishing I hadn't stopped. It was too late, of course. I couldn't 'un-see' what I'd seen. I walked the half mile to our house, and the raw images came with me, no matter how hard I tried shooing them away. Further down the road, I imagined them before the crash, flying the skies, with their bright eyes scanning the horizon. Were they laughing? Were they chatting about the weather? About their family? About the excitement of flying? What had they looked like when they were alive and whole?

Before all of this, death seemed unreal to me, part of the stories my mother read to me when I was five, or ones I'd later read to myself, or even in real life like learning that Nanny had died. It wasn't real. Now it was. Death was lodged inside my head, walking with me, pressing up against my elbows, crawling up and down my back, fidgeting with my shirt collar.

When I got home, I told my mother what had happened but didn't go into the gory details. She eventually realized the impact it had on me when later that week she served up one of her exotic meat dishes for dinner. I looked down at my plate, shuddered, then flew from the table.

Ida seemed to enjoy her time away from the club. Gone were the fancy dresses, the makeup, and the teased beehive. She gained weight and shuffled about the house in her nightgown and slippers, spending most of her time cooking, eating, and reading. My stepfather came and went pretty much unnoticed. Bernard was still living with our grandparents in Georgia, and Gray was staying with a local well-to-do Charleston family, helping my brother financially with his education. Glenn was only occasionally around. It was mostly Ida, her two dogs, and me.

We spent the winter of 1957 on Folly Beach, and for Christmas, my mother surprised me with a paint-by-number set. I tried to seem excited and grateful, but I was confused and disappointed in being given what I considered an utterly stupid gift. What was she thinking? I made a brief attempt at it, daubing a few colors in their designated places but soon gave up on it. I hid it under my bed and retreated further into solitude.

The summer came to an end, and it was no surprise that Ida was anxious to get back to work. She missed the nightlife, her music, and the attention. She'd become bored staying home all day, with her husband at night, and, I'm sure, with her gloomy son.

In 1958, my brother and I were sent back to live with our father. Glenn, however, didn't spend the entire year with us. Ruby couldn't handle him. No one could. He ended up, somehow, back on Saint Simons where he got into trouble. My mother, now at her wit's end, asked the judge for help. Glenn spent the next six months in what then was called a boy's reformatory, part of the Milledgeville State facility where, eighty years earlier, Frances's daughter, Georgie, was left and died. Glenn, fortunately, was released after a few months, and even at such a young age, he was on his own, forced to navigate his life as best he could.

Back in Marietta, things for me resumed as it had two years earlier. I made friends. My school work improved. Breakfast and dinner were always on the table, at the same time, with the entire family present, my father saying the blessing.

When the school year ended, once again, I didn't know what to expect. Would I stay or be sent back to live with my mother? I was afraid to ask, and truthfully, I didn't care one way or the other. As it turned out, my grandparents suggested I live with them in Edison, Georgia. I was OK with this arrangement. I'd spent several summers with them when I was younger. I loved them both, for different reasons, and because Bernard had left for college, I'd have most of their attention, having to share it only with Uncle Ralph, my grandmother's youngest brother. He was a complicated and sad character, unable to hold down a job or stay married because of his drinking problem. My grandmother supported him most of her life.

Edison was a small country town. Most of my classmates were daughters or sons of cotton and peanut farmers. We had one clothing store, one grocery, a bank, one drug store, a post office, an old movie theater, several gas stations, and four churches. Edison was so small that it couldn't decide whether it needed a traffic light or not. Some years it had one, some years it didn't.

The year before, my father had taken me to the local Presbyterian church in Marietta and had me baptized. Once in Edison, however, my grandparents decided I needed to be more than be a Presbyterian. They rarely went to church themselves, but most of their friends were Baptist, and my grandmother would often arrange flowers for Sunday services. This time it wasn't just a sprinkle; it was a proper dunking. Now I was a good Southern Baptist. I sang in the church choir and got myself a girlfriend. My school had mandatory FFA (Future Farmers of America) where I learned the rudiments of carpentry, and everything one needs to know about cows and hogs. I tried to fit in. Because everyone knew and respected our grandparents, and because my oldest brother had been well-liked at school, I was accepted well enough, though I suspect some of the kids thought I was a bit strange. One lanky farm boy found some delight in tormenting me, whenever he had the chance.

Other than my brother, no one had ever physically bullied me. I was always too wary, never getting close enough to anyone or any group to be a target and I'd never thought about what I'd do if anyone tried to pick a fight with me.

The year before, while still in Marietta, when I was a clumsy fourteen-year-old, I discovered I wasn't entirely helpless. I'd come in from outside on a Saturday afternoon and sat on the sofa in the den between my stepbrother and stepsister to watch TV. A few minutes later, brother Glenn came into the room.

"Move. That's my place."

I didn't budge.

"You better move now, boy, or you gonna wish you had."

I didn't.

My brother exploded. He rushed over, picked me up and threw me from the den all the way into the living room, then took my place on the sofa, pleased with himself. Typically, I would have relinquished all territory and anything that was mine, before storming off in bruised silence. Not this time.

I picked up the first object I could get my hands on—it turned out to be a baby walker—and threw it at him with every ounce of strength I had. Glenn managed to get his arms up before it ripped into his face, but the metal legs cut deeply into one of his hands. He turned blue with rage. I took off like a flash. Had he caught me, he would have seriously hurt me. As I bolted from the room, my brother behind me in a roar, Eileen, the part-time housekeeper—sweet Eileen, protector of the innocent—quickly jumped between us. She pushed him away and ordered him to leave the house. He did, and oddly enough, he never bothered me after that.

So, when this farm boy, whose name was Nathan, puffed up and tried to push me out of line, I somehow, without thinking, achieved a natural state of Taekwondo. It seemed a miracle. When he came at me, I gently and effortlessly grabbed his shoulders, pulled him toward me, spun him around and sent him flying backward into a thick hedge of crape myrtle so fast he didn't know what happened. He picked himself off the ground and stormed into the lunchroom, beet red and angry. We stayed out of each other's way after that, for a few years, anyway.

In late summer of 1959, my mother, once again, sent for me to live with her in yet another house, another part of the city, another school. Unhappily, I caught the bus back to Charleston. Ida and 'Mac' were living in North Charleston. She was back on her 'I'm-tired-of-working' schedule and they'd rented an abysmally small apartment, hardly big enough for one person, let alone three, sometimes four, if Glenn needed a place to crash.

For some reason, my mother had become obsessed with collecting tropical fish. It started out with one medium-sized aquarium, but one of anything was never enough for Ida. Halfway through summer, she had twenty forty-gallon aquariums lined up, one after the other, on all the walls in both rooms of our duplex. She bought every kind of tropical fish and water plant imaginable, not to mention all the pumps and hoses needed to aerate the water.

This new fascination consumed her until Hurricane Gracie slammed into the East Coast and knocked out our electricity for nearly two weeks. The fish started dying, so my mother put an ad in the newspaper, and within a day, she sold everything. Would there be a reprieve? A period of quiet? A sense of space? No. A week later, she decided she wanted to be a photographer. She bought herself a Leica and converted our tiny kitchen into a darkroom. She purchased a second-hand enlarger, trays, and chemicals, and strung clothesline throughout all the rooms to dry her prints. We had to dip and duck at every turn. Even her spinet piano disappeared beneath stacks of curling black and white photographs. My mother had an irresistible appetite for making or collecting things—monkeys, fish, photos, clothes, music, sons, and husbands. Everything came and went with the tides of her curiosity.

After a year, we moved into a larger two-story apartment where I had my very own bedroom. A sanctum, finally, of private space I needed for more than a few reasons. I'd just turned fifteen. I also needed to focus on getting back into and through high school. Having to deal with my mother's indecision about her life proved more and more of a challenge. Things began to collapse.

Her pet cockatoo went first. I was getting dressed for school when I heard screams from below. I flew downstairs and found my mother standing in the middle of the living room, tearfully pointing to a trail of gray and yellow feathers, leading from the birdcage on the screened porch, across the dining room, under the table, into the kitchen down a hole beneath the sink. A wharf rat as big as a squirrel had snared the bird and dragged it down into its lair.

Not long after this sad drama, her poodle's new litter of four suddenly and mysteriously died. No one knew why. It wasn't the rat. My stepfather seemed to believe their death resulted from something our once-in-a-while cleaning woman did or didn't do. He never said what but was adamant she was the cause. Within a few days, we forgot about the incident. My mother and I assumed Mac had buried the puppies in the side yard or even thrown them out with the garbage. Not at all. He put them out on the top shelf in our stand-up freezer, all four of them stacked like pork chops. I suppose he was hoping to prove his case when the woman came back. Whether because he was drunk when he did it or was drunk so often afterward—probably both—he completely forgot about the dead puppies. They remained in the freezer for weeks, obscured by a thin fuzz of ice. While rummaging around for some ground beef to make dinner, Ida discovered them one afternoon. She was horrified. Then furious. We didn't have meatloaf that night, and she hardly spoke to my stepfather for weeks afterward.

When I left Edison after my ninth grade, my girlfriend, Diane, sent me letters almost weekly, but I never answered them. I didn't see the point. In my heart, I knew I was only playing a role, what I believed expected of me. Nothing more. I'd known since that summer of 1954 that I wasn't like most boys. I never felt as if anything was wrong with me, nothing broken, just an inability to express my feelings.

By the time I was sixteen, holding everything inside became nearly unbearable. I eventually wrote to Diane and offered some flimsy excuse for needing to break up with her, as if being sixteen and living in another state weren't reasons enough.

That summer, between my tenth and eleventh grade, a woman phoned my mother and wanted to meet. She was a songwriter, so she said, and had heard about Ida's talent on the piano. She wanted to know if Ida would play her music. My mother reluctantly agreed and told her to come to the house. When the woman arrived, she came with her friend, Norma Jean Baltzegar and her son, Rikki. Norma, a chain smoker, was a big woman who spoke too loud and so fast you could barely understand her. Rikki was then about

65

fifteen and apparently somewhat of a local celebrity. His mother acted as his manager, and the songwriter wrote some of his material. Over the next few months, they'd often stop by our apartment, and one day, Norma Jean invited me to visit their home.

Because of the dysfunctional energy between my mother and my step-father, I gravitated more and more to this other family. And in doing so, I became fascinated with the extroverted and impetuous Rikki.

Some months later, the Baltzegars invited me to travel with them up to McKeesport, Pennsylvania. I desperately wanted to go. I'd never been north of North Charleston. I came home, strolled into the kitchen where Ida was preparing one of her complicated meals, and as nonchalantly as I could, I said, "Oh, by the way, Mama, Norma asked me to go with them to Pennsylvania for two weeks. We're supposed to leave mid-June and back by mid-July."

I thought all I had to do was make the announcement and it'd be a done deal. Wrong.

My mother didn't look up; she kept working on whatever dish she was stirring whatever was in the large mixing bowl. After a long silence, she said, "Nope. You're not going, and that's settled. I don't want to hear another word about it."

Shock, anger, heartbreak. I raced upstairs, straight into the bathroom, locking the door behind me. I wasn't thinking, blinded by my emotions. I opened the medicine cabinet and grabbed a container full of pills. I had no idea what they were. I didn't care. "That'll do," I said out loud. I hated my mother. I hated school. I hated my life.

Impulsively, I swallowed about fifty pills, washing them down with tap water. I waited, staring at myself in the mirror, wondering how my demise would play out? What was supposed to happen? Then I started sweating. I turned pale, chalky white. I grew dizzy, then everything inside my stomach wanted out. I dropped to the floor, leaned into the toilet and vomited. When I pulled myself up and leaned against the wall, I felt better than I had in weeks, remarkably so. I seemed to have purged myself of more than just the pills, which, as it turned out were nothing but aspirin, even though, I suppose, that many could have killed me. I cleaned up, went downstairs, into the kitchen, and stood before my mother.

"I'm going. You can't stop me." I said defiantly, standing in the doorway with my arms at my sides, like a gunfighter ready for a show-down.

My mother slowly turned from the stove and stared at me as if she could bite through a 16-penny nail. But she didn't say a word.

I left the room, and two weeks later I was headed north with my soon-to-be adopted family.

Tossing the gauntlet did several things. One, it was the beginning of self-determination on my part, although it would be painfully slow in coming; and two, it severed the psychological umbilical cord between my mother and me. Ida now knew I could and would take care of myself, and this set her free. It didn't take her long to capitalize on this new status either.

In February, my mother suddenly announced she was leaving. This time, much further away. She was off to Texas. Her agent had gotten her a gig in a fancy oilman's private club in Midland, and she was hot to trot for new adventures. One day, she was home, the next, she was gone, leaving me with her husband, her poodle, and yet another mysteriously purchased monkey. This one was a tiny marmoset. I went to classes, Mac went to work, and the days rolled across the calendar.

Two months after she'd gone, she called.

"Honey, why don't you come join me."

"To Texas?"

"Sure, you'll love it here. I can send you a bus ticket."

I didn't have to think too long. "OK, Mama."

I told Mac I was leaving and didn't know when I'd be back. Two weeks later I was in Midland. Ida took me to the private club where she worked. The place was called The Tent Room, made to look like an elegant, upscale circus. I'd hardly unpacked, trying to figure out how and if I could adjust to being in Texas, when Ida announced, "We're leaving."

"What?"

"We're catching a train in two days."

"I just got here. Where're we going now?"

"Hollywood."

Sure enough, the next day we were on a train headed to California. It was my first time on a train and after a long haul through deserts and flat-lands, places I'd never imagined I'd see, we pulled into the train station, were met by some folks, then driven to an obscure neighborhood in West Holly-wood. I wasn't sure I liked the place at all. It didn't matter, anyway, because the next day I was put on a bus and sent north to live with my Aunt Cena and her family in Santa Barbara.

I felt like flotsam in stormy waters.

My aunt taught music and my uncle Bud was a proctologist. They had three beautiful daughters, Camille, Glenda, and Bonnie, and a lovely house.

My aunt, bless her heart, drove me to my new high school, took me in-side, then helped me get enrolled.

She taught me how to play tennis, and we talked a lot about music and art. She did her best to make me feel comfortable, even though I suspect she knew I wasn't happy. I loved them, and they were kind to me, but everything felt so damned foreign. I didn't fit in, and I wanted to go back to Charleston.

After a month of being in Santa Barbara, Cena took us down to Los Angeles to visit Ida. We drove around until we found the address my mother had sent us. It turned out to be a boarding house, with a collection of strange folks floating in and out. My mother looked different, acted strangely. She was thinner, continuously grinding her teeth and clamping her jaws tight. A few years later, when I knew more about drugs, I decided she must have been on 'speed,' something amped up from those diet pills she'd been taking for years. It saddened me to see her like that and I hated to leave her in such a state, but there was nothing I could do or say. She'd have to figure it out all on her own.

A few days later, after returning to Santa Barbara, I went into my uncle's study, sat across from him and told him I was quitting school.

"I don't want to stay here, Uncle Bud. I want to go home. I'll find a job, buy a ticket and fly back to Charleston."

He looked at me, "Son, you're only fifteen. You need to stay in school. I'll tell you right now, if you quit school, you'll never go back. You'll never finish, never go to college. Is that what you want for your life?"

My uncle was a devout Baptist, a stern disciplinarian, and often over-controlling. I looked across his desk and calmly said, "Well, sitting here, right now, I can't prove to you one way or another what I will or won't do, Uncle Bud. All I can say is: I will finish school. I will go to college. I will make enough money to get back to Charleston."

"Alright, son," he said, exasperated, "Looks like your mind's set. I can't stop you."

The next day I searched the classifieds, found a company looking for grunt labor, setting up shelves and polishing glass for a new five and dime store. I showed up, got the job, made enough to buy a ticket. I took my first flight that May of 1960.

Magnolia, 2015

W hen I returned to Charleston, I wasn't sure what I would do. It was too late to get back into school. My stepfather worked as a manager in a fabric plant, and when he'd come home, he'd sit, watch TV, and drink whiskey. He fed the dog, and I fed the monkey. My only friends were the Baltzegars, so I began to spend more and more time with them. They lived five miles away, in a two-bedroom mobile home in a park with about fifty similar homes. Norma would drive over, pick me up, take me back, and feed me dinner. I'd often stay the night, sleeping in the middle room with Rikki, crowded, and never comfortable, but at the time, it was better and less depressing than staying home with Mac who barely spoke a word. Occasionally, Rikki and I would play around sexually, pretending we were asleep, then pretending we weren't playing. It was always clumsy, furtive and futile, never as good as masturbation, but it seemed to release pressure from my escalating testosterone.

A few weeks later, I received a letter from my mother. She'd quit her job in Los Angeles and was now in Alaska. I wasn't surprised, but I wouldn't know for years the reason she left until she felt she needed to confess. I don't think she'd told anyone but me.

Some strange guy came into the West Hollowood club where she worked, sat near the piano for most of the evening, intimating he was with the Musician's Union, trying his best to impress her.

When she finished work, he asked her to sit with him for a drink. She did. Then he suggested they drive somewhere for a late supper.

She accepted.

But once on the road, he kept going until they were miles out of L.A., to a sparse suburban neighborhood in the middle of nowhere. He pulled into his driveway, turned and said, "I thought we'd have a drink first at my place, then go find some food. How does that sound?"

I'm sure my mother was already somewhat alarmed by this time, but also probably a little drunk and careless. She followed him into the house and no sooner had they gotten through the door, he attacked her, grabbing her from behind, wrestling her down, trying to pull up her dress. She was in trouble, but she was good at thinking fast. She faked a loud laugh and said, "Hell, if we're going to do this, at least fix me a damned drink?"

Her plan worked. The guy got up and went into the kitchen. As soon as Ida heard the first ice cube hit the glass, she bolted through the front door, across the yard, and into the street, running as fast as she could in her heels. He easily caught up with her, grabbed her hair and pulled her to the pavement. Ida let out a bloody-murder howl. He let go.

"Hey, take it easy, honey. I wasn't trying to scare you. I just thought, you know, that's what you wanted. "Don't make so much noise. You'll wake my neighbors. Come on. I'll drive you back to the city."

"Not on your goddamned life. Get the hell away from me, you son of a bitch." Ida kept walking, on out to the main road toward the city. She began what she knew would be a long hike back to LA, unsure even if she had the right direction. It was getting light when a city bus passed, slowed, then stopped. The driver opened the door and called out, "Lady, you OK? You need a ride?"

"I don't have a penny to my name. I don't have anything" she said, trying to hold back her anger and tears. "Don't worry, honey. No charge. I'll take you where you need to go. Come on, get in."

A day later, she called her agent. "Hey, this is Ida. I've got to get out of here. I hate this place. Do you have anything? Anywhere?"

My mother could have returned to Charleston, but she'd never do that. She was too stubborn. She waited while her agent checked. After a few minutes, the agent came back on the line, "Ida, I'm sorry. There isn't much happening right now. I've got only one possible gig, but I don't think you'd like it."

"What do you have?"

"The Pastime Bar, all the way up in Fairbanks."

"Where?"

"Alaska. Just below the Arctic Circle."

"I don't care if it's on the other side hell. Just get me out of this place."

Ida finished out her contract in L.A., got her last paycheck, bought herself a plane ticket to Fairbanks, found herself a small apartment in the Polaris Hotel, and made a new life for herself.

Fairbanks is the coldest city in the United States, and in 1959 it had a population of 13,000. It was founded in 1901 as a trading post to accommodate the growing needs of men arriving daily from the lower forty-eight, headstrong to make a fortune. Located in the Tanana Valley at the confluence of the Chena and Tanana Rivers, Fairbanks had only one tall building, the Polaris, but it had a lot of bars.

To my mother, Fairbanks was exotic, the people, characters out of a book. One of the first she met was Irene. No one knew how old she was because she was scarred so badly from third-degree burns suffered while trying to save her younger sister from a burning house. The fire disfigured most of her body, burning away her fingers and much of her face. She spoke with difficulty, and her mind had been affected to such a degree that her parents put her in an institution. Irene didn't like it, and her folks couldn't legally keep her there; she eventually ended up on the streets, homeless, surviving—no one knew how—the brutal Arctic winters, living in a shack made of wood and tin near the city's landfill. She roamed from bar to bar, looking for handouts and free drinks. If you bought her a beer, Irene, short and tough as nails, would laugh and lift you clean off the floor in a bear hug. If you didn't, she'd let loose a volley of language hot enough to smoke salmon. Everyone knew who she was and either stayed out of her way or kept her glass full. I met her on several occasions, and each time I wisely bought her a drink. When she came into the Pastime and discovered Ida at the piano for the first time, she stood there entranced, swaying back and forth to the music.

The Pastime was Ida's kind of place, the characters her kind of folks. She liked being there from the get-go.

Back in North Charleston, Mac called me downstairs one evening.

"I'm leaving on Monday to go get your mother, flying military. I've put in for a temporary leave at the plant."

"How long will you be gone?"

"Two weeks, no more than that."

"What am I supposed to do?"

"You're going to stay here and take care of the house, take care of your mother's monkey. You can do that, can't you?

"Yeah, I guess so," somewhat confused by this sudden news.

Two days later, waiting on the front porch for his taxi, he called me outside and took a few bills from his wallet. "Here," he said, "This should be enough until I get back."

I looked at the money. "Five dollars? That's it?"

He didn't respond, just stared at me with his pale blue eyes, all bleary and sad. He climbed into the taxi and took off. I put the money in my pocket and went back inside the house.

I didn't see him again for two months.

Three weeks after he'd left, my mother called. She knew Mac was trying to find her, but she was dead set on staying hidden. She seemed happy enough in her strange new world, where summer never got dark, and winter stayed dark. She tried to explain what it was like there with so much snow and ice and darkness. I'd never seen snow, and I had a hard time imagining her new world. She sounded happy, though.

"Sweetie, how are you? Is everything OK? Do you have enough food in the house? Are the pets OK? You back in school?

I stalled, trying to decide which question to answer first.

"Well, I don't have any money. Mac left to find you. You know that, right?" I said, changing the subject.

"Yeah, I know. How much money did Mac leave you?

"Five dollars."

"What?"

"Uh huh. It's OK. I've been eating over at the Baltzegars."

There was a long pause of static.

Then I thought I heard my mother say, "Sell the Monkey."

"Do what?"

"I said, sell the damned monkey."

"Your monkey?

"Yeah, honey, the monkey. I'm not there. You gotta make do with what you have."

I let that sink in for a few seconds. "How can I sell it?"

"Put an ad in the newspaper, in classifieds. It won't cost much. Borrow the money from Norma. She'll help you."

"Alright. I can do that. How much?"

"Forty-five. That's what I paid for it. You should get at least that. Don't take less."

"Alright, if you say so."

"It's a marmoset. Don't forget to mention that in the ad."

We chatted a while longer and then she told me to be good, to be careful, and that she loved me, then she hung up.

That evening I went into my mother's and stepfather's bedroom. The monkey, no bigger than a kitten, was in its cage which sat on a small table in the corner of the room. A few half-eaten grapes and rotted bananas littered the bottom along with several piles of monkey shit. I rolled up the soiled newspaper and put new paper inside. The marmoset, crouched in the corner, stared up at me with pitifully sad eyes. Even though I'd been feeding it since Mac left, I never paid much attention to it; I didn't even know if my mother had given the monkey a name. I felt sorry for it.

I called Norma the next day, and she lent me the money for the ad and helped me place it.

Marmoset monkey for sale: Needs new home.
Forty-five dollars. Call: 283-474-4327

It came out mid-week in the paper's morning edition, and by that afternoon, my first call came in.

"Hello,"

"Hey. You the folks with the monkey for sale?"

"Uh-huh."

"How much you asking?"

"My mother said forty-five."

"Forty-five? That seems like a lot."

"Maybe, but that's what she told me."

"OK, I'll buy it. Can you bring over?"

"Yes, Sir, I can. But where? Where are you?"

"My name is Keoga. I'm at..."

"Keoga?" I interrupted excitedly, "I know you. I mean, I've heard about you. You're the guy downtown in the tent, on the radio. I know where you are."

"That's me; I'm Keoga. So, what's your name?"

"Galen."

"OK, Galen. Can you bring me the monkey tomorrow? I'll be here. Not going anywhere for another ten days. I'll have your money waiting."

"Yes, sir, I'll be there."

I put the phone down, pleased to get the money, happy the monkey had a new home, but especially excited to meet someone who seemed to me like a celebrity.

I rose early the next morning, got dressed, went upstairs and put the monkey inside a cardboard box with a handful of fresh grapes, closed the lid and secured it with a string, punched a few holes in the sides for air, then caught the next bus downtown. I sat on the front seat with the box in my lap.

Two blocks from the bus stop, I could see a crowd standing in front of a tent on a corner lot. I pulled the cord, got off the bus and walked up to the guy selling tickets. He looked at me, then at the box.

"That the monkey?"

"Yes, sir,"

"Good boy. I'll tell him you're here."

The guy left for only a few seconds, he came back and said, "Now go on inside and say hello to Keoga."

With the box and the monkey in my arms, I walked through the crowd, to the center of the tented area, toward what looked like a water well, about as high as my waist, four feet in diameter, with a rope, pulley, and a bucket above it. On the far side of the room, the radio announcer sat at a table with equipment, microphones, and a turntable. There must have been about twenty folks who'd paid to see Keoga. I pushed my way through the crowd and peered into the pit. About fifteen feet below, the hole opened to a rectangular space large enough to accommodate the man lying at the bottom on a thin mattress, naked except for a pair of dhoti-like shorts. He was strangely handsome, with pale white skin, dark eyes, and long black hair. Crawling over him were snakes of all shapes, sizes, colors, and patterns—cottonmouth moccasins, rattlers, a few pythons with purple tongues darting in and out of their long, sleek jaws. Three or four other species I couldn't identify filled out the mix. Some of the snakes seemed to be sleeping, others undulated across his torso in slow motion, moving with delicate precision. Small green snakes were nestling around his pillow, weaving themselves into a crown around his hair.

I stood there, utterly transfixed, looking down at this bizarre tableau, the box with the monkey inside tight against my hip. Keoga looked up, smiled, then waved. On either side of his shoulders were narrow shelves on which sat a few old newspapers, a worn paperback novel, a tray holding a glass of water and a half-eaten sandwich. A bare light bulb hung just above and to one side of his head.

"You Galen?"

I nodded yes.

"I'm Keoga. How are you?"

"Hey," was about all I could squeak out.

Keoga traveled throughout the South, setting up his performance in cities and small towns along the southern coast, usually coordinating with local radio stations. Before the crowds arrived, he'd descend into his pit with his reptiles and remain there for two weeks. Or so he advertised. I believed it at the time, but later I decided that, no, he'd more than likely sneak up after the crowds were gone, head for a good meal somewhere and a cheap motel, then back down in the ground before they returned the next day.

It was all carney, plain and simple. I didn't find the scene frightening at all. Snakes had always fascinated me. Three years earlier, I found a dozen kingsnake eggs while digging in the yard at my grandparents. I gently pulled them out and put them in PaChuddy's old cricket box, adding a little straw in the bottom. Every day, I'd check on them. After about a week, I saw movement in one of the eggs, and a few seconds later the shell broke open, the baby snake, no more than four inches in length, pushed its way out. I stuck my finger down through the hole, and it immediately coiled and struck at it. I was delighted, and as soon as all the eggs hatched, I released the babies into the woods, watching them wriggle off into the thicket.

One afternoon, months later, I heard my grandmother yelling. "Galen, come on out here. There's someone here who wants to see you."

I ran downstairs from my room and out of the back door to the patio. A fully-grown shiny black beauty, marked with rings of pale yellow from head to tail, easily six feet long, was curled up next to a large flower pot, in no hurry to go anywhere. I sat and watched it for a while until it finally pulled out of its coil and disappeared into a blanket of pine needles. I didn't know if it was one of the hatchlings, now grown, coming back to say hello, but I told myself it was.

When I was living in Charleston, I was walking home one night through a stretch of marshland, streetlights every two hundred yards or so. Lying on the asphalt was a black snake curled up, not moving. I thought perhaps a car had run over it. Then it shifted its body slightly and moved its head. It was alive. I knew if I didn't help, it wouldn't be alive much longer. I reached down and scooped the snake up, thinking I'd release it further up and off of the road, closer to where the woods began. With two fingers, I grabbed it behind its head, holding it as tight as I could. Immediately the serpent coiled itself around my hands.

I walked along in the darkness for a few minutes, proud of my noble effort to rescue it. When I reached the next light, I could see the snake much more clearly. And I didn't like what I saw. What I was holding was no harmless black snake. It was a deadly cottonmouth moccasin. And ever so slowly and imperceptibly, it'd been slithering out of my grip, its fat, triangular head floating in the darkness, curving back to plant its fangs into the hand trying to save it. Had the snake succeeded, I would have been in trouble. I doubt it would have killed me. Maybe, maybe not. In any case, I didn't ponder on it. My primitive brain took over. I opened and retracted my hands so damned fast, by the time the snake hit the ground, I was twenty yards up the road, jogging at a fast pace.

"Can you show me the monkey?"
"Yes, Sir."
"Go ahead, take it out. Hold it up, so I can see it."
I untied the string, opened the cardboard box, and gently held the

marmoset in my right hand, over the pit so that Keoga could get a good look. The monkey peered over my wrist, down into the hole. It started quivering, its tiny hands tightly clutching my wrist, its head swiveling in all directions. I put it back inside the box. The ticket seller rushed over, took the monkey, then handed me my forty-five dollars.

"Thanks, kid, that's all. You can go now." He steered me away from the tent, pushing me toward the street. I hiked down the block and caught the next bus home.

Decades later, I was telling the story to friends at a dinner I was hosting, with my mother in attendance. I'd shared the experience many times over the years but never with her. When I came to the end of my tale, I looked across the table. Ida's eyes had grown as big as saucers, her face full of shock and disbelief. What had I said? I prodded my brain. Then a rock dropped. Oh...my...God. I'd sold her monkey for snake food. Why this hadn't occurred to me before, I didn't know. I still don't.

My mother didn't say a word. She knew better. Still, she sat there, twisting and pawing her napkin, shooting me dagger-like looks from across the table.

A few weeks after the Keoga episode, my stepfather returned, dark and moody. He didn't say anything about Ida. He'd made it all the way up to Alaska, into Fairbanks, on into the bar to surprise her. She was surprised, but not how he imagined or wanted her to be. He had no idea that the main reason she left the South was to get away from him, to start over, to make a new life for herself.

Three months later, I got a call from brother Bernard, "Hey. We'll be in Charleston in a few hours."

"We?"

"Daddy, Ruby, and me."

I was excited but suspicious. "Y'all are here? In town?" I queried. "Why?"

"We're over at the Palm Motel. We'll zip by and pick you up then take you to lunch. Be ready in an hour." He hung up.

I showered, changed clothes, went outside and waited until their car pulled up. My father stepped out, then Bernard, then Ruby. We hugged and drove off to a local restaurant.

Once inside, we got seated and placed our order. Big glasses of sweet tea came first, then our sandwiches. My father and stepmother filled me in on what had been happening with them. I smiled and sipped my iced tea. Then Sam began asking me questions. He knew Ida was in Alaska and that Mac had finally returned without her. He knew a little about my adopted family, but not much.

"Who are these folks? What do they do? Everybody's worried about you, son. You understand we love you, right?"

I nodded.

"Considering what's happened," he continued, "with your mother leaving and all, we think it'd be better if you come back and live with us."

A litany of reasons why I should go with them followed: school, food, clothing, family, etc. I could already feel myself shutting down. I kept asking myself, "Why now? Where's everybody been?"

It seemed unfair to me. Why did everybody wait so long to see how I was doing? I wanted to express these feelings, but I couldn't. I felt hemmed in, outnumbered. My father was waiting for me to say something but I just looked at my food. "Excuse me," I finally said, "I need to go to the restroom."

They smiled and nodded. I stood and headed down the hall and into the men's room. Once inside, I leaned against the door, desperate for a plan. I looked up and saw a window about five feet from the floor. I climbed on the sink, then hoisted myself up, high enough to crawl through the window. I dropped to the ground, barely missing the garbage cans below and ran all the way home.

Later that evening, my father telephoned the house. I was dreading the call. He agreed to my staying in Charleston, but he wanted me to come to their motel room and talk it over, to try and get things settled. I didn't want to but said I would and hiked over to their motel. We sat around, hashed things out, and my father continued to try and change my mind. I wouldn't budge. Finally, he agreed. He said he was sorry everything had turned out as it had "Alright, son, I promise I'll send you some money every month to help you out. If you change your mind and want to come home, then call me. OK?

I nodded yes. We hugged, and I left, unsure I was making the right decision. Still, I was proud of myself for making one. My family drove back to Georgia the next morning.

When Ida gave up her life in Charleston for Alaska, she left everything she owned. She abandoned her clothes, books and photographs, two or three lovely antique tables, several lamps her father had made, a full set of Spode China, silverware, linens, crystal goblets, paintings, her poodle, the monkey, her third husband, and me.

I moved out of the duplex apartment a week later, and I would never see my stepfather again. I got along well enough with my new family.

A few months later, they bought a small house, of all places, on James Island, where, in middle school, I'd had my epic urination on the bus. Fortunately, I was now in high school, and I doubt anyone would have remembered.

The Baltzegar's modest two-bedroom house was on an acre of land surrounded by pine and oak. I stayed busy in school and helped Mr. Baltzegar on weekends in his construction business. Because I'd quit school in Charleston, and had gone to school briefly in Santa Barbara, then left again, I'd missed too many days. I had to repeat my eleventh grade. I wasn't happy about that.

After a few months, Norma Jean began to question me. "Why hasn't your daddy sent you any money?"

"I don't know," I responded. "I guess he forgot."

"That just ain't right," Norma complained, dragging on her cigarette, blowing blue smoke across the kitchen table.

It wasn't long before she began to apply pressure in not so subtle ways. She started working on my emotions, convincing me that Sam was not only legally obligated to send me money, but he was derelict and irresponsible for not doing so. She called me into the kitchen one day and said, "I'm going to drive you into the city. What you need is legal aid. Five days later we were sitting in the Office of Children's Welfare filing a complaint, suing my father. I was confused and unhappy. The case got filed, presented before a judge in Marietta, and because I wasn't able to be there, I lost. Secretly, I was glad I did.

I got through my eleventh grade the second time around then got a job on a large plantation owned by a wealthy Charlestonian family. They raised thoroughbred horses but also had a successful egg farm. My job, working with the owner's son, was building fences to corral the horses. By hand, I dug the holes for the creosoted wooden posts, onto which we nailed pine boards, and later painted white. It was a long, tedious job in Charleston's summer heat and every few weeks my cheeks and forehead would darken and scab over from rubbing the sweat off my face with creosoted hands.

I left at seven in the morning, catching a bus to and from work, getting home at six pm. On Fridays, I was paid by check about eighty dollars, and when I got back to the house, Norma would be standing at the door with her palm out. I dutifully handed over my wages.

I liked working, and I knew I should be paying something for my upkeep, but I didn't understand why I couldn't cash the checks and keep

Chester and Lucile (PaChuddy and MaUdi) Loback, ca. 1942

a little of the money for myself. The flavor of life with the Baltzegars was getting a little sour.

In July, I turned seventeen. A month later, I called my grandmother. I'm sure she could tell from my voice, I was unhappy. She immediately sent me a bus ticket to Edison.

Once back, MaUdi began to question me, sifting through and translating my hems and haws, doing what I'd hoped she'd do. I was embarrassed and didn't know how to get back into my family. She spoke to my grandfather that evening, and over dinner, they told me to come and live with them, finish high school in Edison, that they'd even help me with college. I was pleased and grateful. I hustled back to Charleston, told the Baltzegars I was leaving, collected my few belongings, and said goodbye.

One of the first things I did when I got back to Edison was to visit my one and only girlfriend from the ninth grade, who'd been so angry with me when I broke up with her in 1960. She was friendly, as sweet as ever, and we remained friends.

I then felt I needed to resolve my guilt for filing legal action against my father. I sat down and wrote a long letter telling him how sorry I was. He called me right away and said he understood and reassured me that he loved me and was glad I was back in Georgia, living with family.

Edison was a small town. Mostly farmers. Everyone knew each other. To call someone locally, my grandmother would pick up the phone, dial the operator. "Hey, can you get me the grocery store? Thank you, Margie." When the clerk came on the line, my grandmother would say, "Hi Mel, How are you? Uh huh. Really? That's nice. I need some milk and eggs, a pound of bacon. Some butter. I appreciate it. Thank you. Bye." An hour later, the delivery boy would pull up in the driveway, carry the bags inside the house, empty everything on the counter, put the milk, eggs, bacon, and butter in the fridge, all of it charged to my grandfather, which he paid monthly. He had an account with every business in town, including the barbershop, where he'd go once a month for a cut, a shave, and a head and neck massage, while an old black man shined his shoes.

I began my senior year of school and did my best to catch up on my studies. I'd never driven a car, so I learned to drive my grandmother's new Buick. I worked on weekends at the grocery store in town, making thirty-five cents an hour.

On Saturdays, I'd often watch a film in the one small movie theater in town. It could seat about 100 folks. No black people were allowed on the main floor, but they could sit in the balcony area, only accessible from a side entrance. Just in front, to the left of the movie theater, above the drinking fountains were the ubiquitous 'Whites Only' and 'Colored Only.'

Years earlier, when I still lived on St. Simons Island, between our house in the woods and the beach, an entire black neighborhood lay hidden, far back from the main road. A few of their oldest residents had been slaves as children. I'd walk past the turnoff, and always wonder what it might feel like to be there, to live there, tempted to hike up into their neighborhood. But I was afraid, and I knew no one would take me. By the time I was in my twelfth grade, I knew that most whites in Edison either hated or just dismissed black people out of ignorance. I also knew it'd be the same for a seventeen-year-old gay boy. I stayed quiet, tried to act straight and get through my last year of high school as best I could.

Chester and Lucile (PaChuddy and MaUdi) met as children in the late 1890s when J.P. Lane invited Frances Fowler and her coastal clan to spend summers with them at their farm in Sowhatchee, Georgia. Frances's daughter, Lilla Belle (Nanny), continued this tradition. At some point, perhaps as early as 1915, my grandparents fell in love, soon married, had two daughters, then made their home in Blakely.

Like my father, PaChuddy was also an alcoholic but was much better able to handle his whiskey than Sam.

When I moved to Edison in 1962, my grandfather was sixty-six and worked as the manager of Edison's local peanut mill until 1970 when he died of a sudden heart attack. MaUdi would live another twelve years until the age of eighty-four when her body and spirit agreed to call it quits. She was ready.

They lived in a house they'd designed and built themselves in 1955. It was two stories, made of concrete blocks, painted pale blue, with a double carport and patio, separating the house from my grandfather's workshop on several acres of land that had once grown peanuts and cotton. By the time I lived there, MaUdi had transformed the two acres into lush gardens of pine tree, azaleas, and camellias, with a sizable vegetable garden in back.

My grandfather was a talented wood craftsman, carving hickory, mahogany, Honduras rosewood, and birdseye maple on his old lathe, mostly turning bowls and lamp bases, spending months on a piece.

My grandparents had separate bedrooms. PaChuddy's had a large walk-in closet in which he kept, in addition to his clothing, an ample supply of food, mostly potted meats, canned soups, boxes of Saltine crackers, and candies. And he never had less than two or three bottles of Old Charter Fine Kentucky Bourbon Whiskey stashed away. My grandfather rarely drank socially. He was a night nipper, beginning soon after he got home from work. Every twenty minutes he'd rise from his chair in the den, amble down the hall to his room, have a nip or two, then back before the TV commercial was over.

Though MaUdi rarely drank, I think she too had a bottle hidden in her closet, secretly tucked behind her clothing. She didn't have any canned or dry food as my grandfather did, but, along with her clothes, she kept a few family photographs and other bits of memorabilia.

I was standing in her bedroom one afternoon, when she dashed into her closet, pulled out a strange contraption, and put it in my hands.

"Can you guess what it is?"

I turned it over several times. "Unh-uh. What is it?"

I could see it was an electrical device of some sort. It had a cord and a plug, a power switch, a dial with calibration on it, and extruding from each side of the box two thin electrical wires ended in small pad-like structures.

"Radio?"

She laughed and held up the pads to her face.

"What you do is put a little bit of this gel on each of these pads. Then you plug the box into the wall, turn on the switch and slowly crank up the power, all the while rubbing the little pads over your face in small circles."

"Why? What's that do?" I asked.

"Takes away the wrinkles," MaUdi said with a serious expression. One wire pulls out the negative energy, and the other puts positive back in. Makes you look younger. Here, let me show you how it works."

"No, thanks." I quickly backed out of her bedroom.

When she and PaChuddy were separated, and she had to fend for herself, she drove around the country selling these devices to women who wanted to reverse the tug of gravity. I can't imagine the contraption did anything more than make you feel good, and I don't think she ever sold too many.

My grandfather was half Finnish and had inherited that peculiar trait known as 'Sisu,' a word I can't adequately translate into English, but it roughly means 'silent with steely determination.'

In the mornings and during most of the day, PaChuddy was about as emotive as tree bark, never smiled, hardly spoke at all. He was like an iceberg on a far horizon. Soon after dinner, after half a dozen trips to his bedroom closet, his 'Sisu' would melt away. He became a garrulous story-teller, his hands floating in the air like a hula dancer, fingers pointing at imaginary landscapes, his mind fired up and spinning out fantastic tales.

When I was a young child, visiting in summer, he'd often regale me with fabulous feats he'd witnessed, or even accomplished himself—long dog-sled trips through the Eurasian Steppes while being chased by twenty ferocious wolves, shooting them one by one, the wolves stopping

84

to eat the last one shot until only one wolf was left. He'd laugh, then look at me over his glasses, no doubt wondering if I was able to process the impossibility of one wolf eating twenty others. I adored his stories. I loved where they took me.

Curiously, PaChuddy never told me anything of his early school days in Brunswick, never spoke about his mother, Nanny.

In the mornings, he'd rise and sit at the breakfast table, stone-faced as a rockfish, slurping his coffee with considerable noise, grinding at my grandmother's usually agreeable mood. She'd frown, shake her head, and hiss, "Chuddy, would you quit that noise!" He loved messing with her.

MaUdi seldom traveled farther than sixty miles in any direction from Edison, hardly ever staying anywhere overnight. But she would occasionally fly out to visit her daughter, Cena, in California. During these extended absences and some holidays like Christmas, PaChuddy migrated from a nightly 'nipper' to a man fiercely dedicated to the art of hard drinking, binging three or four days at a time. My grandmother had no sure-fire way to stop him or control him. She'd lived with it for years, left him once because of it, and her only recourse, and short-term satisfaction was to occasionally rearrange all the furniture inside the house while he was out getting drunk. When he came home, he wasn't always sure he was in the right house. He'd fumble about until he got his bearings, then wall-slap his way down the hall like an old crab until he got to his bedroom, collapsing, fully dressed, into bed. On my grandmother's extended trips, it became my job to keep some sense of order about the place. I wasn't happy at all about that. My grandfather was a handful.

Late one Saturday evening, while she was away, I heard a crash downstairs in the hall. My grandfather, a short man but with a generous girth, was out cold. He'd fallen and hit his head on the corner of the table at the end of the hall where the phone sat. It was a struggle, but I managed to get my arms around his body, drag him like a dead man down the hall, into his bedroom, and roll him onto his bed. I threw a blanket over him, went upstairs and collapsed. I was sure he'd be out for at least twenty-four hours. Not at all.

Early the next morning, I heard his deep-throated singing, an old Hank Snow song, something about Jesus. When I came downstairs, he was waltzing up the hall, toward the kitchen, his bruised and black eye hidden behind a pair of sunglasses, ready for another day of drinking.

Fortunately, he didn't drive during these episodes. That was my job. I took him everywhere. Alcohol sales were illegal in Calhoun County, so PaChuddy would have me chauffeur him across the county line to some bootlegger's house. I'd pull up in the backyard. "Wait here," he'd instruct me. He'd slip in and out in less than a minute, returning with a large brown grocery bag filled with enough whiskey to last a month.

As a boy, growing up on the sea, he ate a lot of seafood. He loved salted cod, fried shrimp, and especially oysters, eaten raw on the half shell. Edison was far from the ocean, and even though it had one oyster bar out on the highway, he insisted I drive him 136 miles to Florida for a seafood dinner. Twenty miles out of town, he spotted a guy selling peanuts on the roadside. My grandfather grunted and pointed. I knew what it meant: Stop and pull over.

The man was standing in front of his table on which twenty or thirty bags of freshly boiled peanuts sat stacked into a pyramid. He shuffled over to the car, tossing a bag in each hand. "These are still warm, Sir. Want one or two?"

"How much?" my grandfather asked.

"Fifteen cents a bag."

"I'll take 'em all," my grandfather said, dropping a ten-dollar bill in the guy's hand. "Keep the change."

PaChuddy chewed on peanuts all the way to Florida.

Once we got to Panama City, we found a room, then a restaurant. We ate oysters, fried shrimp, coleslaw, hush puppies, and pecan pie. I drank sweet tea, PaChuddy drank beer. We spent the night, rose early and by the time I got us back to Edison, I was worn out.

My grandmother returned a month later and resumed her chores. I don't know how she managed to take care of him all those years.

MaUdi was usually in a bright mood, always generous and willing to teach me things. I did my share of stupid teenage stuff, but she never lost her temper. Except once and for something I didn't do. Weeks earlier, she'd hired a guy to fell a pine near her flower beds. He miscalculated. As the tree began to fall, fearing it might crush her prized camellia, MaUdi tried to catch it. The tree snapped her wrist, and she had to wear a cast for a few months, restricting her activity, frustrating her in ways I'd never seen before. One morning, still upstairs in my room getting ready for school, I heard a crash, then loud cursing. I ran downstairs, through the breakfast nook, into the kitchen.

"What happened?" I asked.

My grandmother was kneeling on the floor, fuming. Having to use her left arm to pull the egg shelf out, she pulled too hard; two dozen broken eggs covered the kitchen floor. I was about ready to help when she looked up, scowling. "You lazy, sorry, good-for-nothing child. If you'd been here to help me, like you should have been, this would never have happened."

I was devastated. I'd never heard my grandmother speak like that. I backed out of the kitchen and took off to school without breakfast. By the time I got home, everything was back to normal, as if nothing had happened. I'm sure my grandmother didn't mean it, yet she never apologized. Decades later, while visiting, I brought it up, wondering if we might laugh about it. She just stared at me like I was someone else's grandchild, as if to say, "What on earth are you talking about?"

There was a vast and complicated difference between my libido at fourteen and seventeen. For one, it was now much harder to disguise my fascination with boys. I was a good actor, though. I observed. I mimicked. I stayed under the radar. The one problem, of course, the giveaway, was that I wasn't interested in girls, not sexually, and I wasn't about to pretend otherwise. Not anymore.

I wasn't too concerned about it because once I left for college, I knew I wouldn't be coming back. I didn't plan on living in Edison, getting married, raising kids, and growing cotton or peanuts. What I didn't realize is that a few of these farm boys were sexually curious in ways I couldn't have imagined.

One late Saturday night a few of us were hanging out, traipsing from one house to another. There were five of us altogether. We weren't drinking, but two boys were smoking. The conversation migrated over into sex-talk with the usual teenage goofy jokes. I stood off to the side, as was my usual habit, watching, fascinated with these boys, not quite men but pretending they were. These guys were not the school jocks, the ball players, the tennis champs, but country boys with a bit of delinquency in their blood.

At about midnight, all of us standing around in someone's barn, I turned to the group, "I gotta go home." I said, moving toward the big door. Darrell, who lived beyond my grandparent's house, said, "Wait up, I'll walk with you."

We could have caught a ride, but I felt like walking, and I guess he did too. We started down the road, talking about one thing then another. When it was just another guy and me, I was less quiet, more willing to probe with my questions. Eventually, our conversation drifted back to sex talk.

The sky was full of stars. A yellow moon hung high over the town. We grew quiet. We slowed our pace, veered off the road, and headed into a cotton field, crisscrossing through the young plants. When we came to what seemed like the middle, we stopped and stood, facing one another. We kept talking about nothing in particular, and when Darrell spoke, it was a whisper, not to me, but to something or someone beyond me, far off in the woods. Without one iota of verbal initiation from either of us, we unzipped our jeans, pulled out our dicks, and started masturbating.

An occasional car would turn up the road, its headlights sweeping across the field, illuminating Darrel's face, the light flickering in his dark eyes. Darrell was also seventeen, almost as tall as me. He was slim, with short black hair. His ears protruded slightly outward and his eyes, when he looked straight at you, seemed to swallow you up. We weren't close friends, but we shared a class, and something about him captivated me. What was happening was something I never imagined possible.

Darrell suddenly reached over and held my cock, squeezing it hard at first, then stroking it. I did the same to him, awkwardly mumbling something about size. We let go of each other and finished jacking-off, climaxing at the same time, our breathing synchronized, rushing faster and higher until we seeded ourselves out into the night, onto the cotton plants and the dark red clay. We zipped up, headed through the field, and scampered back on the road. Once we got to my grandparents' house, I turned into my driveway, and he kept walking.

"See you later," he said, over his shoulder.

Halfway down my drive, I turned and watched him disappear around the corner. I went inside, tiptoed upstairs to my room, undressed, crawled into bed and lay there, trying to hold onto what had happened. I knew there was little point in making the experience more than just teenage curiosity on Darrell's part. But still, it was like having the sweetest dessert ever. I held my hands to my face, breathing in his smell that still clung to my fingers. I fell asleep with the image of his face floating in the darkness above me. Afterward, at school, we'd pass in the hallway, nod hello, and that was it.

At school, my favorite teacher was Mrs. Dolen, who taught English and art. She was about twenty-eight, attractive, and popular with the guys. I soon learned why. One afternoon, walking home from school, she passed in her car, stopped, rolled the window down and leaned her head out. "You want to hop in and come to my place? Nobody's there. Ben had to drive up to Macon, won't be home until tomorrow." The way she asked seemed so innocent, and I did like her as a teacher, someone with whom I could share my thoughts about art and music...but I wasn't so naïve not to realize what her intentions were. I felt awkward shaking my head no before she'd even finished her proposition. There was no way I was going to climb into her car. I made a few feeble excuses then turned and made a beeline for home. That was the first time, but not the last that I'd find myself in an uncomfortable situation because of pretending I was straight.

My least favorite teacher was Miss Manry, already a legend of tyranny when my oldest brother had her six years earlier, taught math, a subject almost always beyond my reach. I didn't like it.

In class one sultry afternoon, I couldn't keep my eyes open any longer. Math and her droning on about it brought me only pain and boredom. My eyelids dropped like lead weights. I lay my head on my arms and drifted off, far away from her dry, spiritless world of numbers.

Miss Manry must have been utterly delighted in seeing this, knowing she could use me as an example of a lazy, inattentive student. She kept talking in the same tedious, whiny voice, slowly circling, moving to the corner where she reached down and picked up the metal trash can, worked her way closer and closer to my chair, adjusting her voice accordingly, until she was inches away from my sleeping head. She lifted the can as high as she could, then dropped it to the floor. The noise startled the bejesus out of me. I shot up from my desk and nearly toppled over onto the floor. Naturally, my classmates had a great laugh. They'd seen it all before, and more than a few had experienced it. As cruel as it seemed at the time, I don't think it damaged me in any way. It certainly didn't increase my talent for mathematics, but I never fell asleep in a classroom again.

Toward the end of school, Nathan, the boy who tried to pick a fight with me in the ninth grade, decided we should become friends. I wasn't sure why since we didn't have all that much in common, but, why not? I thought. He was now a tall, handsome, likable seventeen-year-old. In June, several weeks before our senior graduation, he invited me to spend the night at his family's cabin on the edge of a small lake. It was a one-room structure with screened-in porches on three sides, hidden among the trees.

We arrived about five, built a campfire, and sat around shootin' the breeze about getting out of school, what college life would be like, and what we wanted to do when we finished. He wanted to become a lawyer but said he'd probably work on his father's farm. We ate supper, and by ten o'clock, we put out the fire, went inside, undressed down to our underwear and climbed into the only bed in the cabin. We shared a few ghost stories then I turned and curled up on my side. I fell asleep listening to the crickets and frogs, and an occasional hooting owl. The heat of his body beneath the sheet rolled over me like a warm sea.

In the early morning, as light filtered through the trees and into the cabin, I woke with Nathan against me, pushing his erect penis up and down against my backside as if he wanted to fuck me. I didn't have a clue what I should do, or not do. I lay there both petrified and electrified. Was he teasing me? Was it a test to see if I was queer? Was he hoping for sex? Was he even awake? I wasn't sure. I wanted to turn toward him, to touch him. I didn't. I pretended I was asleep. After a few minutes, I heard him sigh as he turned away from me. If this was a test, I passed or failed, depending on what he was looking for.

I've held on to this memory and played it over in my mind many times, wishing I'd been bold enough to let loose my secret anywhere on his body. What a beautiful thing it would have been, two boys making love out in the Piney Woods.

In the long spooling out of things, I guess it hardly matters if it happened or not; one becomes as real as the other, eventually.

"Y̲ou want to come to Alaska and work for the summer? You'd love it up here."

"What kind of work, Mama?"

"Well, a little bit of this, a little bit of that. You'd be taking care of reservations at the hotel, sometimes as a waiter in the saloon. It's yours if you want it. I'll send you money for a ticket."

High school graduation was nearing, and I'd already signed up for my freshman year at the University of Georgia when Ida called me in early May 1963. I couldn't imagine being so far away in a place so different from the South in which I'd grown up, but I didn't have any plans, and I didn't want to work in Edison over the summer. A voice inside me said, "Do it."

"OK," I told my mother, and as soon as I graduated, I headed up to the Arctic.

When I landed in Fairbanks that evening, it was still bright and sunny outside. Ida and her new lover, Don Pearson, met me at the airport. She'd spoken to me over the phone about this dark-eyed, bearded man she'd fallen in love with six months earlier. Was it the real thing? I suppose it was as real as it ever got, even though it wouldn't last more than a couple of years.

Don and two silent partners had purchased an old gold mining camp twelve miles out of Fairbanks, in a small village called Berry, situated on Ester Creek. The settlement, with a population of less than sixty, was later renamed, Ester. Pearson named his new enterprise Cripple Creek Resort, which consisted of an old two-story building, previously used to house the miners who worked out on Gold Dredge #12. In the camp, there were several other wooden structures, one of which had been used to repair machinery and this would become the infamous Malemute Saloon. It was here Pearson planned to make his money (and plenty he did) and where he installed my mother, who'd soon become a local legend at the Malamute Saloon.

Ida Lane with Tom Dooley at the Malamute Saloon, being filmed as 'the lady known as Lou' from the Robert Service poem, 'The Shooting of Dan MaGrew' by a Japanese Production company, ca.1962

When Don and Ida began that first season, she knew nothing about ragtime music. In her mind, it was nothing but 'honky-tonk' music, and she didn't like 'honky-tonk.'

"This is a saloon, Ida. Ragtime music. We need ragtime. Learn it."

"Ok. Damn it; I will." And she did. She advertised for sheet music in a few national magazines. She hit pay dirt. She bought hundreds of original scores, including works by Scott Joplin, twelve years before the movie, 'The Sting' came out and reintroduced Joplin to the world. Ida worked on the music every day until she had most of them memorized—'Maple Street Rag,' '12th Street Rag,' 'Kitten on the Keys.'

That first summer, I checked in guests at the hotel, and worked as a waiter at the saloon, even though I wasn't quite old enough. In the nightly floorshow, I'd sing and play the tambourine. I got used to drinking beer and good bourbon.

I'd be eighteen in July.

Walking into the saloon was a dance with history. Every time I went through the swinging doors, I felt like I'd stumbled into the Wild West of 1850—sawdust floors, burlap bags stretched across the ceiling, an old hand-carved bar brought up from Juneau, and every kind of whacky character one could imagine.

For all of its old-timey charm, the place was a firetrap. It wouldn't take more than a spark to set it off. A year or two later, in fact, in late spring, just before it opened for the season, the saloon did catch fire. I came out of my room in time to see Pearson running frantically back and forth with a garden hose. It was hopeless, of course. The place was nothing but cinders and ashes within a few minutes. We all suspected a disgruntled customer was the culprit, someone 86'd from the bar, who'd come back when the place was closed and tossed a match.

Amazingly, with the help of crew and villagers, a new saloon went up in no time at all. Another old mahogany bar that had been in storage, burlap bags stapled on the ceiling, tables made out of old cable spools, spindle chairs, another old upright piano, and a few truckloads of sawdust from the local mill and the place looked the same.

Ida's first set began at about 8 pm, and she'd play until at least two in the morning, just after the last floor show. The saloon opened every day from three in the afternoon till five in the morning, with each of us having one day off a week. The bartenders and waiters, including me, would stay and have a nightcap, unwind till about six, then head up to the hotel in the bright midnight sun, grab something to eat from the walk-in cooler; then we'd all disperse toward our quarters. The kitchen staff, mostly young women, would usually leave a platter of sandwiches for us, and in return, when they wanted a cocktail sent up from the bar, we'd accommodate. It was a good trade, unfortunately, spoiled when the two main bartenders decided to enact one of their practical jokes. Instead of the usual Tequila Sunrises, they made the drinks from stale dishwater, then had me carry the tray up to the kitchen.

The women never said a peep. They didn't have to. The next morning when we staggered up from the saloon at daybreak, grabbed our sandwiches and just about inhaled them, so ravenous were we, not to mention being loaded on beer and shots of 151 proof rum. Ten minutes after I crawled into bed, I doubled up in a tight knot, then shot for the bathroom down the hall once every ten minutes, until I had to dress and get ready for work.

We learned our lesson: Don't mess with the hand that feeds you. The women made our sandwiches from a spread of delicious roasted meats and mayonnaise. Then they emptied an entire bottle of Cayenne pepper into the mix. Justice served.

Crowds packed the saloon every night. We had a lot of military personnel and college students, mixed in with regular tourists. The floorshow consisted of three or four of the bartenders and waiters performing folk songs with guitar and banjo, and a handful of skits, corny as could be but the audiences loved them. Pearson always followed with recitations of Robert Service, usually 'The Shooting of Dan McGrew' or 'The Cremation of Sam McGee,' and sometimes, 'Bessie's Boil.'

Pearson would stand just below the stage, next to a wooden table, one foot on a chair, with a coal miner's lamp illuminating his face, the house lights down, delivering the poems in a deep, theatrical voice. He insisted on absolute silence. If anyone broke the rule, Pearson would nod once toward the waiters, once toward the door, and the offender was eighty-sixed. Then he'd start over from scratch. Twice a night. Oh, the pain of it; we knew those poems better than he did, better than our faces, I do believe.

Ida worked hard and drank a lot, but it never seemed to affect her playing. She was a seasoned pro. I saw her fall asleep at the piano one night, her head nodding, but her hands never stopped, never left the keys. She didn't miss a note. She'd played these songs so many times the muscles of her arms, hands, and fingers kept going.

The stage floor was made of thick plywood, painted black. At least once a season Pearson would have to replace it where Ida's left foot, clad in high heels, beating out the ragtime, would eventually wear a hole clear through the one-inch wood. The crowds loved her.

When her shift ended, Ida would change into her hiking clothes and head up the road toward her cabin, or she'd hike off into the woods in search of log cabins long abandoned.

When she found one, she'd break in and drag back whatever she could carry—old miners' hats, gold pans, berry pickers, antique soda bottles.

On one excursion, she had no luck and headed back to the village, empty-handed. That didn't sit well with Ida. While hiking on a narrow trail that zigzagged through a field of fireweed, she stumbled over a pile of moose droppings, rolling and scattering in every direction. When she saw them spread out on the ground, she was fascinated with their size and shape. Never one to give up and not wanting to go back empty-handed, my mother knelt down and scooped the pellets of dung into her knapsack. Back at the hotel kitchen, she poured them out onto the counter, then pulled out a tin of flour, and a large mixing bowl. She grabbed a deep skillet, loaded it with grease and lit the stove. She made a thick batter, added a dash of salt and pinch of baking soda, then stirred in the brown pellets of shit, which, if you've never seen, are the same color, shape, and size as a Georgia pecan. Ida dropped them in hot grease until they plumped up like oblong doughnut holes. She drained and sprinkled them with sugar and cinnamon, put them in a straw basket on which she taped a small hand-written sign: "Cinnamon Screamers: 25 cents."

On her way to work that night, she quietly set the basket on the bar between the pickled eggs and dried salmon. Every one sold within an hour. Ida moseyed around the tables on her first break and asked one person or another "What did you think of my Cinnamon Screamers?"

One old miner replied, "They weren't too bad, Ida, leastways, not on the outside. But dry as hell in the middle." She laughed, pulled out a few fresh nuggets from her pocket and dropped them spinning on the table, next to his beer. He looked down, took a deep breath, and shook his head.

"Now don't that just take your god-damned breath away? Shit."

Every afternoon, around six, a few old miners from around Ester would show up and hunker down by the saloon's pot-bellied stove, nurse a beer and a shot of whiskey until the crowds began to arrive. Dirty Earl, one of these characters, was there every night. He usually worked graveyard as a 'sluicer' on the gold dredge. Earl lived in an old travel trailer near the camp. He'd bathe and change clothes only once a year, and when he did, it was always an event much appreciated by those in the saloon.

He'd hitch a ride into Fairbanks in June, buy a new set of clothes, then head over to the local steam house for a good scrubbing.

Pearson sent me to fetch him once. I had to go inside his trailer, dirty beyond belief, and his bed was so filthy and cluttered with trash that I could see the outline his body made where he slept. Earl wasn't there, so I quickly left, happy to do so. The smell was godawful.

Another misfit was Greasy John. He got his name because he'd been a greaser on Dredge #10. By the time I arrived in Ester, Greasy John was a bona fide hermit, in every way. Old-timers in the village told me that as a young man, John was roustabout with an ornery disposition, always causing trouble. The boss finally kicked him off the dredge.

I first saw him from a small helicopter over the Ester gold fields. I looked down and saw someone sitting on the ground surrounded by half a dozen or so bags. He had a cloth sack pulled down over his head.

"Who's that?" I asked the pilot.

"That's old Greasy John."

"What's he doing with all that stuff in the middle of nowhere? Why has he got a bag over his head?"

"He's hauling supplies back to his cache on Ester Creek, about five miles up. He'll come out to the village twice a year, and call a taxi to take him into Fairbanks. He buys half a year of provisions, takes the taxi back to the village, unloads his stuff, picks up what he can carry in both arms, walks only far enough to see still what's left of the other pile. He sets a load down, goes back, picks up another. At no time are any of his bags out of his sight; takes him damn near three days."

"Yeah, but why the sack on his head?"

"He's sleeping. It Keeps the mosquitoes from biting his head. Those things are ferocious up here. Big as horseflies." The pilot veered off and headed back to Ester Creek, setting down in front of the Saloon.

I wasn't sure whether to believe his tale at first but another villager, Ansgar Clausen, who ran the dragline for the gold dredge and did cat work for the local placer mining operations, confirmed it.

"Oh yeah, John's a true-blue weird one, he is. I was pushing dirt around with the D6 one day, looked over my blade and saw a mess of spuds rolling down the hill. I didn't know what the hell was going on. I spied old John scurrying about to catch his potatoes, screaming obscenities at me like I'd tried to kill him. I damn near did."

"In the old days, John would ask one of us to give him a lift in our truck. We'd do it and would have done it for free, but he'd have none of that; always left a silver dollar on the seat of our car when he got out. After that, for a few years, John pushed his wheelbarrow into Fairbanks, loaded it up with his supplies, then pushed it all the way back to Ester, then hand carried his rations up to his cache. Now he's too old. He takes a taxi to Fairbanks, but he still lugs everything from the village, five miles up to where ever in the hell he hides out."

One summer, while I was in Fairbanks shopping, John suddenly appeared in the store. You'd smell him long before you saw him. Greasy John looked to be about sixty. He was dressed in rancid blue overalls, wearing a tattered green parka, dark and stiff with oil and grease. A bit of wolf fur fringed the edge of the hood. When he came through the store, everybody moved out of his way. Once in a while, folks would see John watching a movie at the one theater in Fairbanks, always in the middle of the front row among the children. For some reason, the kids were able to tolerate his fetid odor, or just had no choice.

Greasy John lived miles up Ester creek, in a small cache, built high enough off the ground to keep the bears out. Over time, he'd somehow managed to drag hundreds of discarded items down the trail—old stoves, pipes, broken ice boxes, tin roofing—and laid them out in a circle around the cache, layer upon layer, until he'd made himself a barricade. Anything that tried to climb over it, animal or human, he'd know right away and act accordingly.

One spring, old John didn't show up in the village when folks expected to see him. The only person who knew where John lived, who had seen his cache, drove his snowmobile up the creek to check on him. Jerry climbed over the barricade, crawled up a wooden ladder and poked his head inside. John was stretched out on a thin, dirty pallet. He was frozen solid, his eyes still open, staring at the ceiling as if trying to figure out what day it was and whether he should get up or not. No one knew much about John, what his last name was, where he'd come from, whether he'd ever been married and had children, or if he'd ever had any education. When I heard they'd found his body, I wondered: Did the old man leave anything other than himself and his worn out clothing? Did he meditate? Did he write? Was he a poet who wrote poems in the snow? What did he do all those years, alone, in such cold, dark solitude?

Ida was like a cat with many lives when it came to close calls and guns. You might recall that a young boy shot her in the back when she was but a girl, swimming through her life with the bullet still inside her. It damned near happened again eighteen years later in 1954 when we were living on the Island. She and Lou picked up friends for an evening out. The two guys hunkered in the back seat, one with a shotgun on his lap. The gun discharged, blowing a hole through the front passenger seat, barely missing my mother by just a few inches, exiting the car, leaving a six-inch hole in the door.

Fourteen years later, in 1968, on a crowded night at the Malemute, two men stood outside. They were checking out a newly purchased 30-06 Winchester, when the gun went off, the bullet, with enough force to bring down a moose, entered the front of the saloon, through the wall, hitting the edge of a metal folding chair leaning against the inside wall. Bits of shrapnel flew across the room, slightly injuring several customers. Nothing serious. By the time I arrived, an hour later, everything was as before—waiters rushing about, people laughing and drinking, Ida back on the piano.

I went back outside, stood on the porch in the dark. I could see the narrow beam of light coming from inside the saloon where the bullet had pierced the wooden boards. I bent down and peered through the hole. All I could see was the middle of my mother's back as she sat playing the piano. No one inside, of course, including Ida, had any idea how close she'd come to being shot, yet again. Had the chair been a quarter of an inch to the left, the bullet would have found its mark. I'm sure this third time would have done the job: No more Ida; No more ragtime; No more Cinnamon Screamers.

By early September, it was time to close up the saloon. We swept all the old sawdust in piles and took it outside, strained it through a wire mesh to retrieve whatever bills and coins the customers had dropped during the summer. We divided everything equally—a nice closing bonus.

Pearson drained all the plumbing in the hotel and saloon, boarded up the buildings, loaded his VW bus, and headed back to the lower forty-eight. My mother stayed the winter in one of the small cabins behind the hotel. The bartenders flew back to their respective states in time for hteior winter jobs.

By early September, the snows came in thick blankets of soft, white silence. I headed back to Georgia for my freshman year of college, beginning the University of Georgia around September 15th. I was assigned my dorm room and instructed where to find my classes. My roommate, a rich kid from Atlanta, and I didn't gee-haw at all. We didn't last more than a month. My second roommate, Ben, was an easy-going country boy from a small town near Athens and we hit it off fine.

I wasn't a good student. I didn't know how to study, having so often been moved about as a child. I'd attended too many different schools in too many places. I had difficulty focusing. But I did enjoy my art studies. It was here I met my closest friend, Larry Gray, with whom I shared the same work table in art class. He was a thin boy with red hair and penetrating green eyes. He had a lazy charm about him, and we shared a kindred spirit. Larry was remarkably talented, generous with his ideas and his friendship.

Beyond my art, I took away little that first year. I remember watching the Ku Klux Klan march down the avenue near the university. I remember hearing the Beatles for the first time, and I remember vividly the day our professor came into class and told us someone had just assassinated President Kennedy. We were devastated. Only a week before, his handsome young brother, Ted, had come down to speak to us about participating in American democracy.

At the end of my freshman year, I somehow knew I wouldn't stay in Georgia. My short three months in Alaska had changed me. I wanted to see a real winter, with its long nights, the deep snows in sub-zero weather, to see the Aurora Borealis light up the winter skies.

In May, I told my grandparents I'd be transferring to Fairbanks, even though I had no idea I'd be accepted. MaUdi didn't seem to be too disappointed with my decision. I think, in a way, she was glad I could provide a link between her and my mother. My grandmother never entirely approved of Ida being so far away, and, even though MaUdi wasn't religious or especially prudish, she could never get her head around my mother working in a saloon. I suspect she was mostly worried about what others thought, that the Malamute Saloon was not only a bar, but a brothel as well. When she wrote to her daughter, she always addressed her letters to Ida Lane, in care of the Malemute Club, Ester, Alaska.

A month after I applied for my transfer, I got a note from Professor Charles Davis, Head of the Music Department, congratulating me on being accepted into the music program. I worked a few months in Edison, got my ticket, and off I went.

When I was seven years old, I was standing behind my mother, watching her sew, fascinated with her hands guiding whatever she was making. I wondered how she knew which way to move the cloth, how she kept the mechanical needle from striking the pins that held the pieces together, or her fingers from getting jabbed by the robotic needle.

Without stopping or looking up, she asked, "What do you want to be when you grow up?"

"A painter," I shot back with a child's confidence, "or a singer. Maybe both."

Now, eleven years later, I was entering my second year of college, with studies in music and visual art. The University of Alaska, in 1965, had no art major, so I opted for music, focusing on voice studies.

But the following year I was able to carry a double art Major: Music and Art, spending most of my time in the Art Department, painting, printmaking, sculpture, and then I'd run next door for my voice lessons, choir practice, and music theory. Between these, I took classes in journalism, geology, and psychology. Recalling what a rough time I'd had with algebra, I stayed away from math.

I didn't have enough money to live on campus, so I rented an old travel trailer in Ester for $25.00 a month. I had just enough money from working at Cripple Creek to buy an old Chevy pickup that I named Neurosis; it was always hard to start. I soon traded down and got myself an even older truck, a dark green 1952 Ford panel. This one I liked better.

1965. My first full winter. It turned out to be a doozy. During all of December and half of January, the average temperature hovered around fifty degrees below zero with the last two weeks dropping to sixty below. It was surreal. I'd never experienced anything much below freezing. My truck, like all Alaskan vehicles, had a head bolt heater installed in the engine to keep it from freezing during the long cold nights and still turn over in the mornings.

My trailer was little more than an ice box. I'd crank the oil heater to its highest setting, but it never warmed inside. A pot of water left overnight on my stove would be solid ice by morning. I stayed bundled, slept in all my clothing, inside my sleeping bag, with more blankets on top.

Forget about bathing. I showered on campus.

My toilet was an outhouse, twenty yards from the trailer, half-buried in snow from October until May. Getting to it and using it was a challenge. I had to be quick and delicate. Moisture rose up through the hole, toward the ceiling, forming giant ice crystals coalescing into foot-long stalactites. With the slightest vibration from closing the door or pulling the light cord too vigorously, frozen daggers of ice would break loose and plummet down my shirt collar, sending cold shivers throughout my body. More than once I lay in bed at night dreaming of those warm beaches on St. Simons or hot summer days working in my grandmother's garden, wearing nothing but shorts, sweat pouring out of me.

When I'd finally get the courage to roll out of my warm bed, I'd rush outside, start the truck, run back inside and dress while the engine warmed. I'd layer up in long johns, wool shirts, and pants, a thick sweater, two pair of socks, insulated boots, and the military parka I'd bought at the Salvation Army Clothing Store. Then I'd grab my books and a small pack, and head for school.

I'd usually park near the men's dormitories, sneak upstairs into one of the showers, stand under the hot water until my body warmed, soap up, wash, and rinse again. It was heaven.

Occasionally, I'd stumble upon one of the guys in the shower, his erect penis bejeweled in shiny foam, capping off a potent dream. I'd linger as long as I could, copping looks as discreetly as possible, before drying, getting back into my clothes, heading up the hill to my first class around 10:00 a.m., still dark outside. I'd cut across the parking lot to the music building for music theory, and at about noon, the sky would have just barely lightened up. I'd head over to the cafeteria for lunch, sit around with a few friends for an hour. I'd look out of the windows: twilight. When my last class ended at 3 in the afternoon, it was already dark.

At the end of my first season in 1964, I'd seen my first Aurora Borealis, dancing on the far horizon in fingers of red, purple, and green light. It wasn't until the winter of my second year that I experienced a full cosmic display, shooting across the entire heavens from horizon to horizon. It was breathtaking. I can understand why earlier peoples, like the Dene, believed the Northern Lights were spirits of lost loved ones, dancing through the heavens in divine contentment.

In the summer and fall of 1966, I worked as a carpenter's assistant for the University's physical plant, doing a variety of jobs—construction, driving dump trucks for snow removal, concrete work, and for a few months, a tile setter's assistant.

One morning, I was standing around talking with a few carpenters when one old-timer pointed over my shoulder and said, "See that guy down the hall?"

"Yeah, Who's that?"

"Your new art teacher. He's working this summer to pay for shipping his family here."

"Really? him?" I said, pointing my head toward the guy. He was all togged in white, moving erratically up and down a ladder, alternately spinning left and right, holding a spackling knife, beating out a rhythm on the ladder, bouncing his head to some unheard music.

"Yep. That's your guy."

That first semester, he was Mr. Kesl. After that, he became just Lennie. We quickly gravitated toward each other. Lennie immediately captured me with his exuberance. He'd invite me to his home for dinners, with his wife and two children. It didn't take me long to realize what a remarkable spirit and magnetic teacher lived inside him. Back in the early 1950s, Lennie was intent on becoming a jazz recording artist and managed to get a contract with an L.A. studio owned by Frankie Lane. He was good enough. Lennie was a jazz purist, loved the old school, hated the new jazz of the fifties, so he left his dreams of recording, went back to school and finished his degree. He supported his family by teaching art, but Lennie never gave up performing, and he recorded a few LPs with some notable musicians.

Everyone on campus loved him. Well, not everyone. There were a few, who found Lennie too eccentric. He was that. And unfortunately, because he'd become so popular with his students, the Head of the Art Department became openly hostile and jealous of the student's affection for Lennie. So he fired him. We revolted, wrote letters to the University President, boycotted classes, marched on campus, but it didn't help. And Lennie, to his credit, wouldn't fight what we students felt was a rank injustice. He moved first to Havre and taught at MSU for a year. Ironically, at the same time, my grandmother's brother was teaching music there.

But for us, Lennie was gone, and I was at a loss. He'd kept me focused and without his living life as art, his steadfastness, and energy to guide me, I quickly began to flounder. I grew restless, confused, and more than a little depressed. What the hell was I to do now? Every day I seemed more and more lost, mired in a moody, complicated sexual self, often indistinguishable from my creative center, at least to me. I grew tired of pretending I was straight. I could do it, of course; I'd been doing it damn near my entire life. But I was suffocating, tired of making friends with young men I found attractive and then having to construct psychological fences to protect myself from discovery.

I was still living in Ester in a place a bit more spacious than the old trailer, but it was unfinished, the front windows covered with thin plastic sheeting, raw insulation on the walls still. One funky heater stood in the center of the main room. But it had a poorly designed flue. One late night, I woke with a start to my dog's barking. A thick pall of smoke hung throughout the house with tiny embers like little stars floating in the haze. I jumped up and quickly put out the fire, opened the front door, went outside until the room cleared. I moved out very soon afterward. Too dangerous. I had no idea how much so until three student friends rented the same house after I'd left. The same unusual occurrence happened to them, but, unfortunately, they didn't have a dog's bark to wake them soon enough. When the smoke finally roused them out of sleep, they panicked. Two of the guys flew into the living room then dove through the plastic-sheeted windows into the snow. When they broke the insulation barrier, the frigid air rushed in and fed the floating embers. The interior of the house exploded into flames. The two boys stood outside in the snow screaming for their friend to follow them, but he panicked. Terrified, and confused, he ran into the back room and hid in the closet. He didn't make it.

A month later, I was sharing a rented house with my friend Roy Blackwood and several other students near campus. I spent most of my time, however, in the art studio at school, struggling to do something with my art. I'd often work at night and found myself sneaking alcohol into the studio. I'd load up a coke can with whiskey and sip on it until I could barely see the canvas. I was a mess.

One early evening I returned home drunk. I could hear my roommates inside, laughing, having a good time, but I couldn't get in. The door was locked. I exploded. "Open this goddamned door!" No one came soon enough. I bellowed again, lost it, and punched out the large pane of glass in the door, reached in, and undid the lock, a technique I knew all too well. Blackwood, an ex-marine, finally came out to the porch. He tried his best to calm me, but I was too drunk, and I suppose, more than a little crazy. With no recourse, in a flash, he pinned me up against the wall, holding me six inches off the floor with his left arm. I watched his right fist cock backward.

He punched me in the head so hard I dropped like a rock. When I came to, blood was everywhere. Still, I continued to resist and curse. My roommates finally dragged me outside, wrestled me into the car, and drove me to the hospital. Lying on the emergency table, looking up at the doctor, I let go again. "Get the fuck away from me," I roared.

"OK. I will. I'll do just that. To hell with you," he said. He turned to grab his coat, heading for the door when my three roommates, bless them all, blocked his way. "Sew him up," they ordered. Reluctantly, he did, and the boys carted me back home. What a drunken pain I must have been.

The next day, in spite of a severely swollen head, a brow in stitches, both eyes purple as plums, still somewhat hungover, I felt a sense of relief, as if a heavy rock had slipped off my shoulders. Apparently, I'd unloaded a good bit of emotional pain, and enjoyed my reprieve for a few days. But the relief didn't last long. Over the summer, I began to suffer a strange, neurotic anomaly, expressed in a kind of visual tic. When I looked at objects moving toward me, I felt icepicks jabbing into my head. I had to close my eyes and turn away. It was weird and painful, and dangerous when it occurred while driving my truck.

As the weeks became months, I wobbled more and more out of kilter. I quit going to classes, quit thinking about my art and music, didn't show up for my voice lessons, avoided my friends altogether, and rarely went on campus. I'd become, as my grandfather liked to say, a lost ball in high weeds.

A few months later, in the early spring of 1978, I drove onto campus, parked, and sneaked into the Admin building. It was late; I knew the place would still be open but no one around. I just wanted to walk about, anywhere, out of the cold. The building was quiet. I walked down the hall, gazing into display cases on both sides, filled will trophies and awards, geological samples, posters of events, photographs, even a few paintings. All of a sudden, off to my right, taped on the back wall of one of the cases, was a poster-sized note, written in bold capital letters with a bright blue magic marker.

'WHATEVER HAPPENED TO GALEN GARWOOD?'

I froze. "That's me," I said out loud, wondering how long the poster had been there. Who could have written it? Who would have? Who cared enough to go to the trouble of sneaking it into the building, into the case? At the time, the question on the note seemed almost prescient. Was someone was trying to find me? But who? And why? I felt strangely exhilarated, and I remember asking myself, "What the hell's going on?"

I made it through the winter in my little village, while the world was protesting the Vietnamese war, racial unrest, and social inequities. The Summer of Love, with its long-haired youth, drugs, and sex was flooding across the country like a tsunami. I was never quite part of it, living so far away, but the movement eventually got to Fairbanks and even out to my small village of Ester.

I smoked my first marijuana that year, lying on the floor with my head between two speakers, listening to 'Sgt. Pepper's Lonely Hearts Club Band,' and only a month later, I dropped my first LSD.

I was in my old room at the Ester store when two friends stopped by with some good weed. We got pleasantly high. Then they pulled out a tiny strip of paper and handed it to me.

"What's that?" I asked.

"Acid. LSD. But we're not dropping. You are. We're here to guide you." They smiled.

"I'm not too sure now's the right time."

"Don't be silly, man, this is righteous shit, the best: Orange Sunshine."

I'd heard of it. I'd thought about it, what it would feel like, and where it might take me, wondering if I were capable of such a journey. I did trust these two guys. "Why not?" I thought, slipping the paper on my tongue, and falling back on my cot. We didn't talk, just sat and listened to music. I can still hear Three Dog Night's "One is the loneliest number that you'll ever do. Two can be as bad as one. It's the loneliest number since the number one." The lyrics crawled inside of me and it didn't take long before I was floating inside the music. Suddenly the room fell away and my friends with it. Gone. The room itself was gone. I rose above my body, looking down at my world of everything—memories, beliefs, fears, attitudes, desires. I started emptying myself, like cleaning closets of things long stored and forgotten, and I kept wondering why I had so much shit, why I needed this or that. 'Whys' flew out of me like a plague of insects, spiraling into orbits of space junk. When I was empty, I reached up and began pulling down and putting back only what I needed; things essential and sacred or what seemed so at the time. Eventually, of course, the LSD moved out of my system, but the experience was serenely cathartic. I walked about for days in a dream-state.

Several months later, at a party, someone gave me what they said was mescaline. "Hmmm, my horizons are expanding," I offered in thanks. I didn't know if it was mescaline; I'd never tried it, and didn't know what it was supposed to look like. But I was eager for another mind journey. As it turned out, whatever it was, I experienced something altogether different than with the 'Orange Sunshine.' I swallowed the capsule and drove back to Ester. It was full-on winter, around thirty below outside. I had no guides this time. I was on my own, in my little room, lying in my bed with the lights out, waiting for whatever was to be. After an hour, my whatever came rushing on, and it wasn't one of transcendental glory. No, it was a train of livid terror, looming out of a dark tunnel, quickly becoming gigantic, pulsating orbs of ugliness, as big as stars, pulsing and spinning in infinite space. Suddenly each one grew a face with a massive cavernous maw, opening wider and wider, then vomiting out copies of itself, each new orb of fire spinning toward me, shooting to the left and right side of me, their mouths grinning, belching out more copies.

I was terrified not only of their ferociousness but of trying to fathom my own size. How could I witness such vast immensity in such detail unless I were as large? I jumped up from my bed, switched on the light, thinking the hallucinations would disappear. They didn't. The creatures were as real as the walls of my room. In a panic, I ran to the door, well aware it was dangerously cold outside, but I had to escape. I thought maybe I could find someone in the village who could help me. As soon as I grabbed the door-knob, however, I heard a voice inside my head, "You know, Galen, if you think you need help, then you will, brother. Big time." I sighed and let go, turned back into the room, and fell across my bed, staring up at a burning world. As soon as I did, oddly enough, the creatures disappeared, or rather, they transformed into something else entirely: a breathtaking Aurora Borealis of energy spreading out into geometric colors and patterns, taking me with them.

I don't recall how long the trip lasted. Long enough. Over the following days and weeks, I began to re-gather some sense of purpose. I tempered my alcohol use considerably, and that visual tic with its icepicks of pain disappeared completely.

"Let's get out of here, Galen, let's bum around the globe. We'll start in Japan. I'll write. You take photographs," said Roy.

"Hey, Man, I'm more than ready. Let's go as soon as we can."

That summer I worked long hours at the Malamute to buy the plane ticket, a backpack, good boots, travel shirts, and a new camera.

A week before leaving, I had a farewell dinner with Ida in Ester. By this time, she was living with Ansgar Clausen in his two-room cabin. She wouldn't marry him for another ten years. Ansgar wasn't anything like Sam, Lou, Mac, or Don. That his name had more than one syllable might have done the trick. I don't know, but they stayed together until the end.

I was standing by the wood stove in the kitchen when she turned and said, "You know, I'm pretty sure Buddy (Gray's childhood nickname) likes boys instead of girls."

I already knew that, of course, even though Gray and I had never talked about our being gay. I looked down into my glass, swirling the ice cubes around, trying to find the right words. When I didn't respond, my mother said, "Well if that's he wants, it's fine with me."

I was about to respond, "It's not a question of what he wants, Mama, it's who he is." But I didn't say a word. I'd be giving too much of my secret away. I just nodded and finished my bourbon. Not until two years later did I realize my mother was setting a trap. For me. She was good at that.

Roy and I departed in September 1968, arriving first in Tokyo. What a shock it was coming from the sparsely populated state of Alaska, where there was less than one person for every square mile, to a city where the population density was six thousand times greater.

We checked into our room and began to discuss travel plans. We thought we had a good one. We'd fund our trip around the world by approaching the Honda Corporation, offering to do a series of global travel articles in exchange for a couple of motorbikes and a little money. It sounded good to us. The next day, Roy telephoned Honda's corporate office, and to our surprise and delight, we had an appointment.

The next day, we took a taxi to the heart of the Shinjuku District, jumped out at the Honda Building, went inside and gave our names.

Almost immediately we were escorted into the elevators and taken up to a plush office at the top of the building. Mr. Honda greeted us. He was a pleasant, older man. He looked up from his desk, smiled politely, "What can I do for you?"

Roy pitched the idea.

"So sorry," said Mr. Honda. "We contract such things out to a public relations company. But thank you for coming by." He stood and bowed.

We tried not to look disappointed. I'm not sure whether we believed we could, in fact, pull off such a bold proposal, but we were young and eager. We never expected to be standing in front of the CEO of Honda, that's for sure. We too bowed and turned to leave, slightly embarrassed. As we did, Mr. Honda called to us. "By the way," he asked, "I'm curious. How did you manage to get all the way up to my office?" We had no answer. We rolled our shoulders in an 'I don't know' gesture, smiled once more. Mr. Honda stood and bowed, we bowed, backed out of his office, and quickly headed for the elevators.

Because we had little money, we decided it'd be smart to hitchhike. Unfortunately, no one in Japan understood hitchhiking. Because transportation was efficient and inexpensive, those few who'd stop and pick us up, always drove us to the train station in the city we were trying to leave.

As we traveled through the country, I was astounded at the generosity and friendliness of the people, and never far from my thinking was the conflagration of the war that had occurred less than a generation earlier.

Roy and I landed in Nagoya for a week, staying at one of Japan's many youth hostels. Our second day there, we bumped into a Frenchman who was painting on the sidewalk. He seemed pleased with his success at getting people to stop and drop coins into his box. We exchanged travel stories, and I told him I was an art student.

"You should do this, man. The Japanese love it."

"OK, I'll give it a try," I said. Roy and I didn't have a lot of money and what we had was rapidly disappearing.

I bought some cheap pastels, found a small cardboard box, onto which we taped a sign: "College students from Alaska, traveling around the world. Thank you for your help." We then explored the city looking for a spot, one with lots of traffic. As we passed in front of the train station, I said, "Why not here?"

"Why not?" responded Roy. "it seems perfect."

Getting set up was embarrassing and awkward, having to crouch over and crawl about on my knees with a fist full of chalk. How do I crank up my imagination? But as I began pushing the chalk over the rough surface, I quickly forgot about the people watching. I relaxed. I got into it, and soon an image appeared, a woman's face, surrealistically rendered, starring up to the sky.

Blackwood sat on a nearby curb, reading his book, occasionally looking up. Then he disappeared behind the swelling crowd of onlookers.

Every time I heard a coin drop into our box, I pushed the chalk a little harder, a little more confidently. Soon there was a symphony of coins dropping. The people liked it, giving whatever they could, mostly money, but a few offered us food or flowers. One young man, knowing we were Americans, had apparently gone somewhere and found a hot dog for us, albeit filled with potato salad.

Halfway through my first attempt at performance art, I felt a tap on my shoulder. An older man, short, wearing thick glasses and an official-looking uniform, bent over and politely asked, "Do you speak English?"

I nodded yes.

He handed me a piece of paper, on which was written in English, "So sorry. You cannot do this here."

"OK, OK. Sorry." I said awkwardly, and scrabbled around on my knees, gathering up my chalks. I yelled at Roy to fetch the box of money, the flowers, and the food. We dropped everything into my pack and departed, saying a quick goodbye to the pastel face peering up from the concrete. The crowds quickly dispersed, running off just in time to make their train connections.

I'd apparently chosen the only place in Japan where such activity was strictly forbidden. My first attempt as a street artist was my last.

Weeks later, when Blackwood and I returned to Tokyo, we stopped off for a day in Nagoya. Walking out of the station, we crossed the same area, the same spot. I looked down, and there was my drawing, barely so, but peering up at me, waiting for the rains to set her free.

After Japan, we set our hopes next on Australia, but we didn't have enough money to secure a visa. We tried to book passage on a ship ferrying workers back to India. The agent shook his head, "No, I'm sorry. I can't sell you a ticket."

"Why not?" Blackwood asked.

"The food. You wouldn't be able to eat it. Too spicy. Sorry."

We weren't having much luck. We located a French ship sailing to Thailand, and we had just enough money to secure third-class tickets. We kicked about a couple of weeks until we set sail at the end of November 1968.

We made it across the China Sea in about ten days, stopping in Manila and Hong Kong. Our fellow third-class passengers were mostly students from all over the globe, most of whom spoke English. While third-class fare was the least expensive and offered considerably fewer perks, the shipping line was, after all, French; the food was superb with plenty of French Roast coffee, and wines for lunches and dinners.

Blackwood and I shared a small cabin with bunk beds in the bow of the ship. I took the top, and during rough seas, it was like sleeping on a roller-coaster. Everyone, at one time or another, suffered a bit of seasickness, but I never did.

On one late evening, unable to sleep, I left my cabin and went up to the foredeck. Not a soul anywhere. I crawled over chains, beyond the sign that read 'Do Not Trespass.' I would never usually do such a thing, but I had a compulsion to walk out to the tip of the prow and lean into the tropical wind, like Leo DiCaprio's Jack Dawson on the Titanic, but I was solo. I stood there in the warm wind, watching the moonlit sea breathe, rising and falling beneath a canopy of stars. Silver flashes of flying fish sparkled over the watery plains. Suddenly, I was stricken with an irresistible urge to leap into the sea. It wasn't the same emotional juggernaut I'd experienced years earlier when I was a young teenager, swallowing all of my mother's aspirins. I was at peace, calmly turning over the pages of my life's narrative, from earliest memory until that moment. What would it feel like to let go and tumble into the abyss? It was tempting, incredibly so, but was I serious? Part of me was, but mostly I was curious. That's all.

After a while, I said to myself, with some humor, "OK. Not yet, Galen. Give yourself another year." I turned and went back down to my room, climbed into bed and fell asleep.

After ten days at sea, our ship navigated up the Chao Phraya River and entered Bangkok, a crowded but slow-paced city, filled with exotic smells of incense and spicy foods, the king's palace and temples flashing gold in the distance.

On the journey over, we'd met an Australian rock band hoping to open a nightclub club somewhere near Sukhumvit. They needed someone to manage the place and wanted to know if Roy and I might be interested. We weren't, but we needed money, so we agreed, happily so since they offered to put us up in a small hotel for a few weeks until they could locate the right spot.

Our small hotel, on Soi Lang Nam, was, as it turned out, what's known as a 'short-time' hotel, where men could discreetly bring either prostitutes or women other than their wives. Additionally, a few young men who worked at the hotel floated about in various states of seduction, looking for whatever freelance possibilities might turn up.

Roy and I never discussed issues about sexuality, his or mine. Though once, without telling me, he arranged for a taxi driver to take us to a brothel located on the other side of the city. I think he just wanted to see what I'd do. I didn't say a word during the drive over. I sat and fidgeted. I'm sure Roy sensed my anxiety and discomfort and, at the last moment, he instructed the driver to turn around and take us back to the hotel. I don't know how I would have handled the situation, had he gone through with it. A sudden headache, maybe?

The Australians eventually changed their mind. We were on our own. A friend from Ester wired me twenty-five dollars, and with that, we rented a small one-room teak house, far out of the city. There was no furniture, no beds, so we slept in our sleeping bags on the floor. We sat around and smoked Thai grass we'd scored from one of the hotel boys. We told stories and stared at geckos that scurried about on the ceiling.

It soon got boring, and eventually, with no money, we knew we had to do something. We needed a plan. Before we could come up with one, however, we discovered our visas were nearly expired. We had to leave the country within twenty-four hours. If we didn't, we'd possibly be spending time in Thai immigration prison. Not good. Roy called his parents in Michigan, and they wired enough money for a flight home. We arrived in Los Angeles and headed straight across the Midwest, to Dearborn, Michigan, where I stayed

111

with Roy and his parents for several days. I could have stayed there perhaps and found work, but that didn't fit. I could have gone back to Alaska, but it was even colder there. I finally decided I'd hitchhike south and spend the summer in Edison.

Roy drove me out of town to Highway 41. We said goodbye, and that was the last time we'd see one another. I did reconnect with him in 2005 by email. He'd stayed true to his goals and eventually became Head of the Department of Journalism at a university on the East Coast.

I stood on the snowy edge of the highway with my thumb out, freezing. There wasn't much traffic, but after an hour, a car appeared down the road. I held my thumb up and prayed. A new model Chrysler slowed and pulled over. "Where you headed, buddy?" asked an older man, leaning toward the passenger window.

"Down to my grandparents in southeast Georgia."

"Well," he said, smiling, 'today's your lucky day. I just happen to be on my way to Florida, passing right through your neck of the woods. Hop on in, son."

I smiled and took a deep breath. Buddha Luck.

Y grandmother darted about her small kitchen, stirring the grits, turning over thick slices of smoked ham, cracking eggs into the same skillet, carefully basting them in the grease, just the way my grandfather liked his eggs. She spun around, handed me three plates, and pointed toward the drawer of tableware. "Grabs some forks and knives. Breakfast is almost ready. Get the spoons, too."

"Yes, Ma'am."

"Are you staying?" she asked.

"Ma'am?"

You're transferring back to the University of Georgia, aren't you?"

"No, Ma'am," I answered, putting the silverware next to the plates.

"What then? Aren't you going back to school?"

"I have a job back at the Malamute for the summer. I thought I'd head up to Alaska pretty soon, work for a while until I decide what I want to do."

She shook her head in disapproval, poured up the grits and pulled the biscuits from the oven.

My grandfather, dressed for work in his white short-sleeve shirt and khaki pants, sat quietly at his usual place at the end of the breakfast table, slurping his coffee, staring through the large window at birds fluttering about the feeder in the garden. He usually spoke no more than three words before breakfast, pointing his finger when he wanted something.

I'd been back in Edison a few months, helping MaUdi in the garden, running errands, and occasionally driving PaChuddy about on Saturdays and Sundays. I loved and respected my grandparents, but after living in Alaska and spending time in Japan and Thailand, my world had grown. I'd changed. But not Edison. It was still a small, southern town, charming and friendly if you were a white skin Christian heterosexual, preferably Baptist, and male.

One afternoon, standing in line behind three older white women at the corner grocery store, I heard one say to the other two, "I've told that 'nigger' boy time and time again, "If you wanna to talk to me, you come to my back door, you hear? Don't you ever come to my front door.'"

Her friends nodded in approval.

I was shocked. "Where the hell am I? What year is this?" I asked myself.

I started to say something and should have, but I didn't know what or even if I'd accomplish anything other than creating a scene, something for my grandmother to sort out after I was gone. It was my last week in Edison. I was ready to go and had been trying to come up with a plan, still uncertain where or what I wanted to be. Nothing was coming into focus. Another summer at the Malamute seemed like the best idea.

My grandmother drove me to the bus station a week later. I said my farewells, then headed back across the country, landing first in San Francisco. I had just enough money to survive on until work began in June. I rented a cheap room on Polk Street and spent a week bumming around the city. In 1969, San Francisco's parks seemed to be one grand celebration. People of every age, color, and costume were proudly celebrating peace, love, and sex, the smell of patchouli and marijuana wafting everywhere. I briefly considered staying, maybe looking for work, but finally decided I wasn't quite ready for the big city.

In early May, I caught a ride up to Seattle, took the Alaska ferry to Haines, then hitchhiked up to Fairbanks.

My mother was still living with Ansgar in Ester. Since Dredge #10 had closed, he was working for the Alaska State Highway, operating road graders and caterpillars. Before Ida showed up, his little house of two simple rooms, had only one table, four chairs, a bed and one black-and-white photograph that hung on the wall above where he had his simple meals. It was like a monk's cell. When I returned that spring, Ida had moved in her furniture, her clothing, boxes filled with sheet music, dishes, her mother's paintings, cooking paraphernalia, her old piano, and of course all those items she'd gotten from abandoned cabins over the years.

Ansgar loved my mother, but he preferred the sparseness of his earlier life. He never complained, though. It wouldn't do any good. But whenever she returned to Georgia for a visit, he'd slowly drag all of her 'stuff' outside, around to the back of his cabin, then haul, piece by piece, up the ladder, storing everything in the attic until she returned a month later. He did this for years until he got too old and decided it was easier just to relax and accept life in Ida's world.

Behind his two-room house, he'd built another log cabin for his wood-fired sauna. Every Saturday, families in the village would show up during the day, sit around his kitchen table, drink beer, and gossip until their turn to bathe came. They'd head into the sauna for an hour or two, sweat out the beer, maybe take a roll in the snow, dress, then hike back to their homes in time to make dinner.

My mother loved her simple village life. She played the piano at the saloon only rarely when they needed a fill-in. Ida preferred tending her garden, or she'd paint, crochet, and knit. But her favorite was still cooking. The one thing she'd managed to bring with her from the south was her collection of Gourmet Magazines. She had boxes of them.

On Summer days, she and Ansgar would climb into Ermintrude, his 1939 Ford Pick-up and drive around the village. The gearing mechanism was so antiquated that he could put it in low, step outside and walk along next to it, and pick up litter, the truck driving itself, slowly chugalugging down the road.

One winter morning, while preparing breakfast, Ida heard a noise outside. She looked out of the window and was shocked but delighted to see a moose fifteen feet away, rooting through her garden, digging up unharvested cabbages two feet below the snow.

A new pet, maybe? Thoughts of this possibility drove her giddy. She'd travel all the way into Fairbanks to buy old vegetables from the food stores several times a week. Every morning she'd lay out a feast in the driveway, stand in her kitchen and wait.

"Goddamn it, Ida," Ansgar snorted over his whiskey, grabbing a slice of pickled kohlrabi from a platter on the table, "that creature ain't some little Bambi, you know. She's dangerous as hell."

He knew, of course, whatever he said wouldn't matter a hill of beans. Ida did what she wanted to do, especially on such a mission as this. She kept at it for several weeks until driving into Fairbanks and the feeding chore itself became tedious and too expensive. As quickly as it began, her adventure ended. But not quite.

One morning a week later, a pounding on the door. Then again but much louder, like someone slamming a two-by-four against the side of the house. "Who's making so much racket?" Ida ran into the kitchen, slowly pulled back the curtains and peered out. There stood her moose, hungry and impatient. She opened the door, and the animal pushed its massive head into the room. My mother wasn't sure if she should scream out of fear or from utter delight. She quickly rummaged through the cupboards and the fridge for food. She found some oatmeal, a loaf of bread, and some lettuce, put it all into a large plastic tub, then set it beneath the moose.

115

The giant quickly devoured the food, then slowly backed out of the cabin and disappeared down the trail, beyond the birch trees.

That afternoon the weather changed. A Chinook blew in from the south. With a sudden shift in temperature, the snows began to melt, and the moose never came back. Ida was grateful it didn't. She knew it could be dangerous, to her and the moose as well. A lot of people had guns and used them, whether hunting season was officially open or not.

Even I was guilty of that, though unintentionally. I'd gotten myself an early model Remington .22 rifle that summer, not for hunting, but for occasional target practice with a friend who lived in the village. We mostly shot at old tin cans balanced on a log down at the landfill.

One late September, we were out hiking in the woods, close to the dredge pond, created years earlier by the digging of the gold dredge. The water was crystal clear, icy cold, and covered about five acres or more. Sitting high up on the bluff, I spied a wild duck far out in the center, swimming in circles, diving and dining on pond weeds.

I held my rifle up, aimed in the duck's direction, and even though I was well over two hundred yards away, I shot. I only meant to scare the bird into the air. But it didn't move. It didn't fly off. That's odd, I thought. I scooted down the bluff and around the far side of the pond to get a better look. I could now see the duck floating, its head and neck collapsed into the water. How could I hit something so small from so far away? And why would I even shoot? I had no intention of killing it, but I did. I felt terrible. I looked at my friend. "We have to get it. We need a retriever."

"Unh-uh. Not me, buddy. That water's too damn cold. Go for it."

I stripped down to my undershorts and waded in. The icy water damned near stopped my heart, but the sun had just risen above the hills, giving me enough courage to dive in. I swam out to the middle of the pond, located the duck. My bullet had pierced its neck. I brought it back to shore. I didn't carry it between my teeth, but the thought had occurred to me if I'd needed both arms for swimming. I didn't. I trudged out of the lake, shivering. I dried off, dressed, and we drove back to Ida's cabin in the village. I knocked on her door and when she answered, I held the dead duck up to her.

"Here." I offered.

"What's that?" she asked

"It's a duck."

"I can see that. But it's not hunting season."

"I know, I know. And I'm sorry. But it can't be wasted."

She took the bird and roasted it that evening.

A month later, I was hiking alone, near the same area, close to one of the tributary sloughs feeding the pond. I was surrounded by what the locals called 'the tailings,' mountains of rocky debris left by the dredging process. A few small, scraggly spruce trees had managed to push up through the desolate landscape.

I came to a bend in the trail, and there, just below me, a female moose was standing in the creek, pushing its massive head into the water, pulling up plants on which it feasted. Was it my mother's friend? I wondered.

Beneath the moose, swimming between its legs were three or four ducks, enjoying the leftovers.

I quietly moved down the bank and crouched at the edge of the water. The sun had just risen, cresting above the hillside, silhouetting the bodies of animal and birds, etching them in a corona of light. Droplets of water cascaded from the head of the moose, like a waterfall of golden pearls into the slough. The moose and the ducks, two vastly different species, dined peacefully together, completely unaware of my presence.

I sat for a long while watching this quiet pageantry of sharing unfold.

I found lodging once again in Moody's Mercantile Store, built in the early thirties. It was the closest source of merchandise—clothing, food, and whiskey—for the miners working and living around Ester Creek. My room, a small, windowless space, was upstairs in a maze of others, all connected to a narrow hallway which eventually led out to a porch then stairs down to the dirt road that ran through the village.

My shift at the Malamute began at eight pm. By ten o'clock, the saloon would be jam-packed, with hardly enough room for the waiters to move about with their trays of beer and bags of peanuts. As soon as the midnight show ended, the place emptied, and by three or four in the morning, only a few of us remained. We stood around for a nightcap, and then we'd venture out into the bright sunlight, off to wherever we were staying. Some of the waiters lived in the hotel, some in small cabins on the backside, and I'd head up the street to my little room.

My room was not much bigger than a closet, and the bed was more like an army cot, narrow and thin, the head of it shoved against the wall nearest the door, which I'd leave slightly ajar so a bit of light and air could slip inside.

During these rest periods, I wouldn't sleep at all. I'd drift into a state of what I can only describe as an interior calmness. I was intensely aware of the light entering my room, spreading across to the opposite wall, of sounds—dogs barking in the village, the occasional jet flying over, birds chirping, wind blowing through the birch trees.

I never thought about anything in particular.

After an hour, I'd rise, wholly refreshed, walk to the camp, shower, then dress in my black work pants, vest, white shirt, black western bow tie, and boots, with sleeve garters. I'd chat with the women in the hotel kitchen, have some dinner, then head off to the saloon; this was my routine, every day for three months.

One afternoon, lying in my room in this natural state of meditation, I became increasingly aware that perhaps someone was nearby, standing in the hall, just outside my door. I halfway rose and twisted around, "Who's there?" No answer.

I lay back, but the odd feeling remained. The presence of someone grew more and more intense. I was sure someone was now inside my room, standing above and behind me. I tried to sit up, but I couldn't move a muscle. My heartbeat quickened. Suddenly a hand covered my nose and mouth, squeezing my nostrils shut. I couldn't breathe. I struggled like a man drowning until, after considerable effort, I broke loose. Or did I? Maybe someone or something let go of me. That's how it felt.

Whatever the case, I sat up, gasping and sweating. I spun around looking for whoever was hovering behind me. There was no one, of course. The door was just as I had left it, slightly open, the same wedge of light entering the room. The outside sounds flooded in as before. Everything seemed the same.

I don't take much stock in ghosts, and the mind, I know, can shape our perceptions far beyond our ability to control or understand. Still, at the time, I mused upon the possibility that, perhaps, a disgruntled spirit, some tethered soul, was pleading for release, unhappy I'd taken up residence in this old building, in his or her room. But these thoughts were meant to amuse. It was easier, because, honestly, I couldn't explain it.

More than likely no one was there, no haunted spirit slipping across that threshold of darknesss into my room. Perhaps it was me, trying to break free from my restricted reality, into a higher state of consciousness, escaping what Plato called our 'cave of shadows,' in which we live chained to our limited sensory perceptions. Maybe. Even that sounds pretty far-fetched. At any rate, whoever or whatever it was, I shouldn't have struggled so much. I should have let go, just as I did the year before, in that same room when I was tripping on mescaline, gloriously riding the stellar skies.

This time I couldn't. This time I wasn't in control. Fear of dying was.

September brought the usual freeze and first snows. The Malamute closed for the season, and I moved down to Anchorage, living with my buddy Hank and his wife, Marion. I needed a job, and Hank asked his father, head of Alaska's Labor Union if he could find something for me.

"Absolutely," said his Pop. "I've got an opening down on the Aleutian. Good wage."

"Doing?" I asked Hank when he relayed the possibility.

"Well, you'd be working with a small crew, one or two men only, in a vertical tunnel over a mile down in the ground, something to do with a nuclear test."

I mulled that over for all of two seconds. "Anything else?"

Hank, who taught music in high school, laughed. "I don't blame you, man. I couldn't do that either. Pop said he also has a position stocking sheet-rock, right here in town. Better?"

"Yeah, much better."

The job was in a vast military housing complex outside the city. It was tough work, but I liked it. Six days a week, ten hours a day, an hour for lunch during which I'd eat my two sandwiches and read a few pages in a book, nap for ten minutes, then back to work, stocking twelve-foot long wallboard for almost three hundred units.

One Saturday evening I decided to go out for a little R&R. I headed down West Third Street and heard piano music coming from the Captain Cook Hotel. Inside was a cocktail bar in one corner of the lobby. The pianist, dressed in a tuxedo, played and sang to a group of customers sitting around a table shaped like a grand piano. I sat on the far side, nursing a cocktail, thinking about nothing in particular. Across from me, was an older man, perhaps in his mid-forties, smiling, trying to attract my attention.

Twenty minutes later, I got up, crossed the lobby and went into the men's room to take a leak. The guy followed me in, and stood to my right at the urinal, "Have you been to the gay bar in town?" he asked. I didn't look at him, but my brain did a flip. Gay bar? Here in Anchorage? Then I looked over at him, wondering at first what it was about me that made him assume I was gay. Pushing his luck, maybe? Even so, he had my attention. I was twenty-five. It was almost the beginning of 1970, and I'd never been inside a gay bar. I didn't want to sound naïve, nor confirm his assumption about my sexual proclivity, so I quickly shook my head no.

"You wanna go?" he whispered, in an almost conspiratorial way.

There was nothing about the guy that set off any bells. Still, I didn't want to seem impolite.

"No. Sorry, I can't," I said, drying my hands. But as I pulled open the door to leave, I turned and asked, "What's it called?"

"The Bonfire."

"Where is it?"

He looked at me and smiled. "It's just down the street, on Third, between G and F. Only a couple of blocks from here. Come on. Let's go."

"Thank you, sorry, but I can't. I...um...I have to meet friends. Thanks, though."

I went back to the lounge, listened to another song, finished my drink, then left the hotel. I headed down the ice-covered street, peering left and right, looking for the bar. I was excited but nervous. I'd lived in the 'closet' for so long that I didn't know what I'd find or what to expect or even how to act when or if I did stumble onto the Bonfire. I'd never been around openly gay people, none that I was aware of, other than a few anonymous encounters when there are few words spoken or none at all.

Fifteen minutes later, I saw it: a red neon sign 'The Bonfire,' floated above the door of a concrete block building set back about thirty yards from the street. I walked up to the front and peered through the large plate-glass window. I couldn't see much because of flyers, posters, and the accumulation of snow and ice. All I could see inside were silhouettes of bodies moving to the music. I stood in the cold for another minute, preparing myself. Finally, I opened the door, stepped inside. Men. Mostly young, everyone singing and swaying to Freda Payne's 'Band of Gold.'

The service bar was circular, about ten feet in diameter, with at least twenty mostly handsome guys of all ages leaning onto the bar top or into each other. There were five small tables on the right, and three tables next to the front windows, almost every seat in the place occupied. The bartender, a tall, heavy-set man with a loud voice, leaned across the bar and smiled.

"Hey honey, what's your pleasure?"

"Bourbon, straight up."

I picked up my drink, turned around and caught the eye of a young man sitting alone by the front window. He pulled his green military parka from the empty chair at his table and, with a nod and a smile, invited me to sit. "Hi, I'm Antonio. Call me Tony."

"No, I like Antonio," I said, smiling back. "I'm Galen, Hi."

"You been here before?"

"No. First time. You?

"A couple of times. It's crazy, ain't it?"

"What's crazy?

"I dunno—this place, these guys, the music, old Auntie Wayne."

"Auntie Wayne?"

Antonio nodded toward the bartender.

"Where're you from, Antonio?"

"Los Angeles. I'm L.A. military. My dad was Army. Now, look at me, up here in this god-forsaken cold and snow. You like it?"

"S'OK, I said. "Were you born in California?"

"Yeah, but my folks are from Mexico. We're Latino, amigo." He grinned across the table at me. "You wanna get out of here, go somewhere?"

"Sure," I said, casually nodding, trying not appear too excited as if I had plenty of other possibilities in front of me.

"Where?" I asked.

"I know a place."

We didn't even finish our drinks, just pushed up and headed out of the bar, turned right and after a few blocks, he led me into a small hotel.

Here I experienced my first full-fledged, unreserved, unabashed send-me-to-the moon sexual experience with another person. All my unfulfilled dreams, and those furtive, clumsy episodes—the boys on St. Simons, the spurious moments with Little Ricky, masturbating with Darrell in the cotton fields, wanting so much Nathan's gentle touch—everything became kindling for this beautiful bonfire of sex.

Afterward, utterly exhausted, we lay in that dingy room, smoking cigarettes, quietly talking about our lives, bantering about words and phrases I'd never been able to say to another person. We held on to each other for as long as we could. I didn't want to let him go, but he had to be back on base in a few hours. We showered, dressed, left the hotel and walked down to the corner. I watched him climb onto a bus and head out to Fort Wainright, and then I caught a bus home. I never saw Antonio again.

When my construction job ended, I started bartending at the Bonfire. Soon after that, I moved out of Hank and Marion's apartment and got my own. Only a few months earlier, the Bonfire had been a straight bar with a handful of regulars and not a lot of business. When the owner died, his widow took over until she could sell it. One afternoon a few gay guys came in during happy hour. The next day, a few more and before long, Anchorage had its first gay bar. Eileen seemed to enjoy this new group of men, and they liked her, although she was seldom there, relying on Wayne to manage the place. Disco music soon replaced Country Western, and the money rolled in.

I worked the late shift. It was long hours, and wages were paltry, but free drinks and fleshy perks made up for it. I had more sexual adventures than I could count or even remember, except for those few remarkable ones, like Jack from Amsterdam. He was young, incredibly handsome. I should have, but I didn't check his ID. I took his order, made his drink, and ignored my other customers, all of whom were screaming for complicated cocktails, while all I wanted to do was stare at Jack. I couldn't take my eyes off of him.

He finished his drink, leaned across the bar, and whispered, "Do you want to come to where I'm staying?"

"Sure. I get off duty in about three hours.

"No, I mean now."

"Now?"

He nodded.

I looked around at the crowd, then picked up the phone near the cash register and called Auntie Wayne. I knew he'd be at home watching his favorite TV show.

"Hey Wayne, you gotta come down to the bar."

"I can't, Honey. 'That Girl's' on."

"Wayne, please. Now. Take my shift for a few hours. I gotta leave. That's all I can say. Help me out here."

Wayne showed up in five minutes.

By April, I was exhausted, my libido damned near burned out. Cleaning up the bar late one evening, I realized I'd easily passed my not-so-serious one-year deadline, a promise to sort things out as I stood on the ship's prow above the China Sea. I laughed at how ridiculous it all sounded—I hadn't sorted anything out.

But, hallelujah! I was out.

Chapter Thirteen BIG HAMBURGER

Kenneth was sitting at the bar having his usual tequila and grapefruit, talking about poetry. It was early evening. He was a frequent customer and a wanna-be poet, a bright but unfocused man, relying mostly on the support of his wealthy family back in New York City. His father was a doctor, and his mother ran a successful theater company. Kenneth was on the heavy side, pale skin and light blue eyes. He'd studied literature, had dreams of writing, but that's about as far as he got. Too much 'speed' in his San Francisco days had diluted his creative drive as well as causing most of his hair to fall out. He'd moved up to Anchorage with his partner, and they operated a sign company somewhere in the city. Whatever relationship they had, I didn't know.

I liked Kenneth. I enjoyed his intelligence, his sharp wit, and pithy New York City sense of humor. He kept my work at the bar less tedious, and over the course of a few months, we developed a warm friendship. He knew I was restless, disenchanted with Anchorage, and with the Bonfire. "So, let's head south," he offered one afternoon.

"Like where?" I responded, wiping the bar down, getting set up for the evening crowd.

"I dunno, maybe Laguna Beach?"

Where's that? I asked.

He laughed. "California, man. Sunny beaches and seas of margaritas, no more snow. What do you think?"

"Sounds nice, Kenneth. Why not?"

I turned in my notice, and a week later we were on a flight down to San Francisco, his old stomping grounds, with a brief stop in Seattle, where I'd only driven through on my trip up to Alaska in 1969.

Seattle was known as 'The Queen City,' a phrase coined in 1869 to promote rapidly developing real estate, just before the Klondike Gold Rush, when everyone was heading up toward the Yukon. The name stuck until the gay tsunami came rushing up from San Francisco a century later. Sometime in the early 1980s, Seattle became 'The Emerald City.'

During those two weeks, Kenneth and I met some of the locals and checked out a few of the gay bars where I had a brief but explosive encounter with Scott, a charming young singer/pianist. After ten days, Kenneth and I flew on to San Francisco, then caught a bus down to Laguna Beach. We rented a small house and spent our days loafing about the beach and nights at the Little Shrimp. That was about it. After two weeks, I'd seen enough, had enough. The place was hardly like my childhood island off the Georgia coast: no marshes, no live oaks, no afternoon sweet tea, no lazy walks on a long beach. Here there seemed to be nothing but constant traffic blaring up and down the Pacific Coast Highway. I found the place uninspiring and not at all what I'd imagined.

"Ken," I complained one afternoon, "It is OK here, I guess. But there's not a damn thing to do but bars and beaches. There is only one road, and it's too hard to cross," I said jokingly. "I don't want to stay here. Besides, I need to get back to school. That's why I left Anchorage."

"So, where do you want to go? We could go back up to San Francisco. I have connections there. We could..."

"No," I interrupted, "I liked Seattle. I want to go back. You stay here if you'd like, but I'm out of here. I'm catching a bus up as soon as I can get a ticket."

I knew he wouldn't stay in Laguna Beach. We packed up and caught a bus north a few days later. All I had, the full extent of my possessions, was one suitcase and three small paintings I'd made in Anchorage.

Back in Seattle, Kenneth and I rented a small apartment on Twelfth and Denny. We had little money and no jobs, so I began looking for work the day after we arrived. After a few weeks, I scored work at the Mirabeau, an upscale French restaurant on the fiftieth floor of what was then Seattle's tallest building, SeaFirst Bank.

The Mirabeau took up the entire floor. It was huge. The kitchen had an Executive Head Chef, and below him, the Chef de Cuisine, the Sous Chef, and the Expediter, and beneath these came the head waiters, the waiters, and the dishwasher, and me, the pot washer.

When I arrived for work each morning, pots and pans were stacked four feet high on a large aluminum table next to a deep sink. No matter how fast I cleaned, the skillets, sauté and saucepans, mouse rings, and measuring devices kept on coming. I could barely keep up. It was such tedious work that each morning I'd set a goal to make sure the table didn't get too full. I scrubbed with a vengeance.

One day, I was sent one floor down to the bank's executive suite's dining room to deliver a plastic tub of wine glasses. While stacking them on shelves behind a service bar, I looked up saw an abstract painting on the wall. I knew the work. It was a Paul Jenkins, and a real beauty it was. Jenkins rose to fame in the late fifties and early sixties, part of the New York School. He'd developed an ingenious technique of using tools made of ivory to spread the paint around on the canvas, then drying into luminous veils of colors.

I stood there for minutes, captivated by the painting. It now seems ridiculously naïve, I know, but I remember saying to myself, "One day, you'll have your work in a place like this." I turned and went back up to the kitchen, to my dirty pots.

After a month, I'd had enough. The very next morning, on the bus ride in, I decided, "This is it. If anything isn't just right, if there's any deviation from my routine, anything at all, I'm quitting. I'm out of here." I rode the elevator up to the fiftieth floor, marched into the changing room and began changing into our designated kitchen scrubs. There was only one pair of pants left. When I pulled them on and looked down, the pant legs were at least eight inches above my ankles. "That's It! That's all I needed." I yelled. I pulled them off, threw them in a basket, climbed into my jeans, dashed out and into the elevator, down to the lobby. I ran outside and ducked into the first phone booth I could find. I called upstairs, changing my voice as best I could and asked to speak to the head chef. When he picked up, I said, "Hi, I'm Galen's roommate. He asked me to call you. He told me to tell you he was sorry, that he had to leave last night, had to fly up to Alaska. Some emergency. That's all he said."

"I'm sorry to hear that," the chef replied with concern. "You tell him to hurry back when you hear from him. He has a job here anytime he wants it. He's a good worker."

"Thank you," I almost blurted out, but caught myself.

"OK, I'll tell him." I hung up. I felt good my hard work was appreciated but terrible about leaving the way I did. I guess I should have done it better. I could have.

There was little chance of getting back to school anytime soon. I needed a job, something, anything besides washing pots. I reverted to what I'd done last. A week later, I stopped by The Greek Torch, a gay bar, and restaurant near Pioneer Square and chatted with the owner, Jack Novak, explaining that I'd tended bars in Alaska. I had experience. I walked out with a job, and after a few weeks, I was not only bartending but singing on sets with the club's pianist, a wild character by the name of Jerry Blaine. The job was OK. Jack was OK. But, I barely made enough to pay rent. With tips, I somehow managed, but that was about it.

Early one morning, as I was leaving work, walking toward my bus stop, I spotted a young man leaning just left of the entrance to the bar. He was tall, with blonde hair, and had a thin, agile body. When I looked over at him, he grinned broadly, pushed off the wall and started in behind me.

"What are you doing?" I asked.

"Going with you."

"Me?"

"Yeah. I've been waiting for you."

"For me?

"Why not?"

"OK, why me?"

"I saw you earlier down at the 614 and, well, I wanted to meet you. I asked the bartender, and he told me where you worked. Told me your name. Galen, right?"

I nodded. "What's yours?"

"Bobbi."

He was a freshman at the University of Washington and lived on campus, a military child, originally from Columbus, Georgia, but without a trace of the south in speech or manner. Bobbi was gregarious, had a quick mind with an odd sense of humor. We clicked right away. Within a week, we were spending all of our time together, strolling through the city, going to films and concerts. He'd spend a few nights a week with me, and on several occasions, Bobbi would sneak me into his dormitory room to spend the night, then out again out in the early morning. Before I knew it, he had me. I was in love.

About three or four months into what I thought would be this forever kind of thing, something happened, something I didn't expect, and it changed the rhythm. Bobbi slipped behind me one evening and whispered, "I want you to go to the baths with me."

"What do you mean?" I knew nothing about gay bathhouses. Not then. Once he explained the place to me, I said, "Nope. I can't do that, Bobbi. Don't ask me, please."

He wouldn't let up, kept pestering me like a mosquito until I finally relented. I wasn't happy about it, and I had no clue the bathhouses were such a big part of Bobbi's life.

We went on a Saturday night to a place called the Zodiac. I followed him to the front door, paid the club's admittance fee, and we headed to the lockers, undressed, then wrapped ourselves in towels. He dragged me around the halls, in and out of the dark rooms, or he'd disappear altogether for a lengthy spell. I tried to relax but was too anxious, brittle, and jealous. I'd sit in the corner of the darkened hall, pouting, cringing when he'd suddenly

126

appear with a young man in tow, only to disappear again. I hated it. After an hour, I left and took a taxi home. It shocked and saddened me to learn this had been his pattern of activity all the time we'd been together. I wanted what we had to be different. For me, he was all I needed, but, apparently, for him, I wasn't.

Still, I was helplessly under his spell. Whenever Bobbi was with me, I was putty. When he was away, I was miserable putty, thinking he might be having sex whenever and with whomever. I endured the agony for another four or five months until Bobbi left that spring on a class trip, traveling to Europe for the entire month of May. While he was gone, I began to repair my wobbly emotions, to reclaim my sense of self and was able to break the spell I'd been languishing in for too long. A week after his return, we met for a drink at the 614, a bar in Pioneer Square. "Bobbi, I can't do this any longer. I'm sorry. I just don't have the same feelings I had. We need to break up." He looked at me with hurt and disappointed but nodded OK. We didn't see each other after that, though I would occasionally run into him until he moved down to California in the late 1970s.

A few years later, I was in San Francisco for an exhibition I was having at the Tom Luttrell Gallery. I ran into Bobbi at a dance club in the Castro. We hugged and stood at the edge of the dance floor, trying our best to catch up on our lives. The noise was deafening. The blinding strobe lights impossibly distracting.

He leaned in close and whispered, "I have a disease, Galen."

"What do you mean?" What's wrong? You look OK to me."

"I don't know. Nobody knows. No one's seen it before. People are calling it the gay disease."

I knew nothing about it and wouldn't for another year. After an hour, I had to get back to where I was staying. "Bobbi, please take care of yourself. Let me know how you're doing. Let's stay in touch. I'll see you when I come back next year. Or let me know when you're coming to Seattle."

We hugged and said good-bye. A year later, in August 1983, Bobbi was on the cover of Newsweek. He'd become the official 'AIDS Poster Boy,' a community 'crier,' alerting the gay population and the public at large about the disease's swelling tidal wave. In the photograph, standing on a street in the Castro, trying to appear tough and proud, Bobbi looks bravely into the camera, almost as if he were daring death to take him, his left arm around his lover. The next time I saw him, he was lying in a casket at a small chapel in Tacoma.

Bobbi Campbell was the sixteenth person diagnosed with AIDS. He was only thirty-two when he died.

It was at the Greek Torch where I first met the boys from Villa Mae. They'd drop by the club once a week and spend a few hours during happy hour. I soon got to know all of them—Pat Nesser and Joe McGonagle, the leaders of the pack, Tom Olsen, the intellectual, and Hollis Day, the beautiful one; everyone loved Hollis, including me. Well, not love. Lust. He had an incredible sensuality about him. He never said much, always sitting in the corner, nodding and smiling, usually stoned. He seemed shy, but he wasn't.

There was Kenny, the creative force in the house. There was a tall, handsome guy everyone called 'Madeleine,' and three or four others whose names I don't recall. Villa Mae was known for its laid-back nights of parties, drugs, and sex. Pink Floyd or the Stones flooded the rooms while everyone tripped on Ecstasy, MDA, or LSD.

The year before I moved to Seattle, there was a festive Bastille celebration down in Pioneer Square. Francois Kissel, the owner of the Brasserie Pittsbourg, a local French restaurant, had lent the city an antique cannon to use for the festivities. Someone had the brilliant idea to load it with shredded newspaper so that when ignited, it would explode in a firework of confetti. Unfortunately, they left it outside for several nights before the event. It rained, and when they ignited the cannon, instead of confetti, a lethal and deadly ball exploded into the crowd, striking a young woman with such force, it severed her leg below the hip. She barely survived. Her name was Shelly, and she happened to be a friend of the Villa Mae boys. She eventually moved into the big house, convalescing under the care of a dozen gay men and when she was well enough, they'd take her out to the clubs, cradling her in their arms from one place to another. She adored it.

Shelly would eventually file suit against the City, Francoise Kissel, and the Pioneer Square Association for a goodly sum. She won, and with her settlement, Shelly bought an old building in downtown Seattle, just beneath the Alaskan Way Viaduct on South Washington. The boys had often talked about opening a gay bar, something different from anything Seattle had to offer. She let them use the main floor as the bar. They set about making plans, ripping out old walls, and renovating. Everything was going well. They were nearly done and had come up with what they thought was a perfect name for the place until they applied for their license. The authorizing official asked, 'What are you calling this establishment?"

"Yeah, we have a name. We're calling it, 'The Great White Swallow.'"

"The what?"

"The Great White Swal...."

"No, no, no, sorry guys. Nope, we can't allow that. You understand. Come up with something else."

Disappointed, but not deterred, they all huddled together to find a suitable name. It didn't take long before they had one: Shelly's Leg.

The place became a huge success, the Studio 54 of the Pacific Northwest, if not the entire west coast. Crowds were desperate to get in, lines around the block. Cutting edge music. And not just the gay population, but everybody wanted in. Every night the place was packed.

Conveniently, I had a back-door pass.

By 1979, however, Shelly's had become a haven for illegal drugs. One could buy anything for any state of mind, up, down, or sideways. The dealers, it seemed, controlled the traffic of the place, and the Villa Mae boys weren't happy about it. Pat Nesser called a meeting one evening, after hours. "OK, boys. Here's what we have to do. No more funky blues, no more disco, toss out the R&B and Rock & Roll. What we'll have—wait for it—is good old Country Western. That's all. I'm sure it'll work."

It did. Almost overnight. The drug dealers quickly disappeared. Unfortunately, except for a few gay cowboys from Ellensburg, so did everyone else. Within a few months, Shelly's Leg was history.

A few months before I left the Greek Torch, I received a letter from Ida. I'd written her a few weeks earlier and told her where I was working, though I never mentioned it was a gay club. In her letter, she indicated friends of hers were coming to Seattle and were planning to stop by and say hello.

Oh, Christ, I thought. What do I do now?

What I did, what so many daughters and sons have done, was to write 'the' letter. I sweated over it for a week. It included the usual, "None of this is your fault, don't blame yourself. I'm OK, blah, blah, blah." Two weeks later, while on shift at the Torch, the phone rang. I answered, "Afternoon, Greek Torch. How can I help you?"

There was a long pause. I heard the familiar Arctic static. Then, "This is your Mother," in a voice and tone that suggested no other possibility could exist or that I might have somehow forgotten who she was.

When I tried to respond, she interrupted, "Who did you think you were kidding, anyway?"

I squeaked out "Hi, Mama," but that's about all. There was a pause. Then, I suppose, to lighten her opening tone, Ida changed tenor, sounding less stern. "It doesn't matter, Honey, you know I love you, no matter what."

None of this left much room for discourse, so I just mumbled on a bit, thanking her for understanding. We moved into more mundane topics about weather, family, and holidays, and then we said good-bye. Later I suspected her earlier story about so-called friends dropping by the Greek Torch to

Feeding a Squirrel at Volunteer Park, Seattle, 1971

say hello was only a ruse, another one of her traps. It worked. While I was relieved, even delighted, to have this issue behind me, after it'd been in front of me my entire life, I couldn't help but wonder: Did she understand the definition of 'kidding'? Did she truly believe that lugging around this secret my entire life was a joke? I knew, of course, it was her way—the only way she knew how to make both of us feel comfortable, smoothing out an awkward subject. I wasn't ungrateful, but, still, it stung. I wanted to ask her, "If you knew I was gay, why in the hell didn't you ever speak to me about it? Why didn't you make some effort, even a little, to ease my conflict, since I'm sure it was obvious? And, by the way, just so you know, this pain I've carried inside me so long is not because I'm gay, dearest mother. No. It's because I had no one to express and confirm, or even celebrate, who I was, who I am."

If you're guessing I said none of these things, you're right. I didn't. I should have, but I didn't. I let it go.

A few weeks later, I'm sure after a few stiff drinks to amp up her courage, Ida called Gray, "Just spoke with your brother. He wrote me and told me he likes boys instead of girls."

A long pause.

"Do you?" She asked.

Gray would later call me from New Orleans, where he was teaching at Tulane. "Thanks, a helluva lot," he complained, laughing "I just sent Mama my letter."

A week later, she called her oldest son and told him what she'd learned. I don't know how she said it, what words she used to describe Gray and me. 'Gay' was not yet in her vocabulary, not for that meaning, and I doubt she would have used the word 'homosexual' or 'queer.'

Whatever term she used—Bernard didn't say. But he did say that she paused, then finally deadpanned, "Well, I guess two out of four ain't bad."

When my brother relayed her cryptic comment, I couldn't help but ask, "Which two?"

During this period of 1970 to 1972, while working at the Torch, singing more and more frequently with pianist Jerry Blaine, I decided I'd focus on a career in music. In which direction, I wasn't entirely sure. I began working on the piano, playing mostly by ear, writing ballads, both lyrics, and the music. I'd had years of practice with my voice, some acting experience, having played the part of Emile de Becque in Rodgers and Hammerstein's South Pacific back in 1968 at the University, plenty of practice performing for the crowds in the Malamute floorshows. When I was as young as nine, my cousin Camille and I performed musical skits outside my grandmother's house in Edison, for all her friends and neighbors. I had no problem whatsoever being in front of crowds.

At twenty-six I knew I had to make a choice. I couldn't wait much longer. I thought, why not. Go for it. I made a few demo tapes, had some PR photos taken, and that's about as far as I got. After a few months, I sat down one night and had a chat with myself. I was good at that. I chatted with the me who liked to sing and perform. Then I spoke to the other quieter, self-reflective me, the one who wanted to express himself through visual art, the one who quietly stood in his grandmother's studio when he was twelve, watching her dance around, happily daubing paint here and there on her canvas.

At the end of this inner dialogue, Number Two won. I buried the idea of being a singer or an actor. In some ways, it frightened me. I didn't believe I had the emotional resources nor the stamina to feed that part of the ego. I was afraid of losing something quiet and private. I buried the notion for good.

Soon after my decision, I quit working at the Greek Torch. I landed another bartending job at a place called the Macombo. I still couldn't afford to get back in school, but I'd been making art, mostly collages, in the basement of my funky old house I'd rented on Capitol Hill. Every time I walked about the city, I'd pick up derelict papers and pieces of cardboard that time, traffic, and weather had reshaped. I'd drag the litter back home and into my small studio, fascinated by its texture. It was cheap and had a history.

A bartender needs to be a therapist, a priest, and a confidant.

Customers showed up at the Macombo as soon as their workday ended. Quite a few older, single guys would sit at the bar and drink until they could barely walk, stagger into the restaurant for a meal, then catch a cab home.

I was a good bartender; I listened. I nodded. I smiled.

Not all my customers were older men. More interesting, younger folk would frequent the bar—a street person now and then, a few regular hustlers and the occasional 'tranny,' like Riley Morris, whom I'd befriended while still working at the Bonfire in Alaska. He was short, thin, with scraggly blond hair, a dark shadow of a beard that belied his original hair color. Riley always wore an overcoat that seemed five sizes too large.

"What do you do in Anchorage? I asked after he'd stopped by the Bonfire several times."

"I'm a dancer."

"A what?"

"A dancer. You know. I dance for a living."

"Oh. OK. What kind? I mean, where do you dance?"

"At the Rocket."

"You mean the strip joint down the street? The one for GIs?"

"Yeah, that's right. Come on down sometime and catch my show. My stage name is Sheila Rae," he said. I had a hard time picturing Riley as a Sheila. On my next night off, though, I took him up on his offer.

On stage, Sheila Rae seemed much taller. I suppose it was the high heels and her exaggerated beehive wig. She came out dressed in a see-through something which she quickly discarded, revealing breasts like ripe melons. With her arms out wide, she turned in slow-motion circles, as if to make sure her wig didn't topple over onto the floor. The customers, all rowdy young military guys, were screaming, 'Take it off! Take it off!" And she did. She slipped off her G-string, exposing what appeared to me to be a natural vagina, though admittedly I'd had little experience in that yard. The music ended, Sheila Rae quit spinning, blew kisses at the guys and backed off stage to a chorus of hoots and howls. I discreetly slipped out and went home.

Riley showed up at the Bonfire a few days later.

"Did you like it?" he asked.

"Well, it was impressive. I'll give you that. I didn't know you were a woman, though. "

"I'm not," he said. "I just like to dance like one, dress like one, too."

"Yeah, but, but..." I stuttered, pointing to his crotch.

He laughed. "Oh, that. That's my little mouse trick."

"Huh?"

"Well, see, first thing, I shave my pubic hair. Then I take this ping-pong ball attached to a short piece of fishing line, and the other end I tie to the end of my dick. Then I push the ball up my ass until my penis is tucked tightly underneath, in between. The entire package just...well, it kind of, you know, disappears.

"Finally, I take a little triangular patch of fake hair—my little mouse, I call it—and glue it on."

I wasn't sure I wanted to hear much more, and fortunately, one of my regulars was motioning for a drink. I did, though, halfway try to imagine the procedure. I couldn't help but admire Riley's ingenuity. Except, I wondered what if the little mouse had fallen away and the ping-pong ball popped out while he was on stage. I didn't ask Riley, but I'm sure that possibility crossed his mind more than a few times.

When Riley first moved to Seattle, he needed a place to crash, so Kenneth and I let him stay with us for several months. He'd appear in the kitchen in the late afternoon, sit at the table and begin his transformation. He'd spend three or four hours painfully plucking out the hairs on his face with tweezers, after which he'd apply an arsenal of facial emollients to subdue his tormented skin. There'd be a break and then came the makeup. At the beginning of this complicated and tortuous process, Riley's voice was Johnny Cash deep, but over the next several hours, his pitch got higher, more and more feminine, until, finally, when the big blonde wig went on, Riley was a fully-bloomed Sheila Rae.

Before we departed—the last time I saw Sheila Rae—she confessed that she was still unhappy, confused, and bitter. The physical transformation hadn't brought her what she imagined it would; it hadn't taken her to where she wanted to go. I didn't doubt it at all.

I was also fascinated with Daniel, one of the hustlers who frequented the Macombo on weekends. I doubt that was his real name. When I could, I'd glean as much about his trade as possible—his motivations and techniques, even his disappointments; the latter he'd never discuss. Daniel would sit at the bar and wait for an older man to buy him a drink. He'd smile, but not too much. He'd slip onto the stool next to Bob, or Pete, or Benny. Whomever. It didn't matter. After a little conversation, they'd disappear. Handsome Daniel was as cagey as a Trapdoor spider.

We became friends of a sort, never socializing beyond the bar.

"So, how do you go about it?" I asked. "I mean, say, if I wanted to, you know, how would I go about it?"

He laughed. I persevered, pushing a free drink across the bar. He took a sip, grew quiet, squinting his eyes, looking at himself in the mirror behind the bar.

"First of all, never use your real name. Never. And don't talk about yourself, less they ask. If they do, make up a story.

"And where? Where's the best spot, other than here?"

"Shit, Bro, you want all the answers. I dunno."

"Come on, man. You do, you know."

Daniel laughed. "Try First and Union, in front of Penny's, 'bout 7."

"What else?"

"Make sure he ain't a cop."

"How in the hell do I do that?"

"Ask. Cops gotta tell you."

"Really?"

Yep, if you ask, but you gotta ask right away."

I hadn't thought about that possibility.

"OK…and price?"

He grinned. "Depends."

I stored all of this in my head for a few months, mulling it over, wondering what it would feel like, whether I could pull it off. Then one day, I thought, what the hell, why not? My fascination had nothing to do with having sex. I didn't lack in that department. It wasn't the money. It was just—I don't know—satisfying curiosity, I guess.

The following evening, I took the bus downtown, walked over to the block between First and Second Avenues and stood around. I was wearing Levis, a T-shirt, and a dark leather jacket. Small crowds of people stood here and there, most of them waiting for buses. A few hustlers were already in place, casually walking up and down the sidewalk or leaning against the buildings, smoking, watching the cars slowly cruise up Pike. I staked out a spot by the street lamp and waited.

After ten minutes or so, a long, black Olds pulled up. The driver lowered the passenger window, leaned over and said, "How much?"

"This is it," I said to myself, nervous as hell, stepping up to the window. I answered, but it came out more like a question. "Forty bucks?"

The window quickly rose, and the car drove away.

"Seriously?" I mumbled to myself, disappointed and slightly embarrassed. I was about ready to go home when a smaller car pulled up. The driver leaned over and smiled. "What's up?" he asked, cheerfully.

"Not much."

"Want to go for a ride?"

"Yeah, sure, I guess."

"Are you a cop?" I quickly asked.

"No...are you?"

I shook my head no, and we both laughed.

"What's your name?" he asked.

"Kevin. What's yours?"

"Arnold. How much?"

"Forty," I answered, more confident this time.

"OK. Hop in, Kevin."

Once in his car, we didn't talk until we got to his house. We went inside, sat at the table in his kitchen and he fixed us a drink. The guy seemed pleasant and engaging. We had another round, double scotches. I kept waiting for my cue, not knowing how the arrangement would or should unfold. Arnold, however, wanted to talk—about himself, his job, his hobbies. Then he wanted to know about me—where I was born, how old I was, what I liked, where I lived. I tried my best to say little, to stay in character, but the scotch was messing me up. I was getting off-script. By the end of the second drink, I blurted out, "My name isn't Kevin."

He looked at me with a curious expression. "Really?" he laughed.

"It's Galen. I've never done this before, Arnold. I feel weird, man. I'm not what you think I am. I mean...sometimes I tend bar. Mostly I like...I'm in school, yeah, and, um, I like art. Sorry. I'm little drunk. Man, this is crazy."

I couldn't stop blathering. Arnold just sat and smiled.

If Daniel could have heard my confessions, I'm sure he'd have fallen off the barstool in a hoot-fit.

"That's great, no problem," Arnold responded, without seeming to care one way or the other

"Let's have another drink."

"No thanks, Arnold, I don't need any more alcohol. Honestly, man, I don't. And I need to go soon. Should we, you know, do this?" I asked nervously, having no idea what 'this' might wind up being.

"Yeah, yeah, sure," he said almost apologetically, getting up and putting his empty glass on the kitchen counter. "Let's go."

I followed him out of the kitchen, through the dining room, but instead of heading upstairs to a bedroom where I'd expected whatever was going to happen to happen, he stopped in the hallway by the front door.

"Stand right there and take your clothes off. Will you do that?"

"Here? By the front door?"

"Uh-huh. I'm just going to lie on the floor and look up at you while I... you know...take care of business. You don't have to do anything but stand there. OK?"

"Um...Yeah. I guess so," I stammered, thinking it all pretty damned weird. In a way, though, I was relieved my participation was limited.

In a flash, he was nearly naked, lying on the floor with his left hand tightly wrapped around the bottom baluster, his right struggling to free his swollen penis from his boxer shorts. Arnold looked up at me like a wild goat in heat.

I'd tossed my shirt on the table by the door, kicked off my shoes, and stepped out of my jeans, letting them crumble to the floor at my feet, just in case I might need a quick getaway. I stood there, awkward and naked, halfway expecting a troop of folks to burst through the front door or come cascading down the stairs in some kind orgiastic surprise. I tried pretending I was somewhere else. It didn't help. I stared at the crystal light fixture, while Arnold sweated and pounded away. Once he reached orgasm, his frenzied look suddenly disappeared, his face calmed and cooled down, back to its pasty white. He laughed, pulled himself up, and quickly slipped into his clothing. I jumped into mine and walked into the kitchen toward the back door, anxious to go.

"Where do you want me to take you?" he asked, coming up behind me, reaching around and discreetly slipping two bills into my front pocket.

"Anywhere downtown is great, Arnold."

He drove me into the city and stopped at the same corner where he'd picked me up. The crowds were gone. I opened the door and slid out.

"See you later," I said.

He looked me over for a few seconds, smiled, then said, "Goodnight, you big hamburger."

"Huh?" I didn't understand.

Arnold waved goodbye then drove up Pike Street. I headed over to the Macombo for a much-needed nightcap.

When I saw Daniel in the bar a week later, I didn't say a word about my adventure, nothing about Arnold. I didn't dare. I knew what he'd say: "Big hamburger? Are you kidding me?"

"So, what happened?" asked the detective, leaning over his desk, taking notes, writing in a small notebook.

"I'm not sure," I replied.

He looked up. "You don't remember?"

"No. Not really."

We were sitting in a tiny office at the Seattle police station. I was in a lot of pain and confused, struggling to recall anything from the previous night. Everything was murky.

"All I remember is sitting in my car when some guy suddenly pulled open the door, yanked me out, and started beating the hell out of me."

"Were you stopped? Maybe at a red light?' he asked.

"Yeah, that must have been it. I think. Yeah, I was at an intersection up on Broadway, waiting for the light to turn green. I remember now. The guy pulled me out, pushed me against my car and was pounding my head with his fists. That's about all I can remember. I'm still confused."

"OK, that's enough for now."

My interrogator got up and left the room. I was escorted back down the hall and locked into a holding cell, with about twenty men milling about, mostly young, either drunk, or hungover. I had no idea what time it was, but it was light outside.

An hour later, I was allowed to call my friend, Walker.

"Where the hell are you?" he asked.

"I'm in jail."

"Why? What happened?"

"That's what the detective asked me. I don't know, Walker. I just don't. All I know is I'm hurt. Come and get me. Please."

An hour or so later I was out of jail, being attended to by my doctor, Henry Kuharic, in his clinic up on First Hill.

"In addition to all your scratches and contusions—these are bad, Galen—you've got a severely dislocated shoulder. You'll need to rest for a few days. What about your head? Any headaches?"

"My head? It's a mess. Everything's a bit jumbled up."

Henry treated me as best he could, then gave me a prescription for pain and something to help me sleep. And sleep, I did. I was out for almost three days, waking only periodically. On the fifth day, images began to float in with patches of memory filling in the blank spots. Not until two weeks later, after subsequent conversations with the owner of the Macombo, was my brain more or less able to reconstruct the events of my twenty-seventh Halloween.

I'd ended my shift at the Macombo at 9 p.m. and decided to see what was happening elsewhere down in Pioneer Square. I strolled down to the Golden Horseshoe to have a drink. I stood around and chatted with a few friends, and then everything went dark and rubbery. Did my drink get laced with some potent recreational drug? Maybe. Whatever it was, it knocked me senseless. The bar, the people in the bar, and the music melted into one obscure ribbon of confusion.

The next thing I remember, I'm stumbling up the street, back to the Macombo. The place was locked. I beat on the door, and my boss finally came and opened it. When he saw the state I was in, he immediately called a taxi, and when it arrived, he walked me outside, helped me into the back seat, and instructed the driver to take me to my home address. I climbed in, and within five seconds I passed out, into oblivion. Then, after what seemed an infinity of time, I was abruptly ripped into consciousness. Some guy was dragging me out of what I then thought at the time was my car, pushing me up against the door, holding my neck with one hand, brutally beating my head back and forth with his other. Whatever chemical it is that shoots into the mind in those fight/flight situations came surging forth, shooting across my brain, pulling me out of my stupor, up through sobriety, and on into shock. I had no way to defend myself. I finally managed to break free and took off running down the street in a clumsy, slow-motion gait. The guy quickly caught up with me, tackled me, wrestled me onto my back and with his hands encircling my neck, started choking me while pounding my head against the asphalt.

I couldn't fight; I had no strength at all. I was sure my days on earth were nearing an end. But oddly enough, I wasn't afraid. I just gave in and became curiously observant, watching the end of my life unfold.

It was pitch black outside, except for a few distant house lights. I could hear traffic from a few blocks away, then the wailing of a siren, the loud squeal of tires, car doors opening and slamming shut, shoes running over the asphalt. There was a scuffle, a movement of bodies. I felt a release; my blood suddenly rushed back into my brain. Some neighbor must have called the police. I wasn't going to die, after all. But instead of being rescued, I was yanked up, dragged across the road, and slammed into the side of a police cruiser, my arms twisted behind me, then handcuffed.

The cops drove downtown to the city jail and tossed me into a cell, empty except for one other poor soul. He was a black man, heavyset and tall, about twenty-five, dressed in a blue sequined gown. He was wearing red high heels and a long, platinum wig, his face thickly painted with mascara and lipstick. He was staring at the floor when the two cops brought me in. I walked across the cell and leaned against the wall, trying to fathom it all.

The black man looked up at me with a sad 'You too?' smile.

"What'd they get you for?" he asked.

"I have no fucking idea," I mumbled.

"Uh-huh," he offered, "It's Halloween, that's for sure."

A month later, I had to report before a magistrate at night court.

My lawyer stood and asked my assailant, sitting on the bench in front of me, "Do you see the defendant here in the courtroom?"

The guy, looking a bit like a Neanderthal with bad tattoos, stood and stared around the courtroom, at one point right at me. He couldn't identify me and I sure as hell wouldn't have known him, except perhaps for his size and huge hands. "He ain't here; leastways I don't see him," said the cabbie.

"Mr. Garwood, do you have four dollars and fifty cents on your person?" asked the magistrate.

I stood. "Yes, Sir."

Alright then, go ahead and give it to the man in front of you, the guy who just stood up. The cabbie."

So, this was it: why I'd been arrested, accused of running off without paying my $4 cab fare. The charge, of course, was absurd, since I could barely walk. Still, I knew I'd put myself in this position, and I wanted it to be over. As I reached for my wallet, my lawyer interrupted.

"Excuse me, Your Honor, but if my client agrees to this arrangement, will the charges be expunged from his record?"

"No Sir, not at all."

"Then we decline," my lawyer said.

"Suit yourself," said the magistrate. "You'll be notified when to appear before a regular judge for trial."

Two months later, we were back in court. The prosecuting attorney in charge stood and looked around the room, then at his watch. He sat back down, frustrated, tapping his pen on his knee, looking toward the courtroom door. He was stalling for time. He shuffled a few papers, then looked up at the judge, "I'm sorry, Your Honor, but it appears our witness is a no-show."

The judge, a rather unpleasant sort, impatiently shook his head, then ordered me to stand. "I have a mind to rule in this case anyway," he growled, "I know how tough it is for taxi drivers, what nonsense they have to put up with."

I couldn't believe what I was hearing. I wanted to respond, but my attorney put his hand on my arm. "Wait. Just wait," he whispered.

The judge fiddled with some papers, looked up, then waving me out of his courtroom, said, " I wish I could, but I can't. Not without a witness. You can go."

Some months later, I learned the police had arrested, charged, and convicted this same cabbie for picking up a fare from a gay bar, driving him to some dark part of town, then thrashing him nearly to death, just to satisfy whatever demons festered inside his head.

Two of my regular patrons would arrive between 4:30 and 5:00 every afternoon except Sunday, always sit in the same two stools at the far end of the bar. One, whose name I remember as Bill, was of medium height, a bit on the heavy side with dark, wavy hair, silvery at the sideburns. The other man was Les Whaley. He was older, much taller, thin, and wore a generous mustache that helped soften his long, gloomy face. He smoked as determined as he drank.

Les and Bill were partners in a furniture refinishing business, located in the Maritime Building, down on Western Ave, just beneath the Alaskan Way Viaduct. Whether their relationship was more than that, I had no idea. Les did the refinishing and antique restoration, while Bill took care of the books. Neither man worked too hard, stopping around eleven in the morning for at least two martinis, sometimes three. After lunch, they'd nap for an hour, then work another few before they'd call it quits for the day. They'd head on over to the Macombo just in time for happy hour. Six days a week.

One afternoon, the three of us were tossing about our usual banter, when Les said, "You don't seem your usual self. What's up?"

I told them I was thinking of quitting the bar. I was tired of it, fed up with the drinking, the late hours, the whole damned scene.

"What would you say about working for me," Les said, "I need a strong, able-bodied helper."

"No Kidding?'

"I could use a helper," he said, "I just got a ton of merchandise that needs a lot of work. I need someone to handle the heavy stuff, the furniture stripping, the grunt work. If you want it, I'll train you."

I quit the Macombo the following week.

My new job was messy—paint thinners and furniture stripper seeping into every pore of my skin—but I didn't care. I didn't have to pretend to be interested in boring conversations. I didn't have to watch people drown their sorrows and frustration in alcohol; instead, I could work on my art in my studio at night.

I quickly learned the rudiments of antique restoration, and in no time, I knew one style of furniture from another, where a piece came from, and if it was an original or a copy.

The reason Les suddenly had so much work was that an antique dealer had recently opened a showroom in the same building, bringing in hundreds of items in various states of disrepair. Most of the furniture was either American Empire or Victorian, but mixed in were Queen Anne, William & Mary, a few Jacobean tables, and chairs. Several unusual, very early Italian painted pieces filled out the mix.

The dealer was John Cunningham, more of a shyster than anything. He could locate any style of furniture and always for less money. When he first began, he and his partner operated out of their Volkswagen bus. His clients, mostly local interior designers, would ring him up and ask for a particular style of table, a set of chairs or a sofa frame. A few days later, he'd call back. "I've got it, Bob. Meet me at 14th and Pike at 4:30 sharp." Bob would show up, and John would arrive a few minutes later in his old VW, drag the item onto the sidewalk, negotiate the deal, take the money, and drive off, usually before Bob, or whomever, had time to inspect the merchandise. If the chair turned out to be, well, not exactly the style or the period they thought they were getting, he'd call and complain. Cunningham's reply was always the same, "Don't worry, kiddo, you know me. You've got credit for your next purchase. Trust me, Bob."

And usually, they didn't worry, and they didn't care. With such low prices, they could quickly make a profit and then some.

Within a couple of years, Cunningham had two rooms of inventory upstairs in the Maritime Building and a showroom on the street level.

He soon discovered my talent for restoration, and within a month, he asked me to come work directly for him, while simultaneously terminating Les Whaley. I felt terrible about that, but I had no say in the matter. Besides I needed the work. Les had taught me a lot and Cunningham also, in ways that I found amusing if not valuable. I'd refinished a table

141

for a wealthy client in the Broadmoor area. Soon after we delivered it, the woman called to complain. "John, the color's not right. Too light. I don't like it. Come take it away and re-do it."

OK, Mrs. Fredricks, no problem." John replied.

We brought the table back to the shop.

"What now?" I asked John. Should I re-strip it?"

He looked at me and shook his head. "No, just leave it. Let it sit there for a few weeks. It'll darken by itself. Then we'll take it back."

She loved it.

As the months went by, Cunningham's business grew, and he turned over the bucks; he schemed his way into renting an expensive contemporary mansion on Queen Anne Avenue without paying rent for more than a year. No one had a clue how he managed his operations. He soon got his hands on a vintage Rolls Royce Motor Car and had his assistant, Jeremiah, chauffeur him about the city from one social event to another. Cunningham soon established strong connections to the elite designers in the city and from this finagled a contract supplying all the antiques for refurbishing the Governor's Mansion in Olympia, Washington.

A grand fundraising event was held at a stately mansion on Lake Washington with Governor Dan Evans in attendance.

John stopped by my work area one afternoon and suggested my friend and partner, Walker, and I attend.

I was suspicious. "How much, John?"

"$250 bucks, kiddo."

"$250?"

"A ticket," he said.

"Whoa, baby, that's too heavy for my wallet."

"Don't be silly, Galen. You'll get it back in contacts. Gotta build up your name, people need to get to know you. Trust me, kiddo."

John was short, hair as white as Queen Anne's Lace, and he wore heavy black-rimmed glasses that he was always pushing up the bridge of his nose. When excited, which was most of the time, he'd twitch his shoulders up and down, twisting his body and snapping his fingers. I never saw him still.

He was a born salesman. "You'll more than double your investment, Galen. You'll get new clients, meet the right people—rich people."

I caved in and agreed to go. But it was a lean few months afterward.

Walker and I arrived in our beat-up truck, discreetly parking sev
blocks away. We were escorted by the butler through the house, out
the terrace to mingle with the rest of the donors, all standing aroun
waiting to meet the Governor.

Cunningham, of course, was parked on the corner, sitting in the back
of his rented Rolls Royce, waiting. When the governor arrived, Cunningham had Jeremiah pull up immediately behind, as if he were part of the
official entourage. He never missed an opportunity.

I was slightly uncomfortable in this house of riches. I was also embarrassed because my rented tuxedo pants were too short, just like three
years earlier when I quit my job at the Mirabeau. I didn't cut and run,
though. Not this time.

Governor Dan strode through the front door with his wife. I stood
in the back watching him greet his supporters. Then something brought a
warm feeling to my heart. The Governor's tuxedo pants were even shorter
than mine, ending several inches above his ankles. I smiled, relaxed, and
began to move through the crowd feeling like I belonged there.

At one point during the evening, the governor and I stood off to
one side and chatted, mostly about his love of hiking in Washington's
State Parks. Then he was pulled away to encourage more contributions
for the restoration project. The night ended successfully, with plenty of
funds raised.

A year later, after completion, Governor Dan and his wife held another party, but this time in the Governor's Mansion. Walker and I drove
down to Olympia from Seattle, still in our old Ford van, deciding once
again to park as far away as possible. It was the Governor's house, after all.

Unfortunately, it didn't go as planned. A block away, Washington
State troopers had cordoned off all the streets and were controlling traffic. We were directed to pull up in front of the mansion's porte-cochere
where police officers, smartly dressed in their blue and gray uniforms,
stood, then parked the attendee's vehicles. We had no choice.

It was here, at this moment, one of the trickster gods decided to
satisfy their insatiable appetite for mischief. As soon as Walker shut the
engine, the van coughed and shuddered into what sounded like a death
rattle. A cloud of steam rose out of the radiator, and a torrent of bile
spewed out and across the pavement in front of the vehicle, staining the
concrete shit-brown. The troopers leaped back onto the sidewalk, and
Walker and I tried our best to pretend nothing out of the ordinary had
happened. We undid our seat belt and opened the doors to exit the van.

Except, when I lifted my handle, the entire door came off its hinges, dropping to the street with a loud 'kalunkaty-clunk.' I quickly grabbed the door before it toppled onto the pavement, struggling with both hands to hold it upright. I wiggled my body out, lifted it up and pushed it back into the frame.

"What the hell?" Walker hissed under his breath. We looked at each other incredulously. I raised my eyes, hoping to appease whichever god or gods were tormenting us, while silently cursing them. I mumbled an awkward apology to the troopers, and we dashed into the ceremony without looking back.

Once inside, we made a swift beeline for a young waiter moving through the crowd with trays loaded with flutes of champagne. Eventually, after several, I relaxed and forgot about our embarrassing entrance. I mingled with the designers and the local hoi polloi who stood about in the newly appointed rooms, laughing, gossiping, and waiting to meet Governor and Mrs. Dan Evans.

When I spotted him, I moved in close, shook his hand and said, "Good evening, Governor. Nice to see you again."

He responded as if he remembered me, although I doubt he did. I leaned in closer, "I especially want to thank you for last year."

"I'm sorry?"

"Governor, when we met at the Dulian's home a year ago, I'd been worried about my tuxedo pants being too short. But when you arrived, and yours were even shorter than mine, well, you put me quite at ease. I appreciated that."

He stared at me for a few seconds, perplexed, but then a smile slowly crept across his face. We laughed and emptied our glasses.

A few months later, I was in the workshop coating a chair with paint remover, when Cunningham walked in with a man dressed in an expensive-looking suit. He'd come to look at several chairs he'd purchased from Cunningham, chairs I'd recently restored. I was in my work overalls, wearing rubber gloves that came up to my elbows. Cunningham escorted him over to my end of the room and said, "Don, I'd like you to meet the young man who restored your chairs, Galen Garwood. He's also an artist, by the way.

Don smiled and extended his hand. I scrambled to remove my gloves.

"This is Don Foster, Galen. He owns one of the finest galleries in the Pacific Northwest."

We shook hands, and I turned back to my work.

The two men chatted a few minutes about the furniture, and how business was doing. Don said goodbye, and as he left, he stopped, spun around and asked me, "Do you have any slides of your work, Galen?"

"No, I don't. Just the works themselves."

"Well, if you can, bring a few of those to the gallery, show them to my director, David Mendoza. I'll tell him you're coming in."

He turned back and strode out, with Cunningham a step behind him, snapping his fingers, twisting his body left and right.

My head swam. I could hardly contain my excitement. I was terrified. I felt unprepared. I'd never shown anything to anyone in a gallery. Only to my friends, and to Lennie, of course.

I set up an appointment the next day, headed down to Foster/White Gallery, climbed the narrow stairs to the second floor, my arms loaded with about eight or nine small paper collages. Mendoza was in the back of the gallery. He was cordial and genuinely seemed to like my work. He asked me to leave them for a few days and said he'd get back to me.

A week later, he called to tell me that the gallery wanted to represent me, and they also wanted to give me an exhibition that coming fall. Everything changed. Finally, a foot in the door.

It wasn't long before I had my first real studio. It was a rat-hole of a place in an old building on the corner of First and Pike Street, across from Pike Place Market.

I was on the second floor, behind a T-shirt company, and above a porno theater. Across Pike Street was Gunther's Doughnut Shop and next door was Penny's. My studio had large plate-glass windows overlooking a narrow alley and into the Metropolitan Health Club, where Arnold Schwarzenegger would occasionally work out when he was visiting Seattle. I never saw him, but often there'd be three or four bodybuilders on break, staring through the windows at me as I painted. I'd look up, smile, and they'd smile, offering a thumbs-up before returning to their pumping iron. I'd go back to pushing paint.

It was here I created my first commission, a thirteen-foot-tall vertical triptych collage for C. Davis and Annette Weyerhaeuser, scions to the Pacific Northwest timber corporation. The painting was for their new home in Tacoma, still under construction.

Apparently, Annette had seen my work at Foster/White, liked it, and notified Jean Jongeward, who was the primary interior designer for

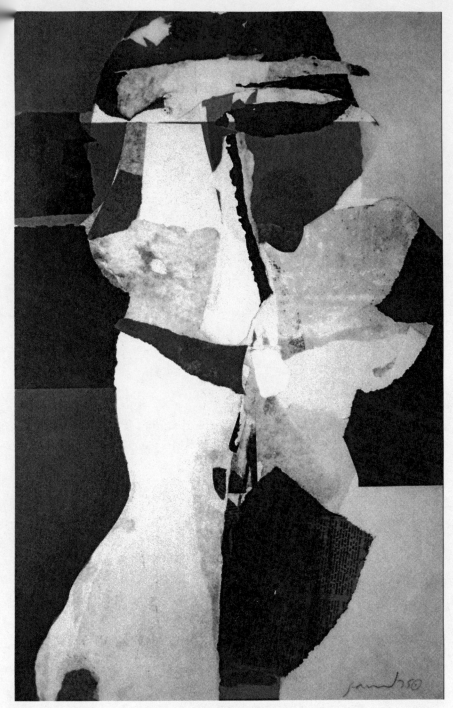

'Elected Angel Walking Away With Sleep,' collage, 34" x 20" 1975

'Yawing,' collage, 28" x 18"' 1980

the new home. Jean was Seattle's premier designer, brilliant but difficult. She sent a message via her staff that I should prepare a mockup of what I would create. I replied, "Sorry. I don't do mockups."

Her 'gofer' phoned me later that afternoon. "Jean insists you do the mockup."

"OK, OK." I threw something together, knowing full well that whatever I final work I ended up with would look considerably different than any mock-up. She didn't like it. She sent a curt note to the gallery: "What the hell is this kid doing?" Don relayed her message to me. I stewed on that for a couple of days and called him back.

"Sorry, Don, I can't do this. I won't do it."

I declined the commission, even though I badly needed the money.

Don called Jean, she called Annette, and a few days later, Annette called me. "Galen, would you reconsider doing the commission, if Jean were out of the picture? Just you and me. Would that work?"

That sounded better. I agreed, and the artwork began the following week. The location for the commission was to be in a high stairwell in their new home under construction in Tacoma. By the time I'd finished, the vertical triptych was too tall to stand upright in my studio; I had to lean it at an angle against one wall.

A week later, Don brought C. Davis and Annette to my studio. I was nervous. Thinking about Mr. and Mrs. Weyerhaeuser having to come to my ratty space, possibly having to side-step a few rats on their way up the stairs made me more than a little uncomfortable. When they arrived, C. Davis wasted no time. He strode into the studio, studied the artwork up close, then walked to the opposite end of the room and scrutinized it from a distance. Again, only inches away, he leaned in close. Then back to the other end. After twenty or thirty agonizing minutes, they left.

That evening Annette called me at my home. She was courteous but wanted to inform me that C. Davis felt uncomfortable with a particular shape. "We like the piece, Galen. We do, but C. David has a problem with something going on in the middle section. He feels it's a bit, well, too priapic for his taste. Would it be possible for you to change it, maybe add something else instead?"

I listened to what she had to say. I thought about it. Priapic forms were not uncommon in my work. Then again penis forms appeared just about everywhere. I couldn't quite grasp the issue.

I didn't want to disappoint or upset Don, and I certainly needed the money. However, I found myself saying, "I'm sorry, Annette, I can't change it." I could have, of course, and perhaps I was too precious about it. But then again, no. I didn't want to, and I still had the taste of

At work in the studio, First and Pike, Seattle, 1979

Jongeward's rude note sloshing around my head. I refused.

"I understand," she said, "and I appreciate your being candid with me. We'll accept it for now, and if we can't live with it, then we'll ask Don to find it another home."

"That's between you and Don, Annette, but I'll hope for the best."

We ended our conversation pleasantly, and the artwork remained covered in my studio for three months waiting for delivery. When their house was ready, a moving company trucked the work down to Tacoma. At the installation ceremony, Annette, Don Foster, Jean Jongeward, her staff, and I stood behind C. David, all nervously waiting for his response. Finally, he turned to me and shook my hand.

"Thank you! I like it, Galen. I do."

I don't know if he genuinely liked it or not. Maybe he did. Or perhaps what he appreciated was my unwillingness to alter it. I have no idea if the work is still there. For me, at the time, I was satisfied with what I'd made and happy with my decision. The entire episode, however, colored my thoughts about doing commissions. I would only do two more over the next forty-three years.

By 1980, I'd outgrown my studio on First and Pike. The place was vexing, depressing, and too noisy. The last straw came one afternoon

149

while looking out of my studio window onto Pike Street. I saw big Gunther, owner of the doughnut shop, drag some poor homeless man up the sidewalk and into the back alley. He opened the dumpster, threw him inside it, and slammed the lid shut. The poor man struggled to crawl out, but Gunther pushed him in deeper, turned and walked back into his shop to make another batch of doughnuts.

"It's time for me to get the hell out of here," I said to the window.

Before I left, however, I wanted to create one last work. It turned out to be a big one, an eight-feet high, thirty-two feet wide collage. I'd ask myself "Why are you doing this?" more than a few times. Partly, there was the challenge of it. I never imagined I would sell it. But I thought I might be able to use it to broker thirteen art credits I still needed for my Bachelor's Degree. To be honest, after having had several exhibitions at Foster/White Gallery, I didn't see much need for a degree, but I wanted to apply for a Prix de Rome that year, and for that, I needed the diploma. I called and made an appointment to see Val Wellman, Professor of Art at the University of Washington and asked if he would give me the credits I needed. "I don't see why not, Galen, but I'll have to see it finished. You know that. And I'll need to like it, of course," he explained.

"Yeah, sure, that's fair," I said, pleased that I wouldn't have to go back into a classroom setting. The next day I began building eight panels, each one four feet by eight feet, then bolted the pairs together, ending up with four eight feet square sections that I hung side by side. After several months, I called Val, and he returned to the studio, studied it for a while and said, "OK, I like it. Congratulations. You've got your thirteen credits."

Fortunately, 'The Wall' sold at my next Foster/White exhibition and the owner lent it to the Seattle Center Playhouse where it lived behind the bar for a few years until he officially donated it to Pacific Lutheran University in Tacoma.

The following summer, I received my diploma in the mail and immediately applied for the Fellowship. I didn't get the Fellowship, but at least I had my Bachelor's Degree.

Did I call my uncle in Santa Barbara, and announce, "See? It took a little while, Uncle Bud, but I did it. I told you I would." Of course not.

In the fall, I moved my studio uptown, leasing six thousand square feet on the second floor of an old building on 12th and Pike. The place was far too big for my needs, but I had this crazy idea I could restore it, divide it up, and sublet smaller spaces. I'd make enough to cover the expense of my studio. It took about six months of hard work. When I'd finished, I was able to sublet all the rooms to visual artists, a musician, a landscape design company, and a dancer. I also leased, for a while, the main central area to the young, chubby guru Maharaj Ji, whose zombie-like members kept enticing me to attend the meetings.

"No thanks," I'd always reply.

The entire three-year episode, thinking back on it, was probably a mistake. It wouldn't have been my first one. Nor my last. The rents from the studio complex at 1205 East Pike did, after all, pay for my space, but the managing of it became too distracting, too many personalities, and ultimately too expensive. Still, I did make art there.

Ida continued her life in Ester with Ansgar. They finally married after living together for more than a decade. She said she wanted to be sure this time. She was fully retired from playing piano, but would occasionally work at the Malamute if they needed her. She spent her days engaged in her various art projects, and, curiously enough, began to study piano again. She'd occasionally fly out to visit family members in Georgia, or me in Seattle. When she did leave, Ansgar, of course, relished his brief but temporary return to bachelorhood.

My father's and stepmother's children, Stephen, Clair, and Sharleen were grown and mostly 'out of the nest,' except for Shawn, the youngest. Sam and Ruby, at one point, moved to Southern California, both still working for Lockheed Corporation. With only one or two setbacks, my father remained sober until his death.

My brother, Bernard, his wife, Sherry, and sons, Reed and Lane, were still living in Albany, Georgia. Glenn was still living in Charleston, South Carolina, married with a son and daughter, beginning a successful career in the insurance industry.

Brother Gray was currently teaching at Tulane University in New Orleans. He'd become a highly respected scientist, a developmental psychologist, researcher, and had authored books on child psychology.

In the early 1980s, Gray received a Congressional Fellowship, left his teaching post at Tulane, and went to work for Democratic Congressman Pat Williams of Montana. Gray became Director of the Select Subcommittee on Education, writing legislation not only for disabled children but, as well, for the National Endowment for the Arts. I never asked him why those two seemingly divergent interests fell together.

151

In 1987, he traveled to Seattle with Congressman Williams and a few other national politicians to hold a conference on Federal Funding for the Arts funneled into city and state programs. Seattle had many enriching arts programs at the time, so it was a perfect model for the study.

I was then living in Port Townsend, Washington, so I drove over to Seattle to attend the conference and observe my brother at work. Gray sat next to Congressman Williams. It was my brother's job, as Counselor, to provide relevant questions for the Congressman to ask members of the panel.

When the conference ended, Gray called me over and introduced me to his boss. The Congressman was pleasant. We chatted a while, then he asked, "By the way, your brother tells me you're an artist. My son has an interest in art. What do you think? Would that be a good career choice?"

I struggled for an answer. I didn't have one, but finally offered up, "Well, Congressman, being an artist is not a choice, is it? It just is." He frowned a bit, looking as if he might ask me to elucidate, but Gray walked up, and the conversation shifted. It was lunchtime.

Gray, Congressman Williams, and the other politicians headed down to Alaskan Way to find a place to eat. I had to catch a ferry back to the Olympic Peninsula. I'd parked a few blocks away, close to the viaduct overlooking Puget Sound. At the time, I was driving an old beat-up station wagon I'd recently purchased from Danny Stewart, for a hundred bucks. Danny ran a small print gallery next to Foster/White, and we'd become close friends.

I used the van mostly to carry small paintings to and from the city. On the top, I lashed a large, coffin-shaped wooden box with a lid to keep any artworks from getting wet.

The vehicle was at least twenty years old. It had formerly belonged to Danny's aging aunt. On a visit to her home a year earlier, to see how she was getting along, he found her in the living room, sitting in her usual chair, facing her garden. She wasn't admiring the flowers. She was dead. Danny would eventually inherit, among a few other items, the station wagon, and in a moment of dark humor, he named the car, 'The Dead Woman.' So here I was, after attending the conference, cruising down Alaskan Way, off to catch my ferry, when I spotted a group of men huddled on the corner, waiting to cross. I quickly realized it was my brother and the delegation, waiting for the light to change.

The question the Congressman asked me earlier about whether being an artist is a good career choice rose up like a clarion as I headed toward the ferry in the Dead Woman. I was hoping I'd make the light before they spotted me. I didn't.

Coming to a stop about twenty feet from the group, I slouched as far down as I could without toppling over. I raised my head up just a little and peered over to my left. Gray and five others were huddled in a group, laughing about something. They didn't see me. Congressman Williams, standing apart, did. He looked first at the car, his eyes moving up from the broken tail lights, to the rickety crate tied to the top. Then our eyes met. A curious smile spread across his face as he raised his right arm, then wiggled his fingers like Curly from the Three Stooges. I waved back, smiling sheepishly while praying for the light to go green.

By the 1980s, I moved away from collage work and began working in oils. I was and still am an 'experimentalist.' I don't usually stick around in one arena long enough for anyone to pin a style on me. I produce a body of work, diving headfirst into whatever it was that excited me. I exhaust myself, take a break, and when I return to the studio, inevitably, my curiosities would have shifted elsewhere.

In 1982, I began a new series of works—animal forms painted on paper, using a medium I'd invented, partly from my furniture restoration processes. I liked the intensity that resulted. These primitive-like creatures came unexpectedly, galloping out of my subconscious. In three months, I had enough for an upcoming show at Foster/White.

I phoned Don and asked him to visit my studio, to look at the work. I had no idea what his response might be since I knew he was expecting something else entirely. He arrived late one afternoon, walked around, looking at one painting then another, nodding, but not saying much. After a painfully long time, he said, "You know, these are OK, Galen, but very different. I'm a bit concerned."

"Really? Why?" I asked.

"Well, because you have an obligation to people who've already collected your work, to those who've invested in you. They have expectations. You need to consider that."

I heard him. I understood what he said, but I didn't like what he said. It didn't feel right. It made no sense to me at all.

I responded as politely as I could, "Well, in my way of thinking, Don, my only obligation is to my search."

153

'Chinese Goat,' oil on paper, 34" x 60" 1980

"Of course, Galen, I understand. I respect that."

I'm sure Don anticipated my answer. He settled the issue by saying, "We shouldn't do the show in September. Let's hold off for a while. Let these works go down to your California show. We'll reschedule."

There were about twelve paintings on paper, approximately 30" x 40" in size, and they were shipped down for an exhibition at Tom Luttrell Gallery in San Francisco later that winter. While in storage, a strange thing began to happen. I came to the studio late one evening, and noticed the beginnings of a kind of crystallization occurring on the surface, probably having to do with the unconventional medium I'd used. I was startled at first. The paintings were changing, breathing on their own. My first impulse was to destroy them, but it then I thought, no, let them live.

Ironically, the show got a reasonably good review from Thomas Albright, art critic for the San Francisco Chronicle. However, he did criticize me for what he called sprinkling them with glitter. I didn't mind the criticism because I hadn't. What he saw, but didn't look at, were those ochre crystals organically growing out of the medium.

To my delight, the paintings did well; they all found homes.

Back in Seattle, after a short break, I returned to the studio. The show in San Francisco infused me with excitement. I got back to work, beating the brushes, pushing around the paint, calling for the animals. I was ready, but where were my animals? Gone. It was frustrating not being able to invoke even a little of their spirit. I had no recourse but to let my imagination out to pasture, to forage for a while. Something, I was confident, would eventually take shape.

Unfortunately, when images did appear, they weren't all pointing in the same direction. I found myself exploring three different possibilities. It was exciting, in a way, but confusing and somewhat aggravating, because I knew I'd soon have to make a choice. I had a show coming up.

Three images, with three different voices, leaned against the walls in the studio, each one demanding, "Me, Me, Me."

One late evening, I was listening to a recording of Saint-Saëns' Symphony No.3. As the first movement unfolded, my attention fell to one of three paintings, the beginning of an abstract landscape. When the *poco adagio* began, with its dirge-like pull, something happened. The music swept me from the room, into the painting, over the darkening plains, toward the stars. There was no longer a choice.

As the landscape paintings evolved over the course of weeks, I began adding a bas-relief grid of small circular points to the surface, using a thick polymer medium. Then I added a visible but subtle underlayment of drawing. Both became secondary illusionary devices, pushing the eye to focus back and forth between grid and far horizon, between one reality and another.

This entire series came during a time I was acquiring a piece of property in the mountains of Eastern Washington. I was driving around the Ellensburg area when I spotted a sign: 'Land for Sale. I had no money, but I took the long, unpaved road up to the property anyway. The parcel turned out to be ten acres of private land high inside the Kittitas National Forest. Everything—the views of the valley, the solitude, the spring-fed creek, the wildflowers, stately Ponderosa pines— seemed incredibly sublime. I had no idea of the price, but as I stood on the little knoll overlooking the valley below, I knew I was meant to be there. After several hours of walking the property lines, getting more and more excited, I drove back down and located the real estate office.

"How much is it?" I asked the agent.

"It's going for twenty-four. You can lock it up for a couple of grand. We'll help you finance it, set up a schedule for you."

'Pneuma-Shift I,' oil on paper, 60" x 40" 1982

"I'll take it," I responded.

And the money? I had no idea where I'd get it, but I knew I would. The land would be my solace and refuge for over a decade.

There were no utilities that high, and the property wasn't accessible during winter snows unless one was energetic enough to snowshoe up, which I did on several occasions. None of that mattered in the least. I drove over to the land as often as I could. That first season, I began creating paths across the steep slopes, building a sizeable wooden platform over the creek, more pathways from this spot to the far corner of the property where I crafted a second, smaller deck. This structure held a makeshift hot tub fashioned out of a cattle-watering container, large enough for two or three people. The water source came from a nearby spring, brought to the inner chamber of a discarded water heater I'd placed it on its side, rocked up high enough from the ground and under which I burned dead limbs from long-felled trees. I plumbed it so I could now run hot and cold water into the tub.

Beyond, the steep meadows and pine forests swept precipitously down toward the valley miles below.

At day's end, I'd hike across from the main deck to the bathing deck, collecting dried limbs as I went, then I'd build a fire, fill the tub and bask in hot water until dusk, sipping wine and reading a book until the sky's light disappeared.

It was from these skies, turning darker and bluer, with the first stars appearing, that I named my retreat, Galax, short for 'Galax Yo Feyes,' an anagram from the last three words of a poem by Plato: *I see you gazing my star, at the stars. If I were but the night skies that I might look upon you with a galaxy of eyes.*

This enshrouding light took hold of me, then carried me back across the mountains to the studio, and into the paintings.

Friend and painter, Ford Crull, and I were dashing out of MOMA one afternoon in the late 1970s. I had to hurry back to my friend's apartment, then do a bit of shopping at Balducci's in preparations for my last night's supper in New York City. I was scheduled to leave for Seattle early the next morning. The crowds were thick with as many people coming as going. Ford and I threaded our way out to the street. I looked up and coming directly toward me, chatting intensely to a woman walking at his side, was my dearest friend, my brother in spirit, Lennie Kesl, oblivious to everyone and everything, except the woman, of course. He loved women more than air. Lennie or L. Kesl or 'El Queso,' (The Cheese) as he sometimes referred to himself, happened to be visiting New York the same time I was.

I hadn't seen Lennie in three years. I began to break stride, preparing to reach out and surprise him, but I quickly saw the danger in that. I had an appointment in twenty minutes. I needed to shop, pack, and help my friend Monty prepare supper for my last night. I couldn't stop and just say, "Hey Lennie. It's nice to see you. Bye now." That would never do. Not with Lennie. The magnetism of his orbit was too powerful. I'd be spinning around him for hours, unable to free myself. I kept walking. We passed one another so close our shoulders almost touched. I was afraid he might look over and see me, but he didn't. I felt terrible, but I had no choice. A year later, on my next visit to his home in Gainesville, Florida, Lennie and I had a good laugh when I told him of our close encounter at MOMA.

It had been my habit since he left Fairbanks in 1968, to fly down every few years, usually during the summer, and spend weeks, sometimes a month or two, with him and his family.

From those earliest days in Alaska, when Lennie was my art professor, we'd talk incessantly about art and the making of it. I mostly listened, but, still, there was always an excitable exchange. In curious ways, Lennie was like a father, a brother, and often a son, yet he challenged me in ways that would ultimately help define who I am.

He was an exquisitely rare creature, a collector of any and everything, all the more so if it were free. Over the course of several decades, after his

Portrait of Lennie Kesl, Savannah, Georgia, ca. 2005

first wife left him, and with his children grown, I watched his 'disposaphobia' surge to the point where it was damn near impossible to move through his house and studios. The place was an impenetrable hodgepodge of paintings, old records, stacks of matte board, bicycles, objects he'd found in the street, dishes, frames, boxes, boxes, and more boxes. Stuff rose up from the floor to the ceiling, blocking out the light from the windows. There was only a narrow, meandering pathway connecting the rooms. When I visited, I almost needed a reservation to get from the kitchen to the bedroom.

Before long his studio became impossibly crowded. He built another, and that too became unusable. Lennie eventually painted works the size of post-cards on his kitchen stove until he rented a studio in a building downtown.

In 2002, I decided to make a film about Lennie, a feature documentary about his life and his work and titled it 'Cadmium Red Light,' his favorite color. It took me about four years and numerous trips back, but I finished it in 2007. It was well received and won First Place for Documentary at the Port Townsend International Film Festival that year. I last saw Lennie in 2010 and had plans to travel back in 2012. We talked briefly by phone in October about my visit. He said, in his parting words to me, "Don't forget about your painting. That's important." Such words from Lennie had always been protein for my soul, even when separated by a continent.

At eighty-six, Lennie was in good health, making art every day and once in a while still singing jazz with various bands around town.

Two or three weeks after our conversation, he'd been working in his uptown studio all day, then had to hurry back to a friend, Barbara's house. In his stocking feet, Lennie rushed up the stairs, holding a drawing in each hand. He slipped and toppled backward, hitting his head on the tile floor. He never regained consciousness.

What a grand life Lennie gave the world, and what a remarkable exit: Art in each hand and joy in his heart.

I was shocked and saddened by the news. I sat for a long while not believing it possible Lennie was no more, having held my friend so long as something unalterable.

If one needs to categorize, I'd say Lennie is a Renaissance spirit, housed in a 'School of Paris' template, often mistaken for a Primitive, but in actuality a Naïve. However, I don't believe Lennie could ever fit into any such definitions.

He loved the paintings of Masaccio, embraced the Expressionists, and was devoted to the Cubists. He cut his teeth on works by Matisse, Modigliani, and Kurt Schwitters. Lennie adored artists like David Smith, Joseph Cornell, and Bruce Conner, all of whom had been his friends. He also championed Outsider artists, such as his friend, Mr. Eddy. And that was just one tap into his visual world. When he veered into jazz, there was no end of Lennie in sight.

On my frequent visits, after dinners, we'd go on long walks down the sandy road that ran in front of his house. We tossed art back and forth like a beach ball.

When he had the ball, it was always bright yellow, or the color of a calm sea, or a boy in a boat, the sun floating in a blue sky, a woman descending, holding a small parachute; this was Lennie's world.

When I had the ball, it was a deep, diminished plum. I wanted to know too much. How do I hold onto art's many sides? How do I define its fuzzy, limitless pathways? How do I control its pull into and out of the darkness?

161

'*Marriage of Lucy Otakeo*,' *collage, 1989*

'*Woman and Cat,*' *acrylic, by Lennie Kesl, 1989*

I never asked Lennie these questions. He would have laughed at such stone-like musings.

In my kitchen, hangs a small collage by Lennie, one he gave me many years ago, one of my favorite Lennie Kesls, created in 1973.

On the bottom half is a frontal silhouette of a man's head with large ears—a self-portrait. Above his head, floats a tiny sun cut from gold metallic paper, and over this, a rainbow. Around the perimeter, in black ink, Lennie inscribed one of his favorite quotes, one he attributes to Modigliani: "Life is a gift of the few to the many, from those who know and have, to those who do not know and do not have."

I've often heard Lennie spin this out like a Shakespearean actor. However, it's not by Modigliani at all, but rather a quote by Gabriele D'Annunzio, one of Modigliani's favorite poets. I doubt Lennie was aware of this, nor especially that D'Annunzio was known as John the Baptist of Italian Fascism.

It doesn't matter, of course. For Lennie, it's those first four words—life is a gift—that meant so much, setting his heart and mind in motion.

About a year after I began showing at Foster/White Gallery in Seattle, Don Foster doubled the gallery's physical size and decided that opening exhibitions would feature two or three artists simultaneously.

Don phoned me one afternoon.

"Galen, why don't you pop by the gallery this week. Let's talk about a show." When I arrived, he suggested I plan on exhibiting some new works in September, along with two artists, one of whom was an American painter recently returned to Seattle after an illustrious career in France, John Franklin Koenig, particularly well-known for his abstract collage work.

I'd heard of him, of course, and was thrilled, even if a bit intimidated. Monsieur Koenig, as it turned out, was not happy about having to share. The show was John's celebrated homecoming vernissage, and he didn't expect to be showing with a young, untested artist. He confronted Don a few days before the opening, complaining that such an arrangement was unacceptable. "I have an international reputation, Don, and that this young man is also showing collage work. It's simply too much!"

I wasn't privy to this exchange, but gossip travels like bad air, and I soon heard about it.

Don, however, was a polished operator, always able to handle the most ruffled of egos. He set to work on John that evening and I, of course, would make every effort to humble myself appropriately. I was intent on learning from John what I could, and there was a lot.

As it eventually turned out, John and I developed a vital, lifelong friendship, one in which we shared ideas about art, people, food, and life in general, and on all of which he had robust opinions.

Some folks found him difficult, and, indeed, he could seem arrogant and stubborn. But he was intelligent, intuitive, and remarkably creative. He was also generous and willing to share his world, one much larger than I'd yet experienced.

A decade later, we would even share property: Galax, the land I'd previously purchased, nestled inside the Kittitas National Forest in Eastern Washington and also land in Port Townsend. Galax was high and steep, dry in the hot summers with vast meadows of lupine, paintbrush, and wild

John Franklin Koenig, Nancray, France, 1993, photograph by Claire Koenig

larkspur. In winter, deep snow and solitude blanketed everything. Frigid water from melted runoff filled the creek that zigzagged down the middle of the acreage.

John adored the place. Right away, he began to build his campsite, in proper Koenig fashion, on a steep incline overlooking the valley. On these first few visits, he constructed a rickety structure suitable for sleeping. The fact that it was far from level didn't seem to matter at all.

In the late 1980s, John curated 'Seattle Style,' an exhibition of eight Pacific Northwest artists traveling to five museums in Southern France. It was a remarkable trip for all of us, and the highlight for me occurred in the small town of Saint-Paul de Vence, near the port city of Nice. Our group of participating artists had been invited to lunch at the legendary restaurant, La Colombe d'Or, hosted by an American artist who now lived in France. The restaurant was in a beautiful old stone building with an open-air terrace on the second level. It originally opened in the 1920s as Chez Robinson but was later renamed.

It quickly became a fashionable spot for locals and celebrities alike, and artists like Picasso, Chagall, Miro, and Braque paid for their meals with art, their paintings hung throughout the restaurant. Our group sat outside on the terrace at a long table covered in white linen, adorned with bouquets of flow-

John Franklin Koenig 'Liebestraum' mixed media collage 10.5" x 9.5" 1974

ers. Handsome, young waiters dashed about with carafes of wine and platters of food. Once we were all sitting, John stood and clinked his glass with a fork. "I'd like all of you meet our generous host: Monsieur Paul Jenkins."

"Paul Jenkins?" I was bowled over. Could it be? It was. Sitting directly across the table from me was the very same Paul Jenkins, whose painting hung in the conference room at SeaFirst Bank when I was washing pots at Seattle's Mirabeau fifteen years earlier.

I told him my story, of course. How could I not?

In the early 1990s, I visited John several times at his Paris apartment across from the Gare du Montparnasse. On my last visit, after a week in this bastion of culture and light, we set out on a road trip to Carcassone, with its famous medieval town, La Cité, still standing in the shadows of the Pyrenees. We were entirely on John's clock, rose late, had a leisurely breakfast, and were on the road by 10 a.m.

We left late morning in John's little white Citroen. I was keenly aware that John had just learned to drive a car, and getting out of Paris with John at the wheel was a nail-biting and perilous adventure. However, once we got into the countryside, one of the most delightful trips I'd ever encountered unfolded. At mid-day, John would mosey the car into some little 12th-century village where we'd procure the right cheese, a perfect patè, and 'Du pain à la boulangerie.' Almost anywhere, we'd find good, but not too expensive, wine. We'd drive on until we found the perfect spot for a picnic, dine leisurely by a quiet copse of trees and a gentle creek, then back on the road by 3 p.m. We'd stop at another small village two hours later and look for lodging.

We would check in to our rooms, have a brief nap, followed by a bath, explore the village, return to the hotel for an aperitif, and finally, a simple supper with more wine and conversation. Bed by midnight. I was in John's slow-paced world. He wrote the manual on 'stress-free' living.

France is a country smaller than Texas and getting from Paris to Carcassonne can comfortably be done in a day. We spent three, meandering through a succession of medieval churches, small museums, and markets, discussing everything from sauerkraut to Kant.

John Franklin had a voracious appetite for all subjects and unswayable opinions about everything. He had little tolerance for the pedestrian mind, but he was passionate for humankind, as excited by Japanese Noh as he was charmed by American rodeos.

Our second day ended in the ancient village of Conques, existing much as it did when the Crusaders camped within the Sainte-Foy Abbey on their march down to Santiago de Compostela during the 12th century. In the morning, a soft rain fell, enshrouding the hillside gardens and darkening the stone roofs. Another leisurely 'petit dejeuner' in the old castle, and off we went in his little, white Citroen, winding through the morning mist toward Rodez.

In his book, The Gift, American poet and essayist, Lewis Hyde, describes the creative spirit as 'gift exchange.' About Walt Whitman, Hyde writes, "Enthusiasts, having received a spirit into the body, having never been hesitant to describe their spiritual knowledge in terms of the flesh, to speak of 'a sweet burning of the heart' or, of a ravaged soul, Whitman is no exception... He takes his own body to be the font of his religion."

Like Whitman, John Franklin's legacy is, to a great extent, a remarkable trajectory of self-fulfilling prophecy.

As John often said to me, "Making art is hard work." That it is, and he meant far more than just making the painting.

John related his only meeting with Morris Graves. It was a dinner for six in Seattle during the early part of the sixties. Morris had been talking about Taoism. John Franklin offered a few comments on the subject but pronounced the word with a T, as in Taos, New Mexico. Morris immediately corrected his mispronunciation with a loud "Tao is with a D!"

John Franklin smiled, nodded politely, acquiescing to the elder master.

After dinner, When Morris and his friend were leaving, John slipped a note into Morris' pocket: 'D or T. Does it truly matter?'

John could weaken a pit bull's grip, so tenacious he was in making right what he perceived as wrong.

We pulled into Carcassonne late on our third day of travel, checked into a hotel and then set out for one of his favorite restaurants, famous for its 'agneau cassoulet.' We were sitting outside, on a stone terrace, overlooking the Old Cité, beneath a starry night, not unlike, I suppose, the one Vincent had painted a century earlier, and Arles was not that far away. Just as the waiter brought our food, John suddenly left the table for a lengthy phone conversation with a representative from the local museum. When he finally returned, twenty minutes later, he took a mouthful of cassoulet, made a face, called the waiter over and complained.

The waiter, a short, thin man with a reedy voice, gestured wildly with his arm. He spewed out an indignant stream of venom while pointing toward the house phones.

"What on earth did you say to him?" I asked.

"Well, I simply complained that my cassoulet was too cold."

He smiled devilishly. "Have some more wine, my dear," he said, holding the bottle to the stars.

Chapter Seventeen **WIZARD OF DIVINE MADNESS**

"Wake up! Get up. We're late. We're supposed to be somewhere in thirty minutes," Gene Ramey sang through the guest room door where I lay compressed in a cocoon of sleep. The night before he'd taken us out to several San Francisco watering holes and God knows where else, places my grandmother couldn't have imagined if she'd lived another two hundred years. Even I had never seen anything quite like these bars, and I'd seen a lot.

It was nearly six in the morning when we got back to his house on Page Street. I do recall our stopping off at Nob Hill Theater to watch a performance by the well-known porn actor, Scot O'Hara. He was impressive. Scot came out afterward, and the three of us stood outside and chatted at length. Eventually, Scot and I became close friends, and he'd occasionally visit me in Port Townsend. Once he even helped me pour concrete for my new studio foundation, from which he took much satisfaction, working with his hands instead of his penis.

While he was undoubtedly a provocative exhibitionist, he was also a thoughtful young man, a good writer, and had a generous spirit. Unfortunately, his chosen profession and longevity were not necessarily good bedmates. I remember receiving a letter from Scot in early February of 1998 in which he wrote, "By the time you read this, I'll be no more."

That was Scot, to a T. He died of AIDS that late February.

I struggled to open my eyes. I slowly focused on the clock. 9 am. "What?" I mumbled from under my pillow. "Why?" I yelled, "it's too damned early, Gene."

"We're invited to a special brunch. Get up lazy bones."

I pried myself loose from the bed, showered and dressed, swigged down as much French Roast as I could before treading down the stairs, out into a morning too bright. I wanted to go back to sleep and cover my head, which felt like it'd been rolling around in a bag of hammers.

Gene crossed Golden Gate Bridge, dropped down into Sausalito, over to the bay, to an area of moored houseboats.

171

Portrait of James Broughton, photograph by Joel Singer, ca. 1982

Don't Trip
on the leaps of your life
Jump
The traces need kicking
over   and over

Trust your inevitable
Trust your ripcord
Jump
into the No
even if it kills you.

James Broughton

By this time, I'd recovered. Somewhat. "Where are we going?"
We're going to Alan Watt's houseboat."
"Alan Watts? The beat philosopher? He's still alive?"
"No, but his home, or boat, is part of the Alan Watts Foundation.
We're going there to celebrate the return of Alan's friend. Mine too."
And who might that be?"
Gene was slowly doling out the information. Wisely so. I was still
drying out my brain.
"James Broughton. Have you heard of him?"
I had not.
"James is a celebrated poet and filmmaker, considered the grandfa-
ther of Avant-guarde Cinema. He and his young companion, Joel Sing-
er, are returning from a lengthy stay in Sri Lanka."
We arrived a bit early. Our host, and also President of the Alan
Watts Foundation, Ruth Costello, greeted us at the door, showed us
inside where we waited for the guests of honor to arrive. At 11 a.m.,
they appeared.

James was medium in height, mid-sixties, sporting a thick white beard, with his 'bright eyes and bushy brows.' He looked as if he'd stepped right out of Tolkien's *Lord of The Rings*. Joel, also bearded, was in his early thirties, dark features and alluringly handsome.

Altogether, there were eight of us sitting around a large table. All day, James regaled us with poems and stories, while Ruth continually replenished the table with food, champagne, and wine, the room glowing with merriment long into the night; we didn't depart for the city until after 11 p.m.

A few days later, I returned to Seattle, my head filled with James Broughton. I knew James would become a significant part of my life. Soon afterward, I collaborated with him on his books, *Graffiti for the Johns of Heaven*, (Syzygy Press, 1982) and *Ecstasies* (Syzygy Press, 1983).

After James and Joel returned to the United States, they moved to Novato, California, and then, eventually, to my great surprise and delight, they left their California nest and relocated in Port Townsend. It was here where our friendship, over the years, mellowed into a lovely Bouillabaisse of art, film, and poetry.

In early 1999, while I was filming 'Cadmium Red Light,' I also made the short documentary, 'Letters from James.'

By then, at age eighty-six, James had already suffered several small strokes and decided he'd had enough. He was tired of what he called his creeping decrepitude. While I was filming in Savannah, that wizard of divine madness, always the director, with his beloved Joel at his side, scripted then directed his final scene.

Late one summer evening in 1979, I was lying in bed, checking out the newest edition of Art in America, when I came across a review of the Northwest Master, Morris Graves. I was familiar with his paintings. I'd heard about him for years, and now we were both represented by Foster/White Gallery. But I didn't know what he looked like, only his paintings. I'd not yet seen those iconic portraits of him by Imogen Cunningham or Mary Randlett. Graves was one of the most celebrated painters of the 20th century, known for his images of birds, his Oriental mysticism, his pranks, and his reclusiveness.

The article, along with half a dozen illustrations, was a review of a New York exhibition showing his newest work: the flower paintings. For some critics, these seemed too radical a departure, so much so that a few even suggested he'd lost his visual power, now painting only 'pretty flowers.' I'd seen many of these at the gallery and later at Seattle Art Museum. I was captivated by the quiet, spiritual luminosity Graves was able to achieve. I didn't think Morris had lost anything.

Midway through the article, I fell asleep, and into a dream; I was in a room where stood an enormous dining table, the largest I'd ever seen. I was on one side and Morris on the other. In real life, at the time, Morris would have been nearing seventy. In the dream, we were the same age—thirty-five.

Neither of us spoke. Strange, magnetic energy filled the room. I felt as if a force emanating from Morris was pushing me away, yet, at the same time, his force-field was pulling me toward him, trapping me in a bizarre stasis. I woke from the dream's intensity, but it bounced around in my head for days. A week later, I ran into Bill, an older friend I'd met in Seattle. He'd known Morris Graves in the early years, knew of the infamous stories, nearly as legendary as his paintings. I told him about my dream. He laughed and said, "You know, you look a little like Morris did when he was your age. Must be the beard."

I couldn't imagine it, but what he said and how he said it touched something inside me. I needed to meet Morris Graves.

I knew he and Jan Thompson, who worked at Foster/White on weekends, were long-time friends. I'd often visit Jan at the gallery on Sundays, usually just the two of us sitting there in the exhibition room. She enthralled me with her stories. When Jan was younger, during the early fifties, she'd travel all over Europe on a motor scooter, something quite unusual to see in those days. Jan was an artist, as well, specializing in portraiture. Though, as far as I know, she never showed her work anywhere. She recounted one story of being contracted to do portraits of a young girl and her younger brother.

"The daughter was quite lovely. I enjoyed painting her. Very charming. The thirteen-year-old son was something else. Wouldn't sit still, kept asking dumb questions, a goofy kid. "

Did you get it finished?" I asked

"I did, finally, but I wasn't sure I liked it. I don't know about the boy or the family, whether they liked it. But they paid me for it. I remember thinking, when I left their house, what a loser this kid's going to be when he grows up."

I shook my head in sympathy.

"I was never so damned wrong about anything in my life," Jan said, her eyes growing wide.

"What do you mean?"

"Bill Gates. That's who the kid was. Can you believe it?"

After we shared a long 'poor me' laugh and caught our breath, I asked her if she thought there was any chance of my meeting Morris Graves, of visiting him.

"Write him. I'll give you his address. There's no telling with Morris. You might be surprised."

I was. Morris replied two weeks later, "Yes, do visit me."

I'd been told, with Morris, one could never just drop in, unannounced. His friend, the avant-garde composer, John Cage, did that once; it ended their friendship. Nor could you schedule a visit too far in advance. Morris didn't like that either. After a second letter, we set a date, and I soon left for Northern California.

Morris lived near Loleta, on the edge of a vast lake, surrounded by a forest of cypress, Douglas fir, and oak. 'The Lake,' as he named it, became his last retreat into solitude.

I arrived in the early afternoon with a friend who lived in Arcata. We approached the front entrance and found a note taped to the door. "G. and L., I'm in the garden. Come on inside. I'll be there soon. M."

We entered, turned right, then walked down a hallway filled with paintings. Side tables stood here and there, full of artifacts, small sculptures of metal and glass by Morris and vases full of fresh cut flowers. At the end of the hall, we turned right into what could only be the dining room. And there it was: the big table in my dream. I stood in the middle of the room, dumbstruck, still shaking my head, when I heard the front door open, footsteps striding down the hall. Morris swept around the corner, dressed in blue overalls, wearing heavy work boots. That was the first time I'd ever seen him, but he looked exactly like an older version of the Morris in my dream. I was amazed at his size. He came up to me, took my hands in his, squeezed them, then hugged me like we'd known one another for years, embracing me in such placid sturdiness, I felt like collapsing into his arms. I didn't, of course, but I did immediately confess my dream. He listened intently and seemed moved by it.

On that first visit to his home, we shared many stories. The day ended with a long walk through his gardens at the edge of the lake where ruins of ancient cypress stumps rose like black statues from the pewter surface of the water. We talked about art, people, and places. I told him I grew up in the rural south, and at seventeen, left for Fairbanks, that I had attended University of Alaska. I explained my fascination with the indigenous culture of Alaska, its art, and mythology. I talked about the paintings of Sidney Lawrence, Paul Eustice Zeigler, and Ted Lambert. He knew about Zeigler because Paul once taught art in Seattle, but he'd not heard of Lambert.

Ted, who'd studied with Zeigler, moved to Fairbanks in the early forties. While Lawrence was the most revered, then Zeigler, to me, Lambert's work was the most compelling, more mysterious. He had, in fact, lived in Ester a few years before I arrived, living in the same small house I briefly rented in 1967. Like Morris, Lambert was reclusive and difficult. His death was as mysterious as his art. He'd left his cabin one winter morning when the temperature was thirty below zero, hiking down a trail from the settlement where he was living; he never came back. No one knew if he'd accidentally frozen to death, or whether he'd planned his demise; they never found his body. Ted could have, I suppose, slipped away, moved to Mexico, or even Northern Thailand. It happens. More than likely though he ended as bear food.

His teacher, Zeigler, was a master draftsman. In 1964, when I first arrived, the University had inherited forty of his copper plates. But since it was such a new art department, no one knew how to print them. The dry-point plates got sent over to the local newspaper. Not a good idea. They didn't have a clue either, covering the plates with newspaper ink, not understanding the patient process of wiping the ink from the copper. What a mess it was. And since they didn't bother to clean the plates afterward, the ink dried on the metal like hard lacquer. That was my first student job: cleaning the Zeigler plates, using a gallon of Putz Pomade and a lot of elbow grease. Then I printed an edition of four of all forty etchings, the way Lennie had taught me. I quickly grew not to like the medium, nor its predictability. However, much

'Cow On Stilts,' monotype, 24" x 18" 1985

The Lake
January 23/86

Reverend Galen,
Your "UNTITLED" monotype —
What a supremely articulated
envisioning of an awesome
phenomenon; compassionate
Kinship — rapport with living
spirit — the psyche —
held (for this passing moment)
in the body of a domesticated
beast.
I hear in my deepest heart
— the tantra-tabla —
reverberations of the
urningism drum: the
tantra-tabla; Love.

Morris

Letter from Morris Graves

179

later, using the etching press and copper plates, I became adept at making monotypes, a reverse painting, if you will. I liked the fact that you could never predict the results; it could be a total failure, of which I had many, or something magical and remarkable.

I once sent an image to Morris, entitled 'Cow on Stilts.' I had no narrative in mind, other than creating a surreal tableau: the impossibility of a cow walking on stilts, wearing a bird's mask, created in honor of Morris's fascination with birds.

He responded in his usual 'Gravesian' manner.

A year later, I sent a similar image to my friend, Hayden Carruth, the celebrated poet and essayist I'd met through Sam Hamill. In this monotype, entitled 'The Secret,' two cows were standing on stilts, facing each other. One cow appeared to be whispering in the other one's ear. After a few weeks, I received a delightful but curious response from Hayden, a lengthy letter about the nature of cows—how they moved and gathered, how they fed. Hayden had lived in rural Vermont for some years, and cows were everywhere in his environment, so beautifully expressed in his poem 'Cows at Night.'

"However," he went on to explain, "two cows will never stand facing one another." I had a grand laugh because he said nothing about whether cows might or might not walk on stilts.

On our walk back from the Lake, it started raining. Morris recalled a time he'd spent in New Orleans when he was a young man.

"I would often go to the open food markets after hours and glean fruit or vegetables left or dropped in the stalls," he said. "On one occasion, as I was nearing one of the tin-roofed sheds, a fierce storm suddenly blew in. I ran toward a long building, open on all sides with wooden tables below a tin roof.

"There was a lone person there, sitting very straight on one of the tables. She was an old, black woman, quite emaciated, but strangely elegant, a fellow gleaner, another soul from the storm. As I walked to the table where she sat, she looked at me and smiled. Rainwater had pooled in the hollows of her collarbones. When she bowed, acknowledging my presence, the rainwater gently spilled out and over her bony clavicles, down her breast like tears."

Over the years, Morris and I communicated mostly through letters, but I did return to 'The Lake' on several other occasions. On one visit, his friend, Robert Yarber, escorted me, not to the big house, but through a long, overgrown trail that led into a clearing on the other side. Nestled within was a Japanese-style bungalow, so close to the lake, it seemed as if it were floating on the water. I walked through a wooden gate into a traditional Japanese garden where, near the front door, hung a bronze gong suspended on a bamboo frame. Robert quietly took the mallet and solemnly struck the brass disk three times. Vibrations rippled through the air. It was so ritualized that I thought perhaps I should fall to my knees and touch the ground with my head.

Morris suddenly appeared at the door and escorted me inside. We spent the afternoon drinking tea, paddling through one conversation into another. His fame and mystical presence could sometimes be a bit daunting. He had a way of weaving stories and postulations then, an hour later, backtracking, asking what thoughts I held about what he'd said, almost as if I were being tested. I suspect I was. I usually responded with some obscure metaphysical nonsense; that seemed to be the safest direction and did the trick.

The man was an intriguing, mysterious puzzle, and over time, through several visits and exchanged letters, I would soon place Morris within my pantheon of mentors, like Lennie, or James, Sam, or John. They were vastly different from one another, but their underlayment was mine. I felt it.

In the early 1990s, I made my final trip to visit Morris, driving down with Richard Svare, who'd been Morris's companion during the 1950s, at 'Careläden,' Morris's second home. Ten years later, they left the United States and moved to Ireland and bought an old castle named Woodtown Manor. Morris spent several years restoring it, but after living there for a decade, he became restless. Morris and Richard ended their long relationship. Heartbroken, Richard moved to Oslo; he founded and directed a successful theater company for a few years until he migrated to New York City, where he worked with Merce Cunningham. He didn't much care for that environment, so he eventually settled in Athens, Greece, becoming a well-known actor in both English and Greek films. Richard retired in the early 1990s and returned to live in his childhood home in Seattle until his death in 2004.

When Morris returned to the West Coast in the late 1960s, he discovered the secluded piece of land in Northern California that would become 'The Lake.' He tracked down a local real estate office, inquired as to the property's ownership, and asked whether it might be for sale. The agent knew the owner and called her; she had no interest in selling. Disappointed, Morris returned to Ireland, but he couldn't get the place out of his thoughts. When he returned the following year, he called on the agent again.

"Ask her," Morris insisted.

"She won't sell it. I can tell you right now. She doesn't need to. She has lots of money."

Morris refused to leave without resolution.

Exasperated, the agent called.

"She wants to know your name."

"Morris."

A long pause…"She wants to know your last name."

"Graves."

The agent turned back to Morris, "She'd like to know if, by any chance, you paint birds?"

"I've painted a few."

After relaying this to the woman, the agent looked up at Morris, confused, apparently not knowing what the woman knew, "She said, of course, absolutely, you can buy the land. I'll get the papers ready."

Thirty years later, Richard Svare would write his book, *MORRIS GRAVES, His Houses, His Gardens*. So endearingly threaded within are numerous historical photographs and Richard's beautifully constrained narrative, modestly told, with almost no reference to their emotional bonding. Sadly, as fate would have it, Richard died before he could hold the book in his hands.

During my visits to 'The Lake,' Morris never spoke about his relationship with Richard. Nor did he ever talk about his even earlier relationship with Guy Anderson. Guy, like Morris, Tobey, and Callahan, represented 'the big four' of the Northwest Mystics. Guy was four years older than Morris, and as young men, struggling to make art in uncertain times, on the cusp of WWII, they held an intimate relationship. By the late 1990s, as their lives were coming to a close, they continued to keep a loving connection.

After both men died, someone told me this charming story:

A friend of Guy's would periodically stop by and check on him, to see if he needed anything. He was living in LaConner, then in his mid-eighties. On this particular evening, she'd stopped by to wish him a happy birthday. As she entered the house, she knew Guy would be sitting alone in his living room, watching TV, as he usually did in those late days of his life.

As the woman stood outside, waiting to knock on the door, she heard his phone ring. The television went silent. She heard Guy rustle from his chair, shuffle across the room to answer the phone. "Hello? Who is this? Who?"

There was a long pause. Then the woman heard Guy ask in his soft, frail voice, "Is that you, Gravy Pie?"

O ver the course of the 'Galax' years, from 1980-1992, most all of my friends came up to visit, to camp under the stars. It was a place of spiritual medicine, just as it had been for the Yakima Indians, who'd inhabited the same hills a century earlier. My home in Seattle was becoming less exciting for me, too noisy, too much traffic, and then, of course, there was always nibbling, somewhere in the back of my mind, my inexorable need for change. It had been twelve years since I'd moved from Alaska, three years since moving into the big studio on Twelfth and Pike, two years since I jumped out of an airplane, falling through the cold, blue skies into the second part of my life.

In 1982, I was invited out to Port Townsend, Washington, a small seaport community on the tip of the Olympic Peninsula. The town became established in the late 1800s with some idea it would evolve, like Seattle, into a bustling coastal city, but the railroad never got out that far, and the settlement never grew beyond being a small town with one street of lovely Victorian buildings. However, it was home to a lot of boat builders and a fishing industry. There was a smelly paper mill, and a cadre of first and second-generation hippies, and quite a few artists.

Port Townsend was an enchanting, laid-back community with a vibrant mix of politics, mostly left-leaning, a quiet place filled with fascinating people.

My visit took me to Centrum Foundation, a multi-disciplined arts organization—music, poetry, writing, and dance—housed in Fort Worden State Park. I was invited there to see their etching press, recently donated by a friend of mine, Ken Snider. The American artist, Laddie John Dill, had just completed the first workshop at the print facility using the new press, and I wanted to see what he'd done.

I drove out for the weekend and fell in love with the town right away. It seemed a perfect size for me. I immediately prepared my exodus out of Seattle, and just as I'd done when I left Alaska, I got rid of most everything—the studio, the cumbersome lease, and too many boxes of things I didn't need. I loaded my VW bus and headed west to the Olympic Peninsula with Greg Mitchell, my partner at the time.

A year before, I'd painted a series of figurative images on Plexiglas in a reverse, reductive process, experimental, different from the abstract landscapes. I suspect they were too dark and erotic for the gallery, though I did sell half a dozen or so. Six months after I moved to Port Townsend, I exhibited some of these in a small space near the Imprint Bookstore on Water Street. At the opening, Tree Swenson stopped in and introduced herself. We chatted for a while and then her partner, Sam Hamill, showed up.

Sam walked through the exhibition, studying the works without saying a word. After twenty minutes, he came up and asked, "Do you have slides of these paintings?"

"I do." The next day I drove out to his office and left him a full sheet of color transparencies.

Sam Hamill, Tree Swenson, and William O'Daly were co-founders of Copper Canyon Press, housed at Fort Worden under the auspices of Centrum Foundation. By the time I arrived in Port Townsend, Copper Canyon already had an international reputation for publishing a broad spectrum of notable poets. In addition to having been the Editor of Copper Canyon, Sam is an extraordinary poet, essayist, and translator of Japanese, Chinese, and Estonian poetry.

Several weeks later, in the mail, I received a poem, entitled 'slide #1." Another week went by: 'slide # 2,' then another, until I'd received twenty altogether, each one in response to images from the Plexi series. Very soon after that, remarkably, the paintings and Sam's poems became one expression. I ditched whatever titles I'd given the images and renamed them after Sam's poems. Our first collaborative project was born: *Passport*, published by Broken Moon Press in 1989.

In 1986, I decided to move 'Passport,' into a multi-media project involving slides of the paintings with Sam's narration of his poems, woven together with a sound score by Jon Brower, a brilliant young composer who'd rented space from me at 1205 East Pike.

I'd lost contact with Jon, and he held the key; I needed his music to tie everything together. I'd last seen him in Seattle several years earlier, but he'd left Washington State. Eventually, through friends and friends of friends, I found him. He was living in Portland, Oregon, still making his music. I called Jon to see if he'd be interested in the project. He was delighted and excited to participate, but before we ended our conversation, he said, "I do have to tell you, Galen: I have AIDS. I'm not in the best of shape.

I was speechless. I knew what this meant. There were no antiviral cocktails developed at this point. "Jon, are you sure?"

"Yeah, I want to do this," he said emphatically. "I need to. Come on down. I just wanted to warn you, so you won't be too shocked when you see me."

A few days later, Fritz and I drove down I-5 to Portland with a CD of Sam narrating his poems.

We arrived at Jon's apartment, and when he opened the door, even with his warning, his appearance was shocking. The last time I'd seen him, Jon was a tall, handsome young man. None of that had changed, but he was pitifully thin now, his body covered with Kaposi sarcoma.

I explained what we were doing, what we needed, and handed him the tape of Sam's narration. Jon brought out cassettes of his music. His entire creative life lay in that small cardboard box. We sat on the floor in his living room. Jon, eyes closed, wearing headphones, listened intently to Sam's narration. Then he would suddenly turn to his archives, flip through the tapes until he found the right composition. He began a sound mix using a small editing machine that sat next to him on the floor. When finished with a cut, Jon would spin back around and play it—one poem with music. I was stunned and delighted. His selection and the editing were seamlessly woven together as if he'd scored the music to Sam's words. By the day's end, I had what I needed, returned to Port Townsend and began working on the entire piece, editing the completed soundtrack to the visuals. When done, I mailed a DVD copy to Jon. I received his letter about how much it meant to him to have been part of Passport. A few weeks later he died. He was twenty-nine.

In 1983, I was fortunate to become the first recipient of Centrum's Northwest Print Project, working on the etching Press at Fort Worden. It was here I fell in love with the monotype process, the spontaneity of the medium. I was allowed six weeks, completed several dozens, and wanted to do more, but my time was over. I decided I needed a press for my studio. I wanted the same model, a French-American Etching Press, and of course, I lusted after, had to have, the largest one they made, weighing over a ton and about as big as a water buffalo.

I put together a campaign to raise the money, held a fundraising event in Seattle, and got most of the funds I needed that night, enough, at least, to order the press. After six months, it arrived. It was gorgeous!

While waiting for it to be shipped from Europe, I discovered and bought an old building previously used as a church, now unoccupied, in

'The Measure' oil on plexi, 1982

The Measure

It is like walking beside a song or a poem
the way moonlight leaps from the shadows,
the way shadows leap over moonlight.
He who has loved has learned of parallel lives.

Finger folded over finger, thumb against thumb,
he counts the small bones of his hands
like prayer beads while around him the streets
glisten with new-fallen rain and shimmer

under oil stains and tar stains and the day's end.
Suddenly, he was in the street and walking,
remembering everything wrong: the aftertaste
of honey, the faint iris perfume

dying of the vase. After the war, after death
has touched us once again or passed us by,
we will lie down together again, and again
listen, silent, for the song of parallel lives.

Sam Hamill

uptown Port Townsend. It was ideal for a studio. But it needed a lot of changes to meet my studio needs. Within three months, however, I was again making art.

Along the sides of the nave, I built work tables, and where the preacher preached, I constructed a painting wall in front of the pulpit. Behind this, was a full-body baptismal, perfect for my shower.

The etching press sat in the middle of the room.

The place worked well enough, at least for a while. I settled in, I painted, made monotypes, and offered workshops for extra income.

After having lived in the building for two years, however, I missed going to Galax, my spiritual retreat in Eastern Washington. Getting there was now more of a challenge, living far out on the Straits of Juan de Fuca. Once again, while rumbling around the area, I stumbled upon a beautifully secluded five-acre piece of wooded property five miles out of Port Townsend, overlooking the Straits.

The price was low, a steal at $45,000.00, but more than I could afford. I called my friend John Koenig and suggested we strike a deal. He took the ferry over the next day, I drove us out to the land, and he loved it. We soon entered into a real estate partnership in which John secured the Port Townsend land, insisting, of course, we call Gala-X. Our friend and attorney, Merch Pease, shaking his head at these two Romantics, drew up the legal papers for what became known as 'The Galaxian Alliance.'

Within a few months, I sold the church and started over. It seemed as if I lived with an almost clinical fixation not only to move every few years, but to find a place that needed reshaping, adding to, or building from scratch. Why? The answer isn't complicated. From birth until I left home, I moved about so often, a pattern took shape inside me, asserting itself every few years. Move, change. Move.

With Uncle Mac, an expert tree-cutter, we cleared an opening in the woods, dropping just enough trees for a building site, then I had a portable mill brought in to rip the trees into rough boards, sticker-stacking the lumber for curing. After six months, I began work on the house. I'd never attempted to build one from scratch. It was a challenge, but the place came together, and before the winter rains began, I had a new home. A year later, a new studio behind the main house. On the front of the property, the bluff side, two hundred feet above the beach, overlooking Canada, I built a small deck on which I'd sit in the late afternoons and watch the sun disappear.

It was here, in 1987, Jesus came calling. I don't mean missionary proselytes had stumbled onto my property, nor did I have an unexpected born-again experience, no dance with the Christian Divine. He came through John Koenig's connection to M. Delaine, Director of the Dunkerque Museum of Art. I received an invitation to submit a painting for 'La Passion de Dunkerque.' I was delighted, especially since the traveling show would have works by artists like Ranier Fetting, Paul Jenkins, Mimmo Paladino, Georg Baselitz, and Andy Warhol.

I wouldn't automatically be accepted, of course. I had to conceptualize an idea, realize it in paint and canvas, then submit a slide to the museum for consideration.

The traveling exhibition was thematic, having to do with events in the life of Christ. The painting could be done in any style one wished and was to be five feet square.

At first, I was at a loss. There wasn't much from my childhood to pull from, so seldom did I go to church. And when I did, the stained-glass windows were about the only thing holding my attention; I'd lose myself in those luminous, saturated colors. Forget about the sermons.

I remembered from art school the medieval painters like Massacio, with his multiple narratives executed in a single painting or series of panels, and a concept began to grow. Once I stretched the raw canvas and started applying the paint, everything fell into place: three events within one image: 'Crucifixion, Deposition, and Ascension,' surely the most iconic in all of Christianity. 'Simultaneous Occurrence' got underway.

When I'd finished, I mailed a slide of the painting to the Musèe de Dunkerque. They accepted it, and I stored the canvas in my studio for a month until the paperwork from French Customs arrived.

A stout, well-crafted crate for shipping was needed, so I contracted my friend, Gary, an excellent wood craftsman to build it for me. A week later, it was ready, and I thought it best to bring the painting to Gary's wood shop. I looked outside to see if the weather was behaving. It was perfect, the skies clear, not a cloud in sight, one of our beautiful Northwest days. I didn't want to wrap the canvas, nor did I want to lash it into the back of my pick-up, so I decided I'd carefully lay the painting in the bed of the truck. "You sure about this?" I asked myself. "No problem. It's only two miles. I'll go slow," dismissing my concern. "Relax, man," I said to myself nervous self.

Carefully, I carried Jesus outside, gently laying him on the back of the old Ford. I drove down McMinn Road, took a left onto Hastings when all of a sudden, my sunny day disappeared. Everything darkened. Wind and rain came roaring in like a freight train. I'd never seen the weather on the Peninsula change so quickly and fiercely. Immediately, I pulled over, slowed to a stop, ready to turn back to the studio. But at that

'Simultaneous Occurrence: Crucifixion, Deposition, Ascension'
oil on canvas, 60" x 60" 1987

precise moment, I saw, in the rear-view mirror, Christ rise up from the bed of the truck, spinning topsy-turvy in the wind, landing in the bushes on the side of the road. I closed my eyes, lay my head on the wheel, and cursed myself for being so damned stupid. I should've listened to my more cautious self. Now, the painting would be scratched, if not torn, possibly damaged beyond repair. I'd have to start all over.

When I opened the door and stepped onto the road, the sky was calm, the wind and rain had followed the storm out to sea. I climbed down a slight embankment and found the painting buried in weeds, face down. Gently, I lifted it, turning it over. Miraculously, not a rip nor a scratch anywhere. Not a bit of dirt nor drop of water stained it. I picked up the canvas and gently laid it back in the truck, and drove on into town.

'Simultaneous Occurrence,' eventually sailed across the ocean and made it to Paris. Weeks later, I received a message that while the painting

190

had indeed arrived safely, French Customs Office demanded a sizable excise duty, which I didn't have and because of the enormous expense of producing two catalogs, neither did M. Delaine. He explained to me that if I immediately faxed him a fake bill of sale, indicating the museum had already purchased the work, Customs would be satisfied. I didn't like this scenario at all, but what options did I have? The painting was in Paris. "OK, why not? It's a simple deception," I said to Merch. He agreed and advised me to let it go. I mailed off the fake document. The painting, released in the nick of time, traveled with the show to four different countries over the course of a year.

When the exhibition closed, I kept thinking they'd return my painting or pay me the five grand we'd agreed upon and that I'd expected. Neither happened. I would ask John occasionally where it was and when I might get it back, but I never got an answer. After a few years, I let go of any hope of seeing it again. Only by a curious bit of correspondence, three decades later did I learned the painting had been living with M. Delaine all this time. Once he retired, he gave the entire exhibition to the Sacred Art Centre in Lille, France. I wasn't unhappy about it, but I thought I should have at least some input. After considerable effort, I managed to locate the retired director and requested that I be allowed to donate the painting to the Centre officially.

"Mai oui," he replied, as indeed he should have.

I'm satisfied. It's enough to know my Jesus is there, stashed somewhere in the dark catacombs of that medieval-looking cathedral, waiting for me to drop by and say hello. Eventually, I will.

We have worlds of time.

"You know, I've only a couple of years left," Ida said, as we strolled down Port Townsend's Water Street. We stopped. It was an out of the blue comment, casually slipped between "That was a mighty good lunch," and "I'll be glad to get these damned shoes off."

"What are you talking about?" I asked.

"I can't explain it. I don't know why I feel this way, but I do."

In 1987, my mother was visiting me in Port Townsend. Four years earlier, she began flying down for a few months each winter, renting a room in a small hotel on the corner of Washington and Tyler. The long Arctic nights had become too depressing for her, especially since Ansgar retired and had nothing to keep him busy. His only hobby was drinking. He'd be soused and cantankerous by mid-afternoon, ready for bed. After spending all day in the kitchen, preparing gourmet meals, she'd ask herself, "Why do I go to all this damned trouble when he's too drunk to eat?"

She loved being in Port Townsend. She walked. She read. She knitted. She cooked for herself, and often I'd bring her out to Gala-X for dinner. Occasionally she'd slip into the Town Tavern on Water Street, just to play a little bit of ragtime on their old piano. And, of course, they immediately wanted to hire her.

"No, thanks, I'm retired." She'd say.

She was only sixty-six, rarely drank anymore and when she did, it was one small glass of wine with dinner. No bourbon. Five years earlier, her heart, enlarged from years of too many diet pills and too much alcohol, and not enough exercise, began to beat in overtime. She thought it was going to explode. Ansgar rushed her to the hospital in Fairbanks and, after a few days, her heart slowed to a more normal pace.

But she'd been careful these last few years, moderating her diet, and walking when she could.

"Mama, don't be silly," I said, not knowing what else I could say. I did wonder, however, if there was something more specific she wasn't telling me. It turns out, there was.

Gray and I would visit each other annually. In early 1989, I spent a few weeks with him in Washington D.C., met many of his friends and learned more about his work with the government. Several months later, he flew out, unexpectedly, to Port Townsend, but only for a brief visit. I didn't understand the purpose of his trip since we'd just spent a good bit of time together in Washington, D.C., nor did he have work to attend to in Seattle.

I was thrilled, of course, that he'd come, and we had our usual chats about the pros and cons of our lives, talking, as usual, about surviving the quirkiness of growing up in Ida's world. He had a tight schedule, so, after a brief visit, he returned.

Two days later, I was working outside, when my phone rang. It was Gray. He seemed unusually quiet; the conversation was awkward. After a long pause, he said, "I've tried to tell you this. I tried when you were here in Washington, but I couldn't…tried when I flew out last week, but couldn't. I couldn't find the words. But I…"

"Tried to tell me what?" I interrupted, with deepening concern.

Another long pause.

"I have AIDS," he said.

His words hit me like a heavy stone. I couldn't find any words to respond, just thinking it should have been me, instead.

Earlier conversations we'd had now came flooding back. We'd been sitting in Gray's living room in D.C., talking about this and that, when he said, "You know, if I were ever to get AIDS, I'd go into my kitchen, stick my head in the oven, and turn on the gas." I assumed he was speaking rhetorically. I said, "Me too."

We'd both lost so many friends to this terrifying disease. It surrounded us like a dark, toxic tide.

I honestly don't remember how or even if I responded to this sad news. Gray kept talking for a good long while to calm me; that would be his way. He told me he was going to leave his position with Congress, that he had accepted a teaching position at Winthrop University in Rock Hill, South Carolina, and would begin almost immediately.

I finally found a few words. "Why don't you come to Port Townsend. Stay with me. You can write that novel you've talked about writing for so long."

"You know I can't do that, Galen. I'm such a damn workaholic. I'd go crazy if I quit working. You know that."

I did.

Gray soon left his position with Congress, bought a house in Rock Hill, South Carolina, and began teaching that fall quarter. Within a few months, his health began to deteriorate, though he was still working. I caught a flight to Rock Hill as quickly as I could. When I got to his home that evening, I tried not to gasp when he appeared at the door. I barely recognized him. He'd lost fifty pounds and looked like he hadn't eaten or slept in weeks.

In his youth, everyone called him Buddy, and he was slightly on the heavier side and teased because of it. His having to wear glasses only made it worse. He grew up into a remarkably handsome young man, studious rather than athletic, soaring through his undergraduate studies at Clemson in less than three years. He immediately went on to receive his Master's then Doctorate with the same speed and dedication.

I followed him inside, down the dimly lit hallway into his living room, illuminated by a small lamp on his desk and the paused movie he'd been watching. We sat and talked all evening. Again, I encouraged him to come out to Port Townsend and stay with me. He wouldn't consider it. We discussed, as best we could, what, if any, plans he had. "Do you have a good doctor here in Rock Hill?" I asked.

"No," he said, "I don't want the school to know. Not yet. I've been flying up to see my doctor in D.C."

In fact, no one knew about his illness in Rock Hill, and he'd told no one else in our family about his diagnosis. Only me. It was evident he was frightened and alone. I continued trying to persuade him to either come live with me or go back to D.C. where he had many friends, but he was stubborn.

I flew home two days later.

He managed to keep going until the school term was over, but in August, I got a call from his doctor telling me Gray was now at George Washington University Hospital.

I returned to D.C. as quickly as I could get a flight. Several of his friends met me at Dulles International Airport, took me to the hospital. In his room, he lay tethered to an assortment of hoses and drip devices, still conscious enough to know who I was, but barely so. The doctors said he was drowning in Pneumocystis pneumonia. The day before I arrived, they'd done a lung biopsy and confirmed it.

I inquired at length of his doctors. Their prognosis was bleak. There was nothing more they could do, they said.

Later that afternoon, I began calling our family. I called my mother in Alaska and slowly, carefully, explained the situation.

"I'm so sorry to have to tell you all of this, mama, but you need to come." There was a long pause. I knew Ida was struggling with the news. I gave her as much time as she needed to pull herself together. "I thought I'd wait." she finally said.

" For what?" I responded.

"Until he gets a bit stronger."

"He's not going to get any stronger. You need to come now, Mama." Silence. Then she said, "OK."

I called my father in Marietta, Bernard in Albany, Georgia, and Glenn, still living in North Charleston. They too wanted to wait, afraid of what their coming would mean. They hemmed and hawed.

"You have to come now," I told them.

That afternoon I went into Gray's room and stood at his bedside. I don't know if he even knew who I was at this point. He seemed delirious, wearing a sorrowful expression under a furled brow as if he were trying to solve all the riddles of the world at once before everything collapsed around him. He seemed trapped at the bottom of a dark lake, struggling to swim upward toward the light. I left and went back to his friend's house where I was staying and tried to get some rest, but sleep was slow in coming.

The next morning, I returned to his room, expecting the situation to be worse. But, strangely, everything had changed. His eyes were luminous and brightly focused. He was no longer underwater. He looked up, motioning me with his finger to lean closer. I knelt by his bed.

"Galen, can we get this show on the road?" he whispered in words so sadly cavalier, it seemed almost humorous. But it wasn't. I wanted to protest, but the look in his eyes was unrelenting. I understood. It was time. As his executor, I knew I'd have to deal with this, his final decision, and the doctors were waiting.

I nodded yes.

I walked out of the room and found his primary doctor, "My brother's ready. Please take him off of everything except the morphine. That's what he wants."

He sadly nodded in agreement, placing his hand on my shoulder. I left the floor and went down to the lobby to wait until my father arrived. There were ten or twelve other close friends, mostly gay, in attendance, including a guy dressed in a rather bizarre outfit, wearing a bright pink wig and eye makeup, something between a tranny-look and a clown, meant as a joke, only to cheer Gray up.

As I sat and waited for my father, I started thinking about something my mother said to me years earlier, right after I came out.

"Don't tell Sam you're gay. He might flip out. When we were still together, he told me about a time when a fellow soldier came on to him. They were on leave, I think, out drinking, staying in the same room at a hotel somewhere. Your Daddy damn near put him in the hospital."

I saw him come through the lobby doors. He walked over and hugged me, and then we sat together with Gray's friends. I tried to get a fix for any negative feelings he might be having, especially when he looked at the guy in the dress and wig. He just smiled. My father seemed entirely at ease with everyone, grateful they were there. He'd seen a lot and gone through a great deal since those early days when he was a young soldier, a new father, struggling with alcoholism, trying to get his life back on solid ground. It was never easy for him.

In later years, I never did talk to my father about my being gay, but he'd met men with whom I'd lived and was always gracious and at ease.

I met my mother at Dulles International. She was in a terrible state, partly because she'd become terrified of flying, but more so from why she'd come. Bernard and Glenn arrived soon after. The five of us met in the lobby and went up to Gray's room together.

By this time, his body had processed then eliminated all the chemicals, the medicines, the AZT, the antibiotics.

When we came into his room, he was lying in his bed, expecting us, happy to see us all. He was nearly his old self, utterly lucid, assisted by sweet Morpheus flowing through his blood, calming his heart. He seemed considerably more together than any of us, especially our mother, who sat biting her lips to keep from crying. Gray took control of the conversation, asking us all questions: what had my father been doing? Was Glenn still with State Farm? How were Bernard's two boys? How was life in Alaska for Ida? Had I finished building my studio?

But we had no questions for Gray.

I sat at the end of his bed looking first at him, then at my mother, my father, Bernard on one side, Glenn on the other. Everyone seemed busy trying to be cheerful, just small talk, trying to get through it all, not knowing what to say or how to act in such a final scene. I fell out of the conversation, leaned back and just observed. How strange, I thought. I'd not been in the same room at the same time with my nuclear family since I was three, the time my father was carted off to jail. Now, almost a half-century later, here we were, all together. What a potent but sad gift my brother was leaving us.

After a while, we stepped outside his room and one by one, his friends went in to say her or his farewell. He greeted them with a beatific smile and tender conversation until they left, each one in tears.

By late morning, Gray was exhausted, his breathing more and more difficult. The doctor told me that by evening, he'd slip into a coma, and then it would be just a matter of a few hours.

My family and I had rooms in nearby hotels, close to the hospital. When I left Gray, I asked the nurse, "Please, call me when he's close. I need to be with him."

The nurse smiled, touched my arm, and nodded yes.

I lay in bed that night waiting for the phone call I knew would come. Finally, I fell asleep. And then the phone rang.

"It's close. You better hurry," the nurse said. I jumped up, dressed, and ran the two blocks to the hospital as fast as I could. When I got there, the nurse was sadly shaking her head.

Gray's heart had quit seconds before I arrived.

A nurse walked me down the hall to a different room, one without all the beeping and gurgling of medical equipment. No windows and only a dimly lit lamp on a table at the foot of his bed. I walked over and sat next to his body. His brow was no longer struggling for answers. It was as smooth as a lake on a windless day, his face the color of alabaster. I sat for a long while by his lifeless body, thinking of our childhood and the times he protected me or teased me. I thought of our episodic bike crash when I was eleven, then later, when, as grown men, we'd gone 'bar-hopping' in Seattle. Neither of us could remember where we'd parked my car and had to taxi back to my apartment at two in the morning, waking up our visiting mother, who stood in the window angrily shaking her fists as she buzzed us in. There was the time we met up on the island of St. Bart's in the Caribbean. We were staying at Les Castelet, where many of the New York ballet dancers hung out. One morning, I nearly ran over Mikhail Baryshnikov in my rented Jeep as I swerved off the narrow road to prevent hitting a descending vehicle. We laughed at what might have been my only claim to fame: Unknown Artist Cripples World's Most Celebrated Dancer.

I thought about the time when all my brothers secretly flew up to Alaska to surprise our mother on her sixtieth birthday at the Malamute Saloon; how happy she was.

Gray's hands lay crossed on his chest, his face glowing in the shadows of the room. I don't know how long I sat there—perhaps an hour—before I headed back to the hotel where I knew Ida would be waiting, depressed and afraid.

The next morning, My father and brothers departed, returning to their respective homes. I drove Ida to the airport for her long flight home. She didn't want to stay for the memorial. Perhaps she did, but both her heart and body were in meltdown. Had I known how ill she was, before she'd flown out, I wouldn't have encouraged her to make the trip in the first place.

She spoke only a few words and said goodbye. I could tell she was on the edge of crying, but she didn't.

I remained in Washington D.C. for Gray's memorial service, touched by the eulogies of his many friends, especially Congressman Williams, who praised my brother's service to education and for writing some of our most important legislation for disabled children. The next day, I stood by his coffin as it rolled into the flames and then, a day later, I placed his ashes, a few photos, and other small items, into his car and drove it across the country, back to my home in Port Townsend.

Gray had stipulated in his will that he wanted his ashes placed into the Straits of Juan de Fuca, in front of Gala-X. In September, I made preparations, removing a token amount of his ashes to ship up to our mother. The rest I put in my backpack and hiked down the steep bank to the beach. It was a lovely, sunny day. The sky above Protection Island was clear and blue, the water, icy cold. I wore a pair of shorts, tennis shoes and a T-shirt. I swam through the currents until I reached a half-submerged boulder, and clambered up to the exposed flat area. I sat for a while, holding the small box in my hands, then I opened the lid and poured his remains into the sea.

Less than a month later, I received a phone call from Ansgar, telling me that Ida was in the hospital. She'd had several small heart attacks, and because of her diabetes, she was suffering from neuropathy, her right leg and foot blackened with gangrene. The doctors told her they'd need to amputate.

I left immediately, arriving a few days before her surgery.

When I came into her room, the first thing she said was, "I'm just like Buddy." I wasn't sure what she meant, but I suppose she was letting me know she was dying. She'd lost a son. Soon she'd lose her leg, the same leg that held the foot that tapped out the rhythm of her music. She seemed unbearably sad and could barely talk.

Still, after five minutes, even in her depressed mood, Ida's dark humor sparked and flared. "Bring me my camera," she said, "I want to document this foot, these toes. I want my grandchildren to see what happened to me could happen to them. It's not enough anymore just to tell them stuff. There's gotta be a picture."

While I was snapping a close-up of her foot, she asked, "You want my leg as a souvenir? Maybe bronze it, something to keep your pennies in, or maybe keep ajar your door?"

"No, Mama," I said smiling.

The pain soon became more than she could stand.

"Cut the goddamned thing off," she cried, "Cut it off! I can't stand it. It hurts too much."

Rising on her elbows, she asked her doctor, "Hey Doc, tell me, and be honest, will I hear the saw go buzz?"

"No, Ida," he said smiling, shaking his head, "I don't believe you will."

"Then tell me—sorry, but I need to know. Will it have its own tiny casket? A box wrapped in string? Or will you just strike a match and burn the damn thing?"

The doctor's smile disappeared.

"You see, Doc, this foot of mine's like a vine; it ties me to sky and earth. Whatever goes up, you know, comes back down wrapped in music. My good foot is the tapper of time. The one you wanna take sustains the line and makes the music flow."

My mother grew quiet. The doctor stood and turned to leave.

"OK, Doc," she said, "Let's go. Let's do it."

Ida remained in rehab for several weeks, and I stayed out in Ester with Ansgar. I built a wooden ramp from the driveway up to the front door, so when she got home, she could come and go in her wheelchair. Ansgar was a complete mess, hardly knowing what to do.

Three weeks later, after she'd spent a week in rehab, getting fitted for a leg, and learning how to use crutches, I brought her home, pushed her wheelchair up the ramp and into the cabin, past her upright piano, and into her bedroom. She was already complaining about the pain in her other foot, watching it slowly turn dark.

I'd done all I could do and had to get back home. The following day I flew back to Port Townsend.

In late November, Ansgar called me. He couldn't cope any longer. Her depression was too much for him. Ansgar called to tell me he'd placed her in a care facility. I knew this would only make it worse. Ida hated the thought of being left to die in such a place. I called the care facility that afternoon, and after several minutes, a nurse wheeled her to the phone. She was bawling, something she'd never done in front of me. Stoic to a fault. She grew quiet, caught her breath, then pleaded, "Get me out this damned place."

I tried to calm her. "There's nothing I can do from here, Mama. But you can. Call Ansgar. Tell him to come and take you home. He will. That's all you need to do."

"Alright, I will," she said.

I told her I loved her and hung up the phone.

My mother did take control. I believe she willed her heart to quit. She died that same night, three months after the death of her second son.

I flew back up to Fairbanks, and as she'd requested, I had her cremated and attended her memorial services. I stayed another ten days out in Ester, dismantling the wheelchair ramp and helping Ansgar deal with her possessions. He wanted only a few things to remember her by, nothing much.

I spent a few days rummaging through the little house in the back, where Ida kept a studio, her private space where she'd make her paintings and craft items. She had a small bed where she'd lie in the afternoons and read for an hour, then nap for a while.

I went through everything—books, photographs, letters, sheet music, dishes she no longer used, stacks of Gourmet Magazines, her old saloon dresses, record albums. I also discovered hidden here and there stashes of Mars candy bars. Every time I uncovered one, I laughed. My mother wasn't supposed to eat sugar. She knew she shouldn't, but she did. I don't know if she'd hidden the candy from herself or for herself; the latter, I suspect.

It was time to leave. I said goodbye to Ansgar, told him I'd come back to visit soon, packed up a few things of Ida's I wanted to keep. At the airport, checking through security, I put my suitcase on the belt and behind it, the small plastic box of Ida's ashes.

"Excuse me, what's inside?" he asked, pointing at the black container. The label, indicating human remains, had somehow come off.

I looked at the agent as if he had no proper etiquette at all, letting a few long seconds tick away before finally answering, "My mother."

He blinked a few times until he realized what I'd said, then he quietly nodded me through. Ida would have approved. I grabbed her ashes, my carry-on, and headed for the plane.

I spent only a few days in Port Townsend then I flew to Blakely where I interred my mother's remains with a symbolic vial of Gray's in the Blakely Cemetery next to MaUdi and PaChuddy. Before flying south to Georgia, I'd kept a small token of their ashes, mixing them together. I climbed down to the beach again, swam out to the big rock and, once again, offered them to the sea. I also brought three red roses, one for Ida, one for Gray, and one for MaUdi, who'd died in the early 1980s. I stood on the large rock and tossed in the flowers, one at a time, watching them swiftly move out toward deeper water toward Protection Island. Then I swam ashore.

When I came out, instead of climbing the bluff back to my house, I turned left. I wanted to walk in the sand and warm in the sun. I didn't want to think about anything, except what a lovely day it was. I hiked along the narrow beach, taking my time, inspecting all those half-buried objects the sea perpetually claims—bone-colored driftwood, broken glass, pieces of plastic, mounds of dying sea kelp, tattered fishing nets, and rusty metal. Decades earlier, the townspeople would truck out their refuse and dump it over the bluff, onto the beach—a modern-day kitchen midden. The sea pulled everything out, and brought it all back over time, altered and etched, to be alternately buried then exposed by the winds.

After I'd gone about a mile, warming in the sunshine, I slowly tacked back to where the small waves rippled over the sand. I looked out. I could hardly believe what I saw. Ten yards from shore, those three red roses were still together, following me down the beach.

B ack in 1969, when I was searching for a way out of the Bonfire, uncertain of what I should be doing, and where I should go, I was sent a message in a dream in which I was walking down a wooded trail. I came upon a small pond, about twenty meters in diameter. A man was standing near the edge, holding a long, wooden-handled harpoon, the kind used in 18th-century whaling. In the middle of the pond, lying just below the surface, seemingly asleep, was a white crocodile, easily three meters in length. The man circled the small lagoon several times, holding the weapon in both hands, furiously thrusting it up and down into the water, trying to rouse the giant, trying to entice it closer to the edge. It worked. The reptile swam toward the man, and when it was within distance, he raised the harpoon into the air, then furiously and repeatedly shoved it down into the water, until he struck deep into the creature's back. I could hear the shaft enter the crocodile's flesh.

It twisted and turned, shot back toward the center of the pond, and, unfortunately, the man refused to let go, desperately clinging to the upper part of the harpoon, his body spinning in the cold air, his legs frantically kicking to keep from being devoured. Hopeless. The croc had him, ripping apart his flesh, one leg at a time.

I wanted to help, but how? I looked about, searching for anything to use as a weapon. No sticks, no rocks anywhere. Frustrated, I began to dig into my coat pocket. Aha! A small handgun. I pulled it out, took aim, and fired at the creature. Instead of metal projectiles exploding from the barrel at twice the speed of sound, tiny green peas exited the gun, floating through the air in slow motion, comically bouncing off the reptile's thick skin, then plopping into the water. I stood and watched in mortification as the man's legs became bloody stumps. I couldn't witness anymore. I turned away, defeated, unable to help. When I pivoted back, both man and crocodile were gone. The small pond was now a vast ocean, the Beretta-like handgun a rifle. I lifted it to my shoulder, aimed at the distant horizon, and emptied the chamber. I stood and listened. After a long interval of time, the sound of the slug penetrating the muddy bank of an unseen shore in a country far away brought me out of my dream.

When I left Seattle for Port Townsend, I was in the second year of a twelve-year relationship, one that would become my longest. Greg and I met at a bar in Seattle in 1981, shortly after I'd moved into my new studio at Twelfth and Pike. I was thirty-seven, he was about twenty-five, and for the most part, it was rewarding; we seemed to nurture the best in both of us. In time, however, the chemistry changed. You don't think about it at first. One day, while you're alone, walking in the woods, working out at the gym, or while painting in the studio, you reflect on your life with this other person and suddenly realize the chemistry of love has died, buried in the ash of habit and convenience. I felt this, but I didn't know how to fix it. It seemed unfixable.

"I have to have more out of this. Our relationship is not working," Greg said one afternoon when I came in from the studio. "You need to try harder. Or else..."

His "Or else?" Ricocheted inside my head all afternoon well into the evening. Is there something else?

Yes, of course, there always is.

I drove over to Galax for a weekend of solitude. When I returned, I confronted him. I had to be brutal, to break it off completely; otherwise, it wouldn't happen. "You're right, Greg. It isn't working. You're only thirty-five, still young, and deserve to be with someone who can give you more than I can. I'm sorry, but we need to end this."

The separation was painful, traumatic, and, in many ways, costly. But it needed to be done.

I packed up and left, letting him remain in the house until we could settle everything. Fortunately, I didn't have to move far at all. Just down the road. I found an old building, still on the bluff. The structure, situated on acres of Douglas fir and cedar, was a multi-garage complex, built to house the previous owner's three vehicles and his thirty-foot travel trailer. Up front was a small two-bedroom apartment with a view across the Straits. It was perfect for my needs. I had a place to sleep, a painting studio, a print room to house my etching press. On the land, I planted a garden and got myself some ducks and geese.

It took about six months of hard work to convert it to a place in which I felt at home. Exhilarated with my new life, I jumped right in. There were many days of doubt, however. I'd turned forty-six that July and here I was, once again, starting all over. Was it the right decision? Should I have tried harder to salvage the relationship, at whatever cost? I didn't know. Once again, however, my crocodile came calling.

Upstairs in my new studio, I heard my front door open. I looked down into the foyer, and there was Greg. We began chatting about something as inane as what vegetables I should plant in my new garden. Suddenly, inexplicably, as dreams will have it, the studio began to fill with water, flooding in and quickly rising. In seconds, it covered the tables and chairs, the bookcases, filling all the cabinets. Unpainted canvases, brushes, and papers rose up, swirling and roiling upon the dream sea. I watched Greg thrash about, trying to stay afloat. Then something ominous beneath the water, something Greg couldn't' see, swam up toward him. I tried to shout a warning, but I couldn't. In a flash, the white crocodile breached the surface, twisting, turning, grabbing my friend in its wide jaws, dragging him down.

Seconds later, the water, churning pink, then red, began to spit up small bits of human flesh and pieces of bone, spinning in a myriad of vortices.

Blessed is the mercy of dream-time.

The blood and body parts quickly vanished, the reptile was gone, the sea was calm. Suddenly, from beneath the water, a newborn infant appeared, his tiny lungs screaming for air, his hands grasping for light.

The dream's message was clear.

Three Turns

December clouds hold us
close to the sleeping light of winter.

I'm touching all the parts
of your body with words.

The winds remember everything
in this beautiful snow.

Galen Garwood, 1992

"Have you been to Athens yet, or any of the Greek Islands?" asked the man sitting next to me.

"No, but I've wanted to go."

"Well," he whispered, leaning in close, "If you ever do, you must come visit me. You'll love it there."

I was having dinner with Merch and Alice Pease, at their home across the Sound from Seattle. My friend Jan Thompson was there, along with several others, including the man on my right, Richard Svare, who, back in the fifties, had lived with Morris Graves.

All during the evening, Richard, sitting next to me, regaled me with wonderful stories about his life with Morris, his few years working with Merce Cunningham in New York, his friendships with Alan Bates and Anjelica Huston, and his living as an ex-pat in Greece, working in film and TV. I had to lean in close to catch most of his tales as he was so soft-spoken. I learned later this whispering technique was meant to pull you into his world.

When the evening was over, as I was leaving, standing outside by the door, I shook Richard's hand, but he insisted on a hug. "If your offer is real and the timing OK, Richard, then yes, I'll see you in several months. I'll be in Italy in November."

"Of course. Absolutely. I'll have the city switched on and ready for you," he said, blowing cigarette smoke up into the wet night.

Several months later, I was in Paris, visiting John Koenig. From there I took a train to Florence, down to Rome for a week, and then headed over to Bari, and from there to Brindisi for my ferry crossing, changing trains in Pescara. Unfortunately, the train out of Rome was late; I missed my last connection. I ran through the station, struggling with too many bags, hoping I could still make it when a man in a dark uniform walked up. "Scusi, signore, it seems you've missed your train."

"It does seem so," I answered, trying to catch my breath.

"No problem, signore, follow me."

He appeared to be an official agent of some sort, perhaps even a conductor, so I grabbed my bags and camera gear and fell in behind him.

He didn't lead me up and through the passenger bridges, but straight through the yard, across the tracks, until we reached the train furthest away. As we boarded, he asked, "Are you traveling first-class?"

"Well, Eurail, but, yes, it's first-class."

He led me through the long train until we got to what must have been the right section. He gestured for me to sit, then sat across from me. "Grazi," I said, and began to settle in, assuming he'd be leaving soon.

He didn't. Out of the blue, he said, "I have a hobby."

"Oh, really," I said, not knowing what else to say.

I love to collect coins. All kinds of coins."

I looked at him for a few seconds, confused. Why was he bringing up such a strange topic of conversation? I wanted only to rest and relax. I waited for him to go, but he continued sitting and smiling. My tired brain finally 'ca-chinked' like an old cash register.

"Oh," I said, slowly nodding my head up and down, while just as slowly, digging down into my pockets and pulling out all of my change, mostly ten-franc coins.

Leaning over, he began to make a selection. The guy had conned this small-town Georgia boy so deftly, so sweetly, I could only smile. I didn't care. I just opened my palms and offered. He generously helped himself to what I would later determine to be about fifty US dollars.

"Signore, do you like wine?"

"I do," I said, anticipating another 'Ca-chink.'

He reached over and took the rest of my change.

"Red? White?"

"White," I said, barely audible. He stood and headed back the way we'd come, disappearing with my money. I had yet to see one other person on the train. After he left, I had a conversation with myself. "Is he coming back? Is this train even headed for Bari? There's always the possibility, you know, it's headed to Rome, back to where you were this morning. Have you traveled much, Galen?" I sighed and closed my eyes.

It was too much to think about, and I was tired. I decided to nap. Just as I was nodding off, I heard singing. I turned, and there was my new friend walking up the aisle, holding a bottle of wine. He set it down, saluted, and left. It wasn't the worst I'd ever had, but close. Still, the guy did come back, and for that I was grateful.

I made it to my ferry, crossed over to Brindisi, and another train into Athens where Richard was waiting for me. He lived in a small but pleasant apartment near the Plaka. Richard was a generous host, a delightful storyteller, and soon introduced me to his close friends. We'd stroll through the ancient part of the city for lunches and dinners. He told me of places to go and places not to go, what to do, what not to do. We took a few trips, one down to the island of Hydra and another to Mytilinyi on Lesbos. But mostly, we got to know one another. We talked a lot, especially about Morris and their lives together.

After the first few days, I began exploring the city on my own, hiking up to the Acropolis and the Parthenon. Or I strolled about Hadrian's Gate, then over to Syntagma Square, where the costumed soldier stands like a statue for thirty minutes, not moving a muscle until another soldier comes to replace him, the guard exchange highly and erotically ritualized.

One afternoon, I decided to visit the National Gardens, a vast, forested area and home to the Presidential Palace. I strolled down a long pathway, its borders lined with hyacinthus, daffodil, and euphorbia, thick hedges, and a dense canopy of trees beyond. I could see no one in the park. It was a quiet and peaceful afternoon. Then movement to my left. A youth appeared, kneeling at the edge of the walkway, holding a wild goose in his arms. How strange, I thought. He was alluringly beautiful with long, fair hair, light blue eyes, wearing a green shirt and white shorts.

He had that delicate Tadzio-look, the boy in the movie version of 'Death in Venice,' but he also reminded me of another youth, or rather statues I'd seen of him: Antinous, that lovely Bithynian Greek so loved by the Roman emperor, Hadrian.

Or might this be Ganymedes, sent to me by Zeus himself?

I stopped.

The boy looked up and asked in English, "Can you help me?"

With what? I wondered. The goose? Was the bird injured? Did he need help taking it back into the forest?

I started toward him, but in midstride, I stopped. I suddenly had the feeling I was walking into a modern-day fairytale. Was this enchantment? The setting didn't seem right; something was amiss. I stopped, then shrugged, as if to say, "I'm sorry. I don't understand," and kept walking down the path.

That evening, sitting with Richard in his flat, having cocktails, I told him about my day's hike through Athens. I went into great detail about my encounter with the youth and his wild goose, his plaintiff plea for help, of my wanting to go wherever he took me, and finally of my reluctance and decision not to follow.

Richard sat and listened patiently, quietly, trying to see the picture I was painting through the smoke of his cigarette. When I finished my tale, he looked at me for a few seconds, rolled his eyes, shook his head, then tsk-tsked. "You fool!" he exclaimed.

"Why?" I bleated.

"He was just trying to get you into the bushes for sex. That's all."

I thought back to the event, turning over things I'd missed. Maybe the goose wasn't wild. Perhaps my Ganymedes was older, ageless even. I looked at Richard, not knowing exactly how to respond, but finally, I offered cryptically, "Some you win, some you don't."

He laughed, then stood.

"Come, dear boy, let's go out," he said, putting out his cigarette, "I know just the place."

Back home in Port Townsend, I thrived in my new seclusion, living alone, working in my new studio, far from the noise of the city. I wasn't a hermit, by any stretch of the imagination. I had my friends in town, my gym, shopping to do, the monthly trip across the water to Seattle, the occasional exhibition.

It was during this last decade of my living in the United States that I entered several embellishing relationships, appearing unexpectedly, and I felt timely, bringing a kind of creative enthusiasm back into my days. That first trip to Greece was still resonating, and it wasn't hard for me to imagine having lived there in a former life.

Early that winter, I read Bernard Sargent's book Homosexuality in Greek Myth, with its tales of male relationships during the Greek Hellenistic period, in which the erastes, or older man and the younger, eromenos, were drawn into a mutually beneficial relationship. More than likely, these evolved from ancient Mycenaean rituals in which the older man would ritualistically abduct a young lad in the village, then take him into the forest for about three months. The ceremony, normalized through millennia, was accepted by parents, community, and the youth himself, and while he was expected to perform sexually with his abductor, he was also taught to hunt and use weapons for warfare, i.e. 'coming into manhood.'

The youth became a man and then he too the abductor. The cycle was repeated over and over again, until a thousand years later when Plato wrestled with ideas of homosexuality, he defined erastes/eromenos as something purely platonic. In practice, however, same-sex expression remained very much part of early Greek society, as it does today, there and everywhere else.

After the battle of Chaeronea in 338 B.C., when Phillip II of Macedonia saw what his army had done against the 'Sacred Band' of Thebes, that legendary, formidable army of male lovers, Plutarch tells

210

us that Phillip admonished his soldiers not to disparage in any way these brave men who died. We know from records when the Sacred Band fell, but we don't know if and to what extent other similar groups existed and how ancient might have been the use of 'homosexual' soldiers in military battalions.

Years earlier, in 1968, I was grappling with the war of my youth. Even though I lived all the way up in Alaska, far removed from the anti-war protests raging through American cities, I felt, like most of my peers, that what we Americans were doing in Vietnam was morally indefensible. Was I prepared to move to Canada? I'd considered it. My draft number came up that summer, and I had to fly down to Anchorage and appear before the draft board. I dreaded it. The idea of being in the military wasn't the source of my anxiety. Fear of discovery was.

I caught a flight and showed up for my scheduled appointment, standing in line with thirty or forty young men, all of us fidgeting, joking, smoking cigarettes.

We were then herded into a large room and told to sit and fill out the initial information form. I thought, here is where I could proclaim my moral objection. I was ready to make my case. But after a few questions, I came to one that startled me. It asked me to respond yes or no: Had I ever had or do I currently have sexual feelings for the same gender?

I was aware of the military's stance on homosexuality, but this was still two years before my glorious 'coming out' party at the Bonfire. The question before made me uncomfortable. I was conflicted, wondering what I should do. But then, staring at the paperwork, my pencil poised in the air, I suddenly realized: just tell the truth. I ticked 'yes.'

I stood, walked up to the front of the room and lay the form on the desk. A minute later, a sergeant sent me down the hall to be interviewed by the military doctor. He was sitting at his desk, perusing my paperwork. When he finally looked up, he referred to the question about my sexual desires by tapping the document with his pen, then asking, "This...um... this feeling you have, do you still have it?

What an absurd question, I thought. Could I have been wrong about myself all these years? Was I just confused?

I thought about the previous evening. I don't remember the hotel I was staying in, but I'd gone out for a walk, nothing really to do, and nothing on my mind except worrying about the next day. I'd had dinner, a few drinks, but couldn't sleep.

I passed a young man about my age leaning against a wall. We locked eyes, immediately sharing some timeless, cautious hunger. I continued for half a block, slowed, and then stood at the corner of the next intersection. He walked up beside me and, with a slight nod of his head, beckoned me to follow. I did. He turned right and at the end of another block, we ducked into a small hotel, the kind of place you never see unless you're looking for it. I stood behind, in the corner of the lobby, while he made arrangements with the desk clerk. When he got the key, he looked at me and nodded toward the stairs. I followed him up to the first floor, down the hall, and into a room. We disrobed and fell across a broken bed. The room smelled of smoke and sex. Neither of us spoke, nor turned on the light. When we finished, we left as anonymous as we'd arrived.

"Yes," I replied to the doctor.

He didn't look up; he merely scribbled something at the top of my form and told me to wait outside until someone called for me. A few minutes later, I walked down the hall, into a room in which an older woman was sitting at her desk. "If you'd like, I can make you up an appointment to see a psychologist," she said kindly, with grandmotherly concern.

"I don't need to see anyone. But thank you." I answered as politely as she'd asked. She smiled, wished me good luck, and I left the building.

On the flight back to Fairbanks the following day, I looked at the paperwork I'd received; 4-F was scribbled across the top of the page, next to my name. I knew what it meant, of course. I was also aware that many straight guys would claim to be gay so they could get the same classification. I guess, for them, it was easier than either moving to Canada or applying for the Conscientious Objector status.

As I looked out of the plane, across the vast Alaskan landscape, I wondered what I'd say to my friends when they asked how things went. Then I remembered: I hadn't told a soul. I was good at that.

It was a Friday afternoon in the winter of 1991 when I drove into Port Townsend for a workout at my gym followed by a sweat-out in the sauna, getting rid of studio poisons—pigments and paint thinner. I was sitting there in a steamy stupor when the door opened and in walked the first of several muses that would light up the end of my fourth decade and into my fifth. He was completely naked, an exquisite and sensual beauty. His spirit utterly consumed me.

212

His name was Ric, and we immediately struck up a such a warm bounce of conversation, I felt as if we'd known each other for years. Though never sexually intimate, we did become friends; he was far too young for anything more than my entwining fantasies. He knew I was gay and because he had a girlfriend, I comfortably accepted his being straight, though it wasn't always easy.

As the weeks went by, Ric and I spent more and more time together. He helped me finish my new studio, and hours each week in the gym. He became like a son, yet a lover I could never touch.

After several months, I told him I'd like to photograph him, suggesting more gym work, enhancing his upper body. He agreed, and together we hit the gym three or four times a week until I felt anymore would have been too much. I rented a large building at Jefferson County Fair Grounds, set up an elaborate set using a large number of rented theater lights. I took hundreds of photographs. In the end, I was only satisfied with a half a dozen, but those few made the project more than worthwhile.

In June of 1992, Ric and I took a long road trip, driving through Nevada and California, surfing the beaches in San Diego, on down to Mexico, then back to visit the Grand Canyon. We canoed down the Green River in Utah and even spent a few nights in Las Vegas, where I tried to sneak him into the gaming rooms. Ric wasn't quite twenty-one at the time, but we found a bar that wasn't so strict with checking IDs, and we celebrated more than we should have on our last night. Returning to our room in the wee hours of the morning, both of us happily but overly inebriated, he came up, hugged me, and said, "I love you."

His words split me down the middle. I'd always kept a safe space between us. I would never violate it. But the parameters were dissolving, slipping away. Too much alcohol. Finally, though, I somehow managed to resist and responded in my best buddy way: "I love you, too, man." I gave him a gentle hug and said good night.

A week later we were back in Port Townsend. Ric soon left for college, eventually met a woman, married her, and started a family. After that, I'd see him occasionally, and then, not at all.

In 1990, I began 'Adagio,' another multi-media project similar to 'Passport,' woven together with poetry and photographs, music by composer, Marcus Duke, and narrated by Richard Svare. It grew into a lengthy, expensive, and exhausting challenge. In 1993, I wrote Richard:

Portrait of a Youth, 1992

"I still have creative blocks in the studio, and it's difficult to determine the source. I'm frustrated with my feeble and failing economic foundation, putting this much effort and hope into 'Adagio,' realizing I was foolish to commit my meager savings for something so financially risky. Now I must concentrate on mending the tear in these day-to-day affairs. I've put all the multi-media equipment up for sale. I tell you this because I'll be sending a note off to Carolyn Kizer to let her know the 'Friendship Project' is off. I'm eliminating art projects for a while. Right now, I'm having a difficult time processing it all. I'm so tired and emotionally drained from what seems like a battle to make art; I question my viability. I'm distracted right now, and I must put away thoughts of doing anything with 'Adagio.' Still, I know my efforts count. I accept 'Adagio' as a project to be completed, as I always do with a painting."

Eventually, I did finish it. In 1992, it premièred at University of Washington's Meany Hall, subsequently traveling to Philadelphia for an international multi-media event. It received a Bronze Award, and a segment of it was included in the 'Xenographia Nomadic Wall,' at the 1994 Venice Biennale, and later in New York at 'Art Affair.' In 1995, I decided to show it locally, at Port Townsend's Rose Theatre.

The day before the presentation, I was once again at my gym, had a rigorous work-out, then hit the heat. The magic sauna. While the sweat poured out of me, I kept thinking about the next day. How would I manage? I needed someone to help.

As fate would have it, my next muse appeared as magically as had Ric a few years earlier. His name was Christopher. In fact, we'd met briefly at the gym the previous year. I remembered he was married and had a young daughter. We chatted a while and then I asked, "Are you free tomorrow? I've got a big party planned at my studio about five miles out on McMinn Road. I need help, mostly bartending. You interested?"

Christopher smiled and accepted the gig.

The performance at the Rose went well, a full house and I invited everyone in attendance to the party, set up with a bar and live music. At two in the morning, everyone had gone home, except Christopher and me. We sat in the kitchen at the table, chatting and drinking, relaxing after a long evening. I thanked him for his work, paid him what we'd agreed upon, and got us another glass of wine.

"Where do you live?"

"I live at the end of Jacob Miller Road, in the woods in a yurt."

I knew where he lived. It wasn't far. But since I didn't want him to go, I said, "Well, I'm not sure I'm up for driving anywhere tonight, Christopher. It's late, and I've had a bit too much wine."

"I don't mind staying."

"Great! But there's one problem. I've got only one bed."

He grinned and pushed his long, black hair back over his shoulders. "That's not a problem, Galen."

And it wasn't. Eros made sure of it. And so did I.

Christopher was twenty-six, brimming with confident sexuality, utterly comfortable with a body so classically Greek, it would have inspired Phidias himself.

I knew right away I wanted to photograph him at some point. I quickly offered the same deal I'd made with Ric, but with a considerably better return. "If you agree to a few months of gym work and allow me to take whatever shots I need for my art, I'll fly us to Greece. I'd like to put your body back in time, against the temples and tombs of the ancients."

I couldn't believe I was saying this. I had no idea where I'd get the money for such an adventure. To this day, I don't know how I pulled it off.

Christopher agreed.

Six months later, with my Nikon, a few sturdy lenses, a good tripod, fifty rolls of film, and heavy backpacks, we flew to Paris, took the train down through Italy, ferried across the Gulf of Patras, another train to Athens, then ferried over to Crete. In Hania, we rented a room, then a Jeep and set about searching the island for ideal shoot locations.

Two days later, hiking through a small village, we stumbled upon the carcass of a goat, its flesh rotted away, but its horns intact.

"Help me yank these out, Christopher. I have an idea."

The horns came away from the skull easily. We cleaned and tossed them into the back seat, then set off toward the mountains.

"I need to find us a cave, as far as possible from other humans," I said.

We headed toward Mt. Ida, and about midday, after climbing an isolated trail, we came to the opening of a cave. It was perfect. There was no sign of any tourists anywhere. We scrambled inside, out of the hot air, into a series of rocky caverns but close enough to the cave's entrance to benefit from available daylight.

I pulled the goat horns out of my pack and with a piece of twine, I secured them into his hair.

"OK, now stand up and take your clothes off." I requested.

Christopher sloughed them off without hesitation.

Standing against the wall, with light from the entrance slipping in across the rocks, Christopher was now Pan, that pastoral god of ancient Greece, seducer of nymphs and patron of the shepherd.

"OK, that's it. That's your wardrobe. Now I need you to become the Great Seducer in earnest. I need action. Give me an erection."

"Easy," he said, smiling.

Before I could even focus the lens, Pan stood there in his wildness, his magnificent nakedness, his beautiful penis, swollen and ripe. It couldn't have been any better had Zeus himself been directing. I got to work and managed to capture two or three good shots when I heard a voice behind me, "What's going on here?"

I spun around. Four tourists were standing in the cave's entrance, blocking the light, coming toward us.

"Fuck! Where in the hell did they come from?" I hissed to myself.

The scene abruptly ended. 'Pan' morphed back into Christopher, Christopher back into his pants, I bundled up my gear, and we hiked back down the mountain and, for my part, frustrated beyond measure.

I didn't know if I'd been able to capture what I'd seen through the camera. 1996 was long before digital cameras were available, and it would be months before I could develop the film and look at a proof-sheet.

As it turned out, I did. The gods were kind and generous.

A few days later, we drove to Sougia, hiked up a steep mountain pass then down into the secluded and ancient settlement of Lissos, on the edge of the Mediterranean. We were the only two living souls there. That night we camped near a phalanx of tombs near the sea, beneath a magnificent sky.

After Crete, we took a ferry to Sicily for a few weeks of shooting, then took a train up through Italy. It was early October of 1996. We arrived in the small village of Assisi in the afternoon on the day of their annual celebration, The Feast of Saint Francis. The entire population crowded the streets, everyone dressed in costume. We were back in the 13th century.

Christopher was enthralled. He loved a ritual of any kind, and I knew right away he'd want to participate. While I rested in our room, he took off to explore the village, returning a few hours later with a bouquet of marigolds he'd pinched from someone's garden and a bottle of wine.

"I'll wear this," he said, grinning madly, and holding up the white fabric I'd brought for various photo shoots, "and you can thread the flowers in my hair. It'll be perfect."

An hour later, we left our room and walked back to the center of the village, but instead of the crowds we'd seen a few hours earlier, no one seemed to be anywhere. The streets were empty. We continued until we heard music and laughter coming from a large tavern further up, around the bend.

"Let's go inside, see what's happening," insisted Christopher, dressed in his toga, his long black hair festooned with marigolds. We pushed

Christopher at Selinunte, 1996

King Selinus

If we should peer beyond what is ours to see,
with deeds and mouth utter blasphemies,
never fear the gods, trespass sacred places,
profane the sea, sky, olive groves, grape vines,
pine, spirit of the fruit of ivy, wild selino,
if we defy justice, stain the good with folly,
fail the feast days, lay hands on tainted
things, how can we dance or holily grieve?
The gods are long gone, their temples ruins
for millennia. Yet look how he turns his toso,
its tragic form, how—no ode to sing, no flute
to follow—he alone's left of the chorus, how his hands
grip his head, hair, how his muscles are taut
with sensual despair, reverent of the rites.

Peter Weltner

open double oak doors and stepped inside. The place looked like the entire village was in attendance, everyone standing shoulder to shoulder, drinking wine and waiting for a roasted pig to be cut and served. But not one soul in costume. Only my friend, Christopher. I turned to look at him, halfway expecting him to bolt, but he didn't. He was grinning from ear to ear, completely at ease. We got ourselves a glass of wine and threaded through the crowd. A group of ten young Italian men, all of whom were extraordinarily handsome gathered around us, intrigued with the man in the toga, wearing marigolds in his hair, looking like some 2nd-century Roman actor. They wanted to know where we'd come from and where we were going.

We huddled close to hear each other above the raucous noise of at least three hundred celebrants. I looked over at Christopher. He was happily surfing the energy that filled the room, entranced with a young man standing to my right. Christopher slowly leaned in, and, quick as a flash, kissed him. The young man bolted backward. The group went silent. Would the Italian youth throw a punch? Would there be a brawl? No, not at all. We were in Italy, not Kentucky, or Georgia. The young man smiled, graciously laughed it off, and the festive mood returned.

I was amused and somewhat envious. I could never be so bold. I also felt a brief pulse of jealousy, enough so that I made a mental note not to let my weaker emotions drag me into places I'd no business going. It was, after all, Christopher's sensual and sexual self, his untameable spirit, that so entranced me. I knew I could never possess it.

We continued our journey north, ending our travels in Germany, then flew back to the United States. Soon after, Christopher moved to his hometown of Louisville, to be closer to his daughter. A year later, we teamed up again briefly in Savannah, and on the enchanted coastal island of Cumberland, Georgia for one final photo shoot. The images gathered at Lissos, however, and those at the ancient temple at Sicily's Selinunte, are the ones I hold most dear.

Where are they now, these handsome men who so captivated me during my last decade in the United States?

Where is my Antinous, my Ganymedes? Is he still in the woods with the wild goose held to his heart, seducing men? More likely, he's sitting in a bar in the Plaka, waiting for some young beauty to walk through the door.

Christopher lives in Louisville, tending to his love of ritual and his family. We stay in touch.

In 2015, I spent a few hours with Ric in Port Townsend. We met for breakfast at what had once been the Salal Cafe, a co-op restaurant owned by a hand full of writers.

In middle age, Ric still has that seductive charm that once entranced me so. We sat and reminisced. He filled me in on his life—his work, his wife, his three children. Was he happy? I wondered. In spite of his bright smile, there was a sense of sadness about him, something unresolved, perhaps even lost. We finished breakfast and stood to leave, but I still had questions. I wanted to know what might have happened, what could have happened, that night in Las Vegas? Did he know how much I loved him, that I still do? But I didn't ask.

We walked outside, said a few last words, and shook hands. Ric crossed the street, and headed toward his motorbike, but stopped in the middle. He ran back, hugged me, kissed me on the cheek, and told me he loved me. Then he quickly sprinted across the road, jumped onto his bright red bike and headed home.

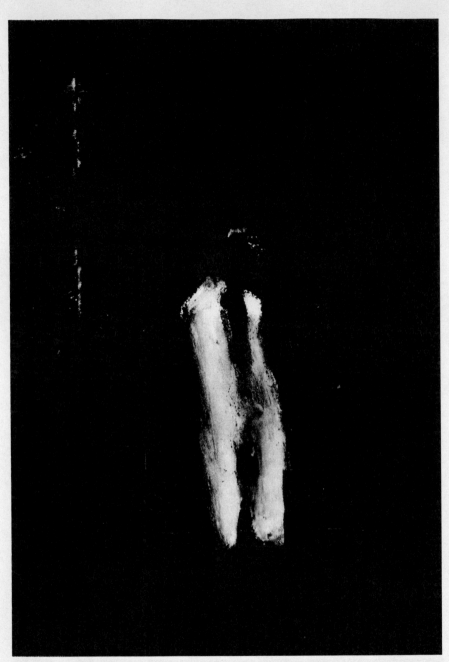

Figure 1, monotype, 18" x 12" 1984

Chapter Twenty-three THE SCENT OF GARDENIA

It was after midnight when the ringing woke me for the third time. I got up, grabbed the phone and buried it under the cushion of an old Victorian chair that sat nearby, adding extra pillows from the four-poster bed. I knew who was calling.

I sank down into the mattress, just drifting back to sleep when another unpleasant buzzing came from downstairs. "Oh, shit," I cried to the ceiling. "He's gonna wake up the whole damn house." I crawled out of bed, jumped into my clothes, and loped down the narrow stairs to the back door. I could see him in the window, smiling broadly, hands in his front pockets. I opened the door.

"What's up, Wade? It's late."

"Hey man, I know. Sorry. Can you lend me twenty bucks? I have to take my baby girl to the drugstore and get her some medicine."

"Baby? You mean like a real baby, an infant? You need how much? Twenty bucks?" It was all coming at me too fast. I was still half asleep. I scratched my head, doubting his story. "I'm not sure, Wade, if I..."

"Wait a sec, Galen." He disappeared around the corner of the house, through the side gate, and reappeared in a few shakes holding a black baby; Wade was as white as a magnolia blossom.

He put the baby in my arms. "Hold her, OK? I'll be right back."

"No, Wade. I don't think..." But he was gone again.

The baby looked up at me with wide eyes and a dimpled smile. She seemed perfectly healthy to me. I bounced, turned, and 'cooed.' I knew it was a setup—the baby, the medicine, the 'hold her for a second'—nothing but a ruse, Wade's trick to scam money out of me. I'd have to pay the twenty bucks just to get rid of him. "Whose baby are you anyway, and where the hell is Wade?" I grumbled. Then just as suddenly he reappeared, took the baby from my arms, and stood there, looking like someone waiting for their Big Mac at MacDonald's. All I wanted was sleep. I pulled out a twenty, Wade plucked it from my hand and slipped it into the back pocket of his jeans. "Thanks, man. Catch you later," He said, already halfway through the garden with the baby in his arms.

"Yeah, no problem, Wade," I mumble, locking the door, climbing to my room and collapsing into bed.

So, who was this Wade character? And where was I, exactly?

I'll explain. But let me back up the story, all the way to Seattle in the fall of 1978.

I'd received an exhibition announcement from Foster/White Gallery: an upcoming exhibition for an artist they'd just taken on. I was fascinated with the image on the card—a vast, brooding sky with only a sliver of a landscape. By the time I got to the gallery the following Thursday, the place was packed. The paintings, more like skyscapes, were indeed extraordinary. I was impressed with their color and mystery.

I heard my name called. I turned. My friend, Jan Thompson, was pulling someone toward me. "Galen, I'd like you to meet the artist," she said. "He painted these magnificent works. Aren't they spectacular?"

I smiled and moved to shake his hand. In mid-stride, I froze, stunned. "Larry? Larry Gray?"

"Galen?"

So long ago. I'd forgotten. But those piercing green eyes and red hair, that charm, and sweet southern accent I knew so well. I doubt either one of us had thought much about the other since we'd been at the University of Georgia in 1963. We laughed and hugged. What an incredible happenstance after so many years. It was unbelievable, but here we were, both showing at the same gallery.

Larry and I chatted the rest of evening, catching up on our lives as best we could, between ongoing interruptions from people wanting to speak to the artist.

Months after his first Seattle show, I drove down and visited Larry and his wife in Northern California, where he taught art at Humboldt State. Larry and Harriet, or 'Harry and Larriet,' as close friends called them, had been together since undergraduate days. They seemed happy. She managed the business side, and Larry made the art, and sales were doing better and better.

They were a good match, except for the fact that Larry is gay. In his youth, either he wasn't aware of it—if that's even possible—or he found life more comfortable in a traditional, heterosexual relationship. He seemed to love Harriet. But truth struggles to bloom; Larry came out. Harriet initially accepted his being gay and even tolerated his affair with another man. The three would often travel together. But this arrangement was impossible to maintain; separation followed. Larry, now single, moved back to Georgia, not to his hometown of Warner Robbins, but to the charming old city of Savannah.

He'd done well with his art. He bought a lovely 19th-century brick house on Monterey Square, around the corner from Mercer House, where Jim Williams, made infamous in John Berendt's novel *Midnight in the Garden of Good and Evil*, threw his lavish parties. In fact, the book had been published just before my first trip to visit Larry in Savannah in 1994.

Even though I'd spent my childhood sixty miles down the coast on St. Simons Island, and part of my teens in Charleston, South Carolina, two hours north by car, I'd never spent time in Savannah. I liked the place. It was different, a bit like New Orleans in some ways, similar and smaller than Charleston, but it has a charm about it, all its own. In addition to being the oldest city in Georgia, Savannah, established in 1733, was the first State Capitol. It sits on the Savannah River, twenty miles from the Atlantic Ocean.

On the second day of my first visit, Larry and I strolled down Liberty Street for coffee. We stopped at a favorite café on Liberty Street, sat at a small table outside and he told me about his new life, extolling the benefits of living back in the south, the warmth of the city, his new friends. Suddenly, looking over my shoulder, he called out, "Hey Wade, come and meet my friend, Galen." I looked up and saw a handsome young man moving in our direction. Wade smiled, nodded at us both, and sat at the table, though he said little, mostly nodding yes or no to whatever questions asked.

Larry leaned over and whispered, "You'll like him. He's one of Alvin's boys."

"Who's Alvin?" I asked.

But Larry was already up and paying the bill, walking away with a sly grin on his face. "I'll see you back at the house. Y'all have fun."

Wade, as it turned out, was one of the 'Savannah bad boys,' hustling flesh as twilight fell in the city. They usually plied their trade around the old city squares. They'd stand on the corner or sit on the wrought-iron benches, beneath the tall marble statues of Savannah's heroes. Most were local, but a few, like Wade, drifted down from up north, preferring the slower, more relaxed pace of the city and its laid-back clientele.

I had, of course, known guys like Wade from my bartending days at the Macombo. I'd even once, out of prurient curiosity executed a clumsy attempt when I was barely young enough to pull it off.

Now, in 1994, I was fifty, sitting across the table from a charming hustler who wanted nothing from me but to procure his services. He had the same shtick as Daniel had: charmingly evasive. While I was no stranger to sexual encounters, I'd never paid for it; never thought about it. But on such a lovely afternoon, in such a charming city, I thought: I'm here. Why not? We got up from the table and headed over to his room, more like a one-car garage, on Montgomery Street. We made it through the initial awkwardness, the sex, the brief after-chatter in about an hour. I quickly dressed,

left to right: Alvin Neely, Lennie Kesl, Gainseville, 2010

chalking off another first-time experience, then enjoyed the rest of the after-noon, exploring the city.

The following day, Larry suggested we visit his friend, Alvin.

"'The' Alvin?"

"Yep. The one and only. Alvin's somewhat of a legend in Savannah."

After a twenty-minute walk, we arrived. The magnificent Queen Anne mansion, known locally as the Baldwin House, was built for George Baldwin and his family in 1887. It looked somewhat like a castle with massive turrets, terracotta motifs, and eccentric roof lines.

We climbed the stone steps and rang the bell. The door swung open and a man in his early sixties with brown, thinning hair, wearing glasses, dressed in a white Polo shirt and Khaki pants, greeted us.

"Y'all come in," He said in a soft-spoken, genteel accent.

Alvin had been a professor of English literature, retiring early, investing in Savannah at a time when it was foolish not to. It'd only been little more than a century when the city elders rode out to bargain with Sherman, pre-senting the General with a symbolic 'key' to the city, which he then sent to Lincoln. It worked. Unlike Atlanta, Savannah survived the war intact.

By the early 1960s, in an economic slump, the city was on the verge of demolishing many of the old buildings, replacing the historic district with new, cheap, commercial structures. Fortunately, a few smart investors were paying attention to what was happening up in Charleston—massive restoration programs feeding a fast-growing tourist industry, hungry for anything old and everything quaintly elegant.

Entrepreneurs swooped in from Atlanta and other cities, converting many of the antebellum houses into small hotels and B&Bs.

Alvin led us through the main foyer, into the dining room and out onto a large screened porch where we sat and drank gin & tonics until dinner. He'd filled his home with art, lovely antiques, cabinets full of crystal and silver, and furniture from various periods.

The red-brick house was spacious. In addition to the main floor, the second floor had two bedrooms, and a small suite presumably occupied in the early days by the staff. This room was my usual accommodation when I'd visit. Additionally, there was a rental apartment in the attic, two in the basement, and two units in the carriage house outside.

I visited Alvin several times on my first two few trips to see Larry, then many times afterward, especially when Larry moved elsewhere.

In 2000, I spent one entire season helping Alvin restore his living and dining rooms to their original state, or as close as we could imagine it. There were no extant photographs or plans from its early days when the Baldwin family lived there, so a good bit of creative invention was needed. For almost a decade, every year, I came to visit. Alvin's home became a place in which my southern roots got nourished, albeit his house was far grander than any I'd ever lived in during my childhood.

There was never a dull moment at Alvin's. Beneath this quiet Victorian atmosphere, intrigue and chaos bubbled up with unending drama from an endless stream of quirky characters, many of whom John Berndt wrote about in his book. I met most of them, including the infamous Lady Chablis, who would later play himself (herself) in the film, directed by Clint Eastwood.

These colorful and aging misfits would show up unannounced, at all hours, sometimes at the front door, usually at the back. It wasn't only the local misfits who came, but also the well-established, the wealthy, the writers, artists, and architects. And always bubbling into to the mix, were the 'Savannah bad boys.'

Before the laws changed, hustlers stayed close to the old squares, much like they did around Penny's in Seattle or Santa Monica Boulevard in Los Angeles. Savannah's city fathers put a stop to this when tourism took off.

Now the hustlers had to learn new techniques, like collecting phone numbers and polishing their social manners.

During my visits, I met a good many. I was fascinated with their country boy charm and always amazed at the way Alvin dealt with them, almost fatherly, with a good measure of discipline. Of course, they only showed up

227

'Portrait of a Young Man, monotype, 18" x 24" ca. 1995

whenever they needed a little cash. He knew them well. A few he'd known for decades, and even though they'd long lost their arsenal of beauty, they were part of that prismatic mix in Alvin's multi-layered, fascinating life.

The one I knew best was Johnny.

After my third or fourth visit, always within a day or two of my arriving and getting settled into the guest suite on the second floor, Johnny would mysteriously appear at the front door. He seemed to know when I was in Savannah and I always wondered how.

The pattern was the same: Johnny knocks on the door. Johnny comes inside. Johnny, Alvin, and I sit in the small library, sipping on cocktails. Johnny spins out his alluring web. Alvin and I watch and listen, intrigued by his technique, amused by its transparency.

Within half an hour, Johnny and I trundle up the stairs to my room. He immediately hops into the shower, reappears, wrapped in a towel. Like peeling a ripe pear, I slowly pull the wet cloth from his body, revealing his pale nakedness. Johnny falls across the bed. His blue eyes butterfly toward the ceiling. I don't kid myself; this is sex for money and money for sex, emotionally unencumbered. That's all. No endearments. No expectation, other than mutual participation in an explosion of sexual fireworks. Still, a tenderness and unspoken affection breathe between us.

Afterward, we both shower, then dress. Johnny offers a brief bit of conversation as if we'd just finished a game of eight-ball at the local pool hall on Broughton Street. He walks to the mantle, picks up the two twenties I'd left, tucking them into his wallet.

"Tell Alvin I'll call soon," he says, tiptoeing down the stairs.

Johnny's gone. I dress, go outside, and relax in the garden next to the house, sipping a glass of tawny port. The night is dark and warm, the air thick with the scent of gardenia. Somewhere, in the alley a few houses down, I can hear two men talking about 'The Perfect Storm,' a movie they'd seen that night at the Regal Cinema.

Stain

In the King's palace, the lovely children,
dressed in colorful silk, their hair
braided and banded in gold and silver, sing
of the ancient, white elephant
wise and revered,
 the Buddha reincarnate.

While in the fields, the mahouts,
for production's sake, spike
bananas with amphetamines and feed them
to the giant beasts.

Their tusks grow brittle and break.
Their hearts thicken and convulse, a great
hurt settles in their eyes and dark
runnels of tears stain the dust
on their beautiful feet.

One more stain of human consumption.

Galen Garwood
1998

Chapter Twenty-four **ELEPHANTS**

It all began that summer of 1998. I was sitting in front of my Port Townsend home and studio, enjoying a glass of red wine, the last rays of the sun sinking beyond the Straits of Juan de Fuca. I was flipping through a recent publication of Smithsonian Magazine and came across an article about the plight of the Asian Elephant. By the time I finished reading it, I was crying. I don't know why this affected me so. Perhaps the essay touched something long forgotten, pricking my hypothalamus like a balloon, switching on my tear machinery. But elephants?

I do recall, when I was six, my mother took me over to Brunswick to see the circus. Toward the end of the big show, six elephants were trotted out under the spotlights to perform with what seemed like toy humans glittering on their back. The creatures were huge. They lumbered about, or reared up on their back legs, trumpeting, kneeling, then rolling over like a trained dog. One old tusker placed his foot, as large as a wash basin, inches above a performer's head as she lay on the ground. Closer and closer the foot descended, all the while drums beating. When it looked like it touched her nose, the elephant reared back, circus music filled the tent, and the elephants made one full circle around the ring, bowed, trumpeted, then shuffled off, head to tail, through the opening at the far end of the tent.

I sat next to my mother, terrified, yet fascinated by their immensity, their dusky, hairless skin, and strange shape. When the circus was over, the crowd rushed out to their parked cars. It was getting dark and time for supper. In the crush of people, I somehow got separated from my mother. Terrified, I ran back and forth between the cars, afraid I'd be forgotten. She found me crying, led me to the car, and drove us home.

Elephants didn't enter my thoughts again until 1965 when I was living in Ester, Alaska, where the last gold dredge was still in operation. Dredge #10 was a massive, seven-story metal monster floating on a pond, feeding on the earth below. Like an elephant, it had a protruding snout-like device on which was attached fifty or more pronged, cast iron buckets, each one weighing half a ton, all held in place by a four-inch thick rubber conveyor belt. This 'digging ladder' would dump the pay dirt into a perforated steel cylinder, about twelve feet in circumference, inside the belly of the dredge. It acted as a filter, like a metal stomach, spinning from pressurized jets of water, pulverizing large clumps of earth into small pieces of stone and gravel. The system was designed to filter out the gold and move it to a locked pay-room so that none of the workers could touch it, discreetly slipping a nugget into their pocket. I was told, however, that a worker up on the tailing deck would occasionally see a chunk of gold as big as his fist hurtle up from below, into the air, then get buried beneath mountains of rocky debris.

Only a handful of men were needed to operate dredge #10. It ravaged the landscape day and night, from the first thaw until the pond froze in November. As it fed, twisting and grinding into stone and ice, you could hear it from miles away, sounding like a symphony from hell.

In addition to dredging, another method used was placer mining. Water from Ester Creek was pumped through large hoses under enormous pressure directly into the hillsides. The water would melt the permafrost, disintegrating layers of earth into a thick sludge from which the gold would be sluiced out, along with other minerals and the remains of hundreds of woolly mammoths. These prehistoric creatures, buried for millennia, migrated during the Pleistocene age, across the Bering Land Bridge connecting Asia and Alaska, surviving on grasses, fleeing humans who ate the mammoths. Proboscidean graveyards were everywhere below the permafrost.

During the summer of 1966, I worked for Wien Alaska Airlines, loading and unloading cargo on the Fairchild F27Bs that Wien flew to and from Seattle and all across Alaska.

The F27B was a small, twin prop aircraft in which cargo and passengers shared the same level. Its design, a kind of upscale bush plane, was well-suited for getting in and out of the isolated settlements that populated the Alaskan landscape, from Juneau to Point Barrow.

My co-worker and I were on break in the cargo shed when a message came in that a flight from Seattle on its way to Nome had to make an emergency landing in Fairbanks. We were needed immediately on the tarmac, with a forklift and a water truck. "A water truck?" My co-worker and I looked at each baffled, wondering what the problem could be. The boss told us a baby elephant had been shipped to Nome as a promotional gimmick for the town's first major grocery store.

The baby more than likely had been leased to the grocery chain from Morgan Berry, an elephant trainer who'd once worked for Seattle's Woodland Park Zoo and then later began breeding elephants on a tract of land in Kalama, Washington, supplying various zoos with stock.

The plane landed, and we drove the forklift up to the side cargo door, unloaded the baby, and placed it on the tarmac, about fifty yards away. The little elephant, squeezed into a crate, hardly bigger than herself, bellowed and whimpered. Some not-so-bright person in Seattle or Anchorage, we were told, had fed her green apples, which led to a nasty case of diarrhea. The bottom of her cage, filled with a thick fecal slurry, was leaking out and into the aisle of the plane, causing a good deal of distress for the few passengers on board. We brought up the water truck and hosed down the cargo hold, then the baby and her cage. She rocked her body from side to side, slipping her trunk in and out of the crate searching for food and affection. We had nothing to give her—no tasty bananas, no sweet stalks of sugar cane, no bunches of grass.

Is it possible, I wondered, this little elephant, so far away from its natural habitat, from its mother and family, terrified under the bleak Arctic sky, could sense the presence of her ancestors buried in the ice below her? Probably not, but elephants do have an uncanny ability to detect the bones of their long-dead relatives. In any case, it was a pitiable sight, and to me, it seemed cruel and pointless.

We loaded her back onto the aircraft, and the F27B took off toward western Alaska.

When I'd finished the article in the Smithsonian, I went into my office, switched on the computer and sent an email to 'Friends of the Asian Elephant Hospital' near Lampang, Thailand. "I'm coming to help. I'm on my way."

Later that evening, standing in the kitchen preparing my dinner, my second self, knowing me and my impermanent nature all too well, challenged me. "What could you possibly do to help elephants in a country so far away?"

"I could, um, I suppose, make a documentary," I answered.

"What are you talking about, Galen? You've never even held a video camera."

"Yeah, I know. I know." I countered. "But it couldn't be that hard."

"But then what? You have no money. You have this beautiful studio and home, admittedly, with a sizable mortgage. You have your French/American etching press you worked so damned hard to get and haul around every time you moved—to what, three places now?"

"Fair enough," I said. "OK. Here's my plan. I'll sell the studio and the etching press. I'll sell as much art and furniture as I can. What I can't sell, I'll give away. I'll buy myself a camcorder, learn how to use it, head for Asia and everything else will fall into place."

"You're out of your mind, Galen. But, hey, who am I to try and stop you?" My alter ego knows me as no one did or ever could. I wouldn't change my mind. Not now.

And so, I began my new adventure. I had to refinance my studio and home before I could sell it. I went to my bank. They refused.

"Why?" I asked.

"Well, Mr. Garwood, your place is unconventional. Too hard to sell. We're sorry." They weren't, of course.

I found a small mortgage company who agreed to work with me. I sold it in six weeks. Before leaving, I held several studio sales, getting rid of most of the objects I'd accumulated—my etching press, my art collection, things I'd inherited from my brother Gray, my grandfather's oak table and turned lamp, most of my books. I still have the photograph of that last event: All of my Port Townsend friends milling about, my young friend Josh helping with sales, my friend Ed Cain standing in the corner pointing at my prized Goya print I reluctantly sold. I moved into temporary housing, bought a Canon XL1 video camera, taught myself how to use it, and headed for Asia.

I'd lived in six places in or near Port Townsend since leaving Seattle. I'd been in the area longer than I'd been anywhere. It seemed time to go, and the elephants were as good a reason as any. Better than most. And truthfully, I'd become disenchanted with what I had long perceived as the 'banality' and over-commercialization of art. Sure, this might have been more a perception than anything real—though I don't believe it was—but my retreating to a place and time for better perspectives on why I made art in the first place seemed like a good idea to me. So, after twenty-five years, I ended my relationship with Foster/White Gallery and left the country of my birth.

It had been three decades since I first experienced Thailand with my college buddy, Roy Blackwood. The country had changed considerably, especially in Bangkok. Too big. I headed north to Chiang Mai, the second largest city, and, in fact, closer to the elephants. I bought a handful of maps, rented a Jeep, and hired a young man to act as my translator.

In the beginning, I traveled back and forth, visiting elephant camps, elephant hospitals, interviewing various groups and individuals responsible for the welfare of captive elephants. I collected video footage and interviews from as far down as Phuket up to Mai Sai, on the northern border with Myanmar, from city to village. On my return trips to the United States, I collected more interviews at Woodland Park Zoo in Seattle. I no longer had a home so I'd either house-sit or stay with friends.

By 2002, I had enough material to begin editing.

Like 'Passport' and Adagio,' this was an independent, self-funded and, as it turned out, profitless project. There were times I'd wake up in some small guest house in a village on the border between Thailand and Myanmar and question my sanity. Wasn't I supposed to be in a studio making art? I'd chew

234

on this consideration for a few minutes, have a cup of coffee, eat breakfast, climb into my rented Jeep and head for the next elephant camp.

I spent seven years alternately working on the elephant film and the other documentary projects I'd begun in the United States—'Cadmium Red Light,' 'Letters from James,' 'Ed and Ed,' 'Anne Hirondelle,' and 'The Letter,' a short work on John Franklin Koenig.

Between film projects, traveling within Thailand, back and forth to the United States every few months, adjusting to a new culture and language, I managed, somehow, to make a few paintings.

The elephants were also painting. When I arrived in the winter of 1998, there was an explosion of hype in the Thai tourist industry with elephants making art. I ran into this at the Elephant Conservation Center in Lampang, where I first began to collect data for the documentary. As an artist, I wanted to know more about it, so I arranged an interview with Richard Lair, Project Director for the Center, and I even participated in an afternoon painting session with several mahouts and their elephants.

I wasn't so much interested in when they paint or how they paint but do they paint, i.e., are they making art? My job was to mix the colors, load the brush with pigment, give the brush to the mahout, who in turn placed it in the elephant's trunk. The elephants would paint on the paper or canvas until the mahout took away the brush. I'd dip it into another color, and then back it goes to the elephant. The mahout often, though not always, influences the actual process by pushing the trunk left or right, guiding a tusk with his hand or occasionally using vocal commands.

It did appear as if the elephants were involved in some kind if conscientious deliberateness. However, what seems and what is are not necessarily the same thing.

Pong's interest in creating enclosed, parenthetical shapes was consistent throughout his painting career, and his stroke application was very different from Wanatee's Cezannesque, vertical slashes, which looked uncannily like the forest in front of her. Like human painters, several of the elephants appeared to be eager to make art, but some found the activity rather uninteresting. The elephant does it, but is it because he or she knows there's always a bit of food on the back side of the work? If so, I can't argue that this choice appears to be smarter than many human painters, who, without alternative means, would starve. I speak from experience.

If elephants like to paint because they get depressed from being in captivity, as some argue, then they surely must get bored from repetition. These creatures paint for the tourists twice a day, seven days a week.

I wondered whether Prathida would have continued painting as long as I gave her a brush loaded with paint. Would she ever be able to express

Elephants and Mahouts, Lampang, Thailand, 2001

herself in a finished work, as I try to do? And would she want to make art without encouragement? These might seem like ridiculous questions, but are they?

Many of the elephant paintings are stunning, and quite a few have fetched high prices at auction houses over the last few decades. Some of the images have the vibrant spontaneity of a Cy Twombly or a Joan Mitchell, but, then again, the works are not dissimilar to paintings by children. And children's art is not adult art. We understand this—or we should—because, otherwise, we'd be exploiting the innocence of the child's spirit. A child's painting might be mistaken for an adult's, but the child is not necessarily trying to paint like an adult. On the other hand, as Picasso famously said, "It took me four years to paint like Raphael, but a lifetime to paint like a child."

An elephant making art is entertaining; so is an elephant playing football. Neither are activities the animals would perform in their natural environment. We defend it by insisting that it provides a bit of exercise and relief from the tedium of being chained and caged. It doesn't hurt them.

But what does it do for us? What does it do to us?

While we readily fly the banner of supreme intelligence, we could easily suffer an inglorious disappearance from our indifference and greed. I hope not, and I hope, for theirs and our sake, elephants remain with us. But they shouldn't have to paint to do so.

I completed 'Panom, a Story of Elephants and Humans' over a decade ago and went on to write several children's stories about elephants. In the course of making the film, I fell in love with the country, and the people of Thailand, and decided to move here permanently. Of course, I miss many of my friends in the United States. I miss my etching press now and then, and I'll reach for a book I no longer have but wish I did. Or I might wonder whatever happened to a particular painting. But not often.

Now and again, I reflect on whether my efforts might have made some slight difference in the life of an elephant, even if only igniting a flicker of awareness in at least one other human. I hope so.

The beautiful rub is, though, I'll never know. And that's OK.

For the first several years of filming 'Panom,' I returned to the United States for half the year, living in Port Townsend or visiting friends throughout the country.

In July of 2001, my brother, Bernard, made plans to fly out to Port Townsend for a visit, arriving at SeaTac International Airport in the late morning. It takes a few hours to get to the airport from where I was living on North Beach, which lies at the tip end of the Olympic Peninsula, so I rose before sunrise, early enough for coffee and a light breakfast before heading out of town, southward down the Peninsula through several small farming communities.

The weather was gray, wet, and foggy.

As I drove through the small community of Hadlock, a van barreled up behind me, its headlights blinding in my rearview mirror. On the narrow, two-lane highway, it's difficult for cars to pass. and since I had plenty of time to get to the airport, I slowed and turned off the road to let it go around me. When I pulled back onto Highway 20, I could see the van's taillights disappearing into the fog.

I drove another half mile when I saw something in the middle of the road, too far away to discern what it was. At first, I thought it might be a cow that had wandered up from the pastures. I gently started braking, and at about two hundred yards, I could see it was a car, obliquely angled in the direction I was traveling, dead on the road. I stopped and stepped out.

A gentle rain began to fall. Approaching, I could now clearly see the car, its front end demolished, smoke rising from the engine. The windshield had exploded from the impact; tiny fragments of glass were scattered across the pavement, glittering like jewels in my headlights. The driver's door was twisted open, barely attached. A young man or a boy—I couldn't tell—lay still, his head lying on the wheel as if he were sleeping.

Was he still alive? Should I pull him from the wreckage? Was his back broken? Might leaking gas explode any second? Should I turn and run like hell? And how had it happened? There was no other vehicle but his and mine.

I backed away, uncertain what to do, then a car drove up. The driver jumped out and ran toward me. "Jesus, what happened? Are you OK?"

"I'm fine. I just got here. Do you have a phone?" I asked.

He nodded, pulled it out, and called 911.

Standing about fifteen meters from the crash, waiting for help, we heard a noise that sounded like muffled cries but from where we didn't know. We looked at each other in confusion. My first thought was that someone had been thrown from the car. I ran from one side of the road to the other, looking up and down and through the bushes, until I came across an area where vegetation appeared to have been recently plowed over. "Over here," I yelled.

We scrambled down a steep bank, through the bushes and undergrowth, and discovered a second vehicle, still upright, the front end crushed, the driver barely conscious, pinned beneath the steering column. There were three other young men inside, all badly injured, crying "Please, please, get us out."

Impossible. The van lay pinched between several small trees, the doors severely crumpled.

"Hang on. Help is on the way. Just a few more seconds."

It wasn't long before a team of emergency personnel and firefighters came swarming down the bank like ants. I quickly moved out of their way then climbed back to the road. There was nothing else I could, so I got into my car and headed for the airport.

It had been too chaotic at the crash scene to make the connection at the time, but after about five miles, I suddenly remembered: the van was dark red. It was the one I'd let in front of me minutes earlier, now lying mangled at the bottom of the bank near the pasture. Had I not slowed and let it pass, had I kept on driving, more than likely it would be me lying there, trapped. I doubt I would have survived such a crash in my small car. The head-on impact was so intense it altered the direction of both vehicles 180 degrees.

The next morning, I learned from the local paper that the men in the van, all Hispanic, were on their way to work. They survived. The driver of the car, only eighteen, was thought to have fallen asleep at the wheel, dying on impact. The article also indicated that he was on his way to get his father and then off to the airport to pick up his brother flying home for a visit. I shuddered as I thought about it, wondering if my being alive and the boy being dead were purely serendipitous, nothing more than the fall of the dice. Or is someone or something else at play, moving us like pieces on a chess board?

A few months later, I drove out to visit my friend, Ed Cain, on his five-acre parcel of land not far from my old studio. It was Monday morning, September 10th. Ed lived in a modest two-room house and studio he'd built with his capable hands. He tended a sizable vegetable garden and kept various breeds of chickens.

I'd met Ed eighteen years earlier through my friend Sam Hamill. He'd married twice, had children from both, and even though his second family lived on the opposite corner of the acreage in a house he'd built for them, he preferred his solitude. He lived alone.

He greeted me at the door with his usual good-natured "Get on in here," sweeping his right arm out into the room as if to say, "OK, you found me."

Ten feet across the room we stopped and stood before one of his newest paintings, a large silver and black abstraction that nearly covered one wall. I smiled and nodded appreciatively. Then he led me across the room, around an old platen press, through his kitchen and out the back door to a small porch where we settled down to a lengthy conversation. Trees towered above us on all sides.

We hadn't seen each other for weeks and, as usual, were soon discussing our inescapable, irresistible tether to art, the joy we found in making it, and the various ways in which it entered and affected our lives. Our newest topic, however, was Ed's participation in several of my film projects.

Some months earlier, I had interviewed him for 'Cadmium Red Light.' Previously, I'd introduced Ed to Lennie Kesl, and they quickly became friends. It seemed fitting that Ed should add his two cents to the film's already rich collection of interviews. He was happy to do so, but what he ultimately offered surprised me: someone else emerged; not the gentle Ed I'd expected but an off-the-wall, slightly cantankerous character with sharp-edged humor. I was fascinated with what whirled out of his imagination, and I immediately sensed another project on the way. I asked him if he'd be willing to let me continue the interviews, not about Lennie, but about him or 'whoever' happened to appear when my camera was rolling.

What developed was a delightful fable. Ed split into fictional identical twins: Edward and Edwin. In the spooling-out of this enchanting yarn, Edward was contemplative and artistic. Edwin was cranky and countrified, a man who loved his chickens.

Being interviewed first, Edward explained that family tradition dictated the first-born son be named Edward. When twin boys arrived, their parents decided to call one Edward and the other Edwin. When they were children, they were known as the little 'Eddies.'

"OK," I said, "I'm game. Let's see where this fairy tale takes us."

Edward explained that his twin had fallen from a horse while trying to jump over a feed trough and landed on his head. "Edwin is a bit slow. When Mom died, I took him in. I take care of him. He helps around the yard, tends the chickens, stays out of trouble."

When I interviewed Edwin, however, the story reversed. In his slant, it was he who took care of Edward.

"Edward ain't good for much. He can't make a living. He don't do nothing but write poetry. Never did. And those pictures? Hell, nobody can understand them things. If he'd get himself a decent job, he might do OK."

On the surface, this unfolding invention seemed like a delightful comedy, but there was also something unsettling, something I couldn't quite put my finger on. After four or five interviews, the title of the film, conjured up by Edwin, asserted itself: "Ed and Ed."

In reality, the Ed Cain I'd known since moving to Port Townsend didn't have a twin. He'd grown up in the American West, part cowboy, part farmer and, eventually, he tried his hand at cooking, landscaping, and working in general construction. Ed was competent at just about everything —a jack-of-all-trades. But mostly, he was an artist and poet. He designed and handset the type for his limited-edition books, printing them on that old printing press he had dragged around for decades. His paintings are figurative abstractions, of birds mostly— loons and crows—or the human female body often expressed in bold, child-like strokes of black and white.

A big, tall man, Ed was quiet-spoken and possessed a gentle, generous heart. He loved to tease his way through conversations. He made you feel comfortable.

Our talk migrated from art in general to the specifics of setting up our next interview. We talked all afternoon. The sun moved beyond the clearing, behind the fir trees. The air grew cold. Ed's light bantering slowed, his usual bright disposition darkened. He seemed to collapse in on himself as he leaned both arms on the table, clearing his throat as one might do when wanting to change the subject. He paused, looked at me, and softly asked, "What do you think I should do with my work? With my paintings?"

"What do you mean?"

"Well, I don't think anyone much cares about them, one way or the other," he said, looking down at his hands clasped together, fingers twisting in fingers as if in agitated prayer. "I thought you might have some ideas."

I looked at Ed, still unsure of what he was asking. I didn't take the question too seriously, because, while generous to a fault with his friends, he was perhaps the most independent, self-reliant person I'd ever met. Returning a favor always required subtle ingenuity. I stuttered for an appropriate response until my awkwardness left a gap in our conversation. He felt my discomfort and quickly changed the tenor to his usual light bantering.

After another ten minutes, we stood and wandered back inside, through the kitchen, walking around the press, toward the front door.

I explained that I'd be leaving soon for Thailand, to resume work on the elephant film. I told him I would think about his questions and offer the best advice I could before leaving the country. I said I'd return in a few days to get more material for "Ed and Ed." I was excited by what we had, but we both agreed it wasn't nearly enough.

Ed smiled, walked me to the door. We laughed and shook hands. I got into my car and drove home.

On Wednesday, like most every other person in the world, I was still staggering from Tuesday's unimaginable destruction: planes crashing into the World Trade Center, bodies burning or falling from those iconic buildings, another plane crashing into the Pentagon, and yet another plunging into the woods near Shanksville, Pennsylvania.

No one had ever witnessed anything like it on American soil, not since the bombing of Pearl Harbor. 9/11 was a catastrophic event that irrevocably changed the way we think, spawning a new matrix of fear and hatred.

That early evening, I received a phone call from Lana, Ed's estranged wife. She was in Oregon and had been trying to reach Ed but couldn't. She was worried. I told her I'd call him. When I tried, I got no answer. Lana returned the next morning, and having to go directly to her office, she phoned me again, still concerned, and asked if I would drive out and check on him.

"OK, Lana, I'll drive out. Don't worry."

Ed lived out of town, not too far from my old studio. I drove out Hastings Avenue, left on Jolie Way, then onto his graveled driveway through the trees until I reached his house.

On the way, driving out Hastings Avenue, I found myself imagining a rather dark 'what-if' scenario. I don't believe these thoughts came from any feeling I left with after seeing him on Monday but more likely from Tuesday's disaster.

When I arrived, I saw his old, silver van parked in its usual place. The front door to his house was open. I got out, stood by my car, and called his name several times. No response. I called louder. Still no answer. The morning was bright and sunny, with a slight breeze.

I walked up and stood on the bottom step of his front porch. "Hey, Ed, are you there?"

The chickens started fussing louder, the way they do when hungry.

I heard a voice coming from inside. But I didn't think it was Ed's. It sounded more like a TV. Then—I don't know why—a darkness jolted me. I realized I was about to walk into something I didn't want to see.

But I had no choice. "Just go in," I told myself.

I could tell the door had been open for a good while because leaves from

'Figures' monotype 1995

outside had swirled into and through the room, scattering about into small drifts across the floor. Between Ed's front door and kitchen, the printing press stood in quiet obstinacy.

Little clay sculptures of birds lined the shelf beneath the windows. The large painting I'd seen on Monday loomed more intensely, its black and silver strokes piercing the room's dark interior.

Just to the right of the front door, he lay on his narrow bed, wearing only a white undershirt, twisted and bunched above his stomach. Ed was still holding the rifle, his right hand loosely cradled around the stock.

A small portable TV sat on a crate next to his bed like some strange intensive care device, attending the body that lay before it. The bullet, entering his mouth, exploded the skull's parietal bone and left a large, irregular pattern of blood and flesh against the wall. His face seemed strangely tranquil as if he were merely in repose, eyes shut, calmly listening to the newscast. I stood there, transfixed in the aftermath of mayhem—the strange juxtaposition between Ed's lifeless body and the droning television spooling out tragedy to the world.

I'd entered a wholly new kind of experience and seemed to be operating, almost autonomously, as if from a script. I picked up the phone from the table near a window that looked out into the yard. I knew I needed to call 911, but first I called my friend, Anne Hirondelle. It seemed crucial I speak to someone I knew. I told her what happened, what I'd found.

"Call Stephen. Please tell him to come over right away."

Then I dialed the emergency operator, turning away from the tragic scene. I looked out of his window, into his garden, thinking how beautiful and green everything was. I could hear the clucking and crooning of chickens. "I need to report a suicide," I said to the operator.

"Are you certain he's dead?"

"Yes, I'm sure of it."

"How far are you from the body?"

"I'm close...maybe fifteen feet. It's a small room."

"Can you take the phone to another room?"

"No, I can't."

"OK. But I need you to stay on the line. Keep talking to me. Stay on the line. The sheriff is on his way. He should be at your location momentarily."

"This is hard for me."

"I know it is, sir, but I need you to stay with me."

After the initial shock—the mind's processing of death, a friend's death, of seeing what the force of a bullet does to flesh and bone, and of seeing his nearly naked body slumped against the wall on which his last thoughts remained, painted in blood and bone—I turned away.

245

The overwhelming horror ignited chemicals in my brain that helped defy my frailty. The body mercifully does that. Strangely, I became emotionally detached.

As I waited, I held the phone to my ear, my eyes wandering everywhere but toward the bed.

"Are you still there, Sir?"

"Yes, I'm here. I'm here," I kept repeating, assuring the voice on the other end of the line.

On the windowsills and table, lottery tickets had been scratched, crumbled, and tossed. Stacked bills unopened. On the bedtable was an empty wine bottle. In the middle of the room, a dark-red upholstered chair lay overturned, and beyond, a closet door stood open.

There's no way to be sure exactly when Ed pulled the trigger. But while I waited for the sheriff, and to keep from bolting—I thought I might—I began to paint his last scene: A man is lying on a small bed, trying to swim out of darkness, desperate to ease a sorrow he can't name. His entire world is collapsing, and a voice on the television confirms it. He makes a decision. End it all. Don't hesitate. He rises, stumbles toward the closet. He knocks over the chair, grabs the rifle from the closet, falls back in his bed. Don't think. Pull the trigger.

"Are you still with me?" asked the woman.

"I'm here."

"The sheriff is heading up to the house."

"OK."

"Now, listen carefully. Here's what I need you to do, Mr. Garwood. Put the phone down. Place it on the table, OK? But don't hang up. Then I want you to calmly and slowly walk outside with your hands—both hands—over your head. Do you understand?"

I did. I got it. Completely. Instantly. Uncertainty surrounded me. I could have been the shooter.

I walked out with arms raised. The sheriff approached warily, apparently trying to get a read on any possible and unpredictable move I might make. I thought I heard him say, "It's OK." I relaxed and let my hands fall. Quickly, he reached for his weapon. Back up went my arms.

A moment later, the county prosecuting attorney arrived. "He's OK, I know him," she said, moving between the sheriff and me, on into the house. The sheriff followed her inside, and after a few more minutes, an emergency vehicle arrived. Two paramedics rolled out a gurney, and they went inside.

From behind, Ed's wife and fifteen-year-old son suddenly appeared. I turned. Horror and disbelief clouded their faces.

246

They wanted to go inside, but I stopped them.

I knew this could have devastating consequences, especially for the boy. I pleaded, "Go home. You do not want to see this. You mustn't."

In tears, they turned and left.

After a few minutes, the sheriff and county prosecutor walked out of Ed's house, got into their cars and drove off. The medics followed with Ed, encased in a body bag.

No bright yellow tapes cordoned off the house. The sheriff had given me no instructions. I stood in the yard, wondering what to do next. I assumed the county officials considered Ed's death self-inflicted, and that I was expected to go home as everyone else had. But, how could I?

I went back inside. Ed was gone, the rifle, gone, and the TV, silent.

When Stephen appeared, we went to work, searching around Ed's kitchen for rags and cleaning supplies. We scrubbed the floor and the wall behind the bed. I dragged the mattress into the yard, searched through Ed's studio and found paint thinner to pour over it. I set it aflame.

We did our best to put the place into some semblance of order, as if Ed were merely out for the afternoon, getting supplies. Stephen washed the dishes. I put the empty wine bottle and the stained towels and bedding in plastic bags. We set the dark-red chair upright, shut the closet door, and swept the dead leaves out into the yard. Then we left.

A week later, I headed back to Thailand.

By November 2006, I'd finished "Cadmium Red Light" and had nearly completed the elephant documentary. I began to think about the scant video footage I had for "Ed and Ed."

The mini-tapes had lain undisturbed in their tiny, plastic box on a shelf in my office, gathering dust. I couldn't look at any of the material. But those three one-hour tapes kept nagging at me.

As winter drove on, every time I went to my office, I could feel Edwin pulling at me. It was time to edit the twins.

Admittedly, I helped define the two characters by shaping my interviews to accommodate either Edward or Edwin.

Nonetheless, as I began to study the raw material, I wondered to what extent. Ed orchestrated the entire scenario. It was his invention, his fable. "Ed and Ed" was his. I was only shadowing his imagination.

I began to assemble what material I had. There wasn't much. I wanted to stay close to Ed's Ed, but I needed to understand why. I needed to know how. My job was to make sure the story would ultimately pass the honesty test.

There's a scene in which Edward talks about bringing his brother to live with him after their parents died. He talks about going to Cenex, a local garden store, to buy fertilizer for his vegetables, and he takes Edwin with him.

When they've finished shopping, and are back in the van, Edwin has a box of baby chicks on his lap. Edward says, "What do you have there?"

"Baby Bafarmingtons," answers Edwin.

Now, as far as I know, Ed never studied acting, yet he tells this fabrication with such conviction, his voice breaking, tears welling up in his eyes, that one feels genuine brotherly love.

As I struggled to develop a narrative, it became apparent that Ed's alter ego, Edwin, represented everyone who didn't or couldn't understand Edward, (i.e., Ed) dismissing his paintings, his poetry, and his need to make art. The challenge for me was weaving together a story with such limited material, achieving the necessary balance. It needed a beginning, an ending, and a purpose. It also needed to be collaborative, to be what I imagined Ed would have wanted. For the viewer and the integrity of the documentary, it seemed necessary I stitch the brothers together, back into Ed Cain, to resolve it as history.

After completing the first draft, I showed the film to a test group. I wanted feedback, to know not only whether I'd successfully created the illusion of twins but, more importantly, whether the fable could transcend itself to become real. Would the film offer some lesson—a parable's gift—the viewer could grasp?

Of those ten subjects who viewed the film, only one was uncertain while the others fully believed Edwin and Edward were twins, at least until the ending when the Eds became one. In the film's beginning, he reads one of his poems:

In winter one loon stays
just short of the farthest old piers.
Perhaps it is not always the same loon
The light in this sun-diminished season
seems continual and it makes
little difference if it's dawn or evening.
In reflection, the loon seems not so cold.
The window mirrors my eyes against haze.
The loon stills the air between us.

In the final scene, Edward is sitting on a metal stool in front of his platen press. As the interviewer, I explain that his brother Edwin has dismissed his version of their lives together. That Edwin, in fact, had been taking care of him. Edward quietly laughs and says, "That's amazing. I'm surprised you got that much out of him. He usually doesn't talk that much. I don't know whether I want to dispute what he says or not."

He slowly stands, walks toward the viewer and disappears. We are left alone in the room with the printing press and the little clay sculptures in the window. We see a message scrolling up and over the final scene. From these few words, we learn there was only Ed. The viewer now understands the truth in the fable's revelation.

I was the last person to have seen him alive, and the one who found what he'd left us. I would later ask myself, "Was I not listening close enough on that Monday afternoon? Was I overly concerned with my projects, my preparations for travel to detect his pain?" Whatever clues he might have given me on that Monday, I missed them entirely. Then Tuesday came.

Much later, however, going back through my last day of filming, I discovered in one sequence, Edwin talking about their lives, his and Edward's. He says, "We don't have a desire to get involved with one another now," adding, "It's almost door-shuttin' time." Did his colloquial humor merely refer to being old and shuffling off naturally, or did it reveal darker thoughts? Ed was only sixty-six. And was it possible, as he lay in hopelessness on that Tuesday night, what came spewing out of the TV was the proverbial straw that broke him beyond repair? Was Ed another victim of 9/11?

It's been fifteen years since he asked me about his art and what he should do with it. I think about his question still. Ed understood that only time and human capriciousness determine art's durability. If perhaps he felt his paintings and poems tethered this world to another, then sure, he'd want to know. I would, too.

Thinking back on that Monday afternoon, as we sat beneath the trees, the sun falling into the sea, I don't believe Ed was asking a question at all. He already knew the answer. He was merely offering an awkward, oblique farewell, stilling the air between us.

'The Path' galenograph, 2018

Afterlife

Now we share everything—
seven petals, seven seas,
seven words like moths
wet with the night. You give me something
I give you, feeding doubt, faith
obscured by the living rain.
Leaves gather what we make
of the yellow bells at dawn,
the horizon ringing us
plural. Seven clouds oblivious
to the seven cathedrals of the sun—
we struck an accord, you and me,
with the scent of an orchid, a shape
we discover in nearby nebulae.
Shattered beauty, unravel with me.
Every day rings in seven songs without a name.

William O'Daly

Chapter Twenty-Six *SLEEPING WITH MY BROTHER'S KILLER*

The most prodigiously pushy life form surrounding my house surely are those large red ants that patrol the perimeter of my garden. They inhabit every tree, constructing their nests by rolling up leaves, gluing the edges together with material manufactured within their body. The ants are always on the march for food, blazing trails through thickets of dense undergrowth, navigating superhighways of electrical wires, and the bamboo fences that enclose my yard. They don't bother me unless I stumble into their territory. Then, of course, the warrior ants attack, relentlessly and aggressively, surging from the ground or parachuting from the trees, delivering painful bites, injecting their venomous *Solenopsin* into my blood. I stay out of their way, as best I can. We understand our boundaries, but occasionally I intrude, or they intrude.

It's difficult to know the ants have attacked until they've done their damage. They rip through the skin with powerful jaws and thrust their stingers into my flesh. I try to slap them into oblivion, but after the first bite, it's too late. I prefer to think of them as one organism made of limitless, self-replicating parts, each part designed to perform specific tasks, like biting into human flesh. My flesh. Thinking this way helps absolve my guilt when I occasionally find and destroy a nest of hundreds, even thousands of ants. I suppose I should learn to cook them up as the Thais do. They delight in eating almost every kind of insect.

After a long day in the studio or the garden, I lie in bed and contemplate another organism, too small to see without powerful microscopes. It inhabits my interior universe.

A decade ago, I was visiting my friends, Walker and Jim, in Palm Springs. They weren't home at the time; they were in other states visiting their families for Thanksgiving. I had their magnificent home to myself, a car, a sizable pool, and hot desert air. I had nothing to do but swim and read, watch TV, go to the gym, visit a few friends and sleep.

For the first few days, I exalted in this 'do-nothing' schedule. By the end of the week, however, something changed, coming on suddenly, like a bad cold, then quickly picking up momentum, moving into my lungs, tearing at my energy. I moped around the house. I couldn't sleep. When I lay down, I felt as if I was drowning, my lungs filling up with water. Eventually, to get any rest at all, I had to sleep sitting up. I should have gone to a doctor, but I didn't. At the end of the month, I'd lost considerable weight.

My friends flew home, took a taxi back to the house and when they saw me, they were stunned.

"Galen, I don't know what's going on with you, but I'm taking you to the hospital. Now. Let's go." Walker insisted.

I didn't argue. I was too tired and grateful the guys had returned. In the emergency room, after a series of tests and five hours of waiting, the doctor returned, telling me I had acute pneumonia, but that, additionally, I was HIV positive.

Like most humans afflicted by an illness that suddenly interrupts our day to day routine, altering our entire connective sense to everything around us, including and especially time, the news sent me reeling, tossing me into what felt like a sea full of hungry sharks. The doctor put me on a heavy dose of Bactrim until I could return to Thailand a week later. Once back in Chiang Mai, after another blood workup, my Thai doctor decided on the best course of antivirals. He informed me that I'd need to take them every day at the same time for the rest of my life. My first concern, strangely enough, was how in the hell could I afford this without insurance. I knew that HIV meds were expensive. I had no choice, of course.

On my first night of taking the drugs, the side effects were frightening and destabilizing; I felt as if I were on a bad LSD trip. I didn't think I could handle it, so I returned to the hospital the next day, looking for some alternative. My doctor informed me that there was none, except death, of course. He assured me that my body would eventually tolerate and adjust to the drug, that I should take it just before sleeping.

"Sleep," he said, "somewhat masks the intense effect." It does, and it doesn't. My dream world became razor-sharp. It's OK, most of the time.

I take my meds each night, crawl into bed, and wait for sleep to enclose the drug's intensity. Even in sleep, I can sense the conflict between the virus and the anti-virus. My body is a battleground upon which everything—composites of water, biological catalysts, enzymes, hormones, acids, electrical impulses, minerals, gases, human debris, symbiotic bacteria, virus, fungi, and even desire—struggles for balance. I witness this fortress of urgency, every element, event, and expectation pitching in to maintain the body's integrity, its desire for homeostasis, for longevity. But HIV is never part of the team.

These tiny sputnik-shaped orbs with their lethal docking prongs are dead set on replicating themselves by subterfuge, converting their RNA into DNA.

If they can, they attack my body's agents of defense. They destroy my T-helper cells, my CD-4 coding, obliterating millions of years of cellular negotiations. Systems of immunity fail.

When my brother was dying of Pneumocystis pneumonia, his doctor explained to me that the fungi, *Pneumocystis Jirovecii*, live in all of us, in our lungs, safely corralled by our primary immune system. When HIV hacks into our CD4, however, demolishing our lines of defense, the fungi multiply to such an extent they inflame then destroy our lungs. We drown.

Two years ago, I decided to quit taking my meds. I was weary, to be honest, of the hassle, the side-effects, the residual sluggish feeling I have every day at about noon. And, of course, the cost. I Googled. I researched. I studied what I could about people who'd gone off treatment. Many have, so I made myself believe I could as well, that I'd survive without the drugs. And, as a backup rationale, I told myself that even if I were wrong, it wouldn't matter all that much. After all, I was entering my seventh decade. So, I quit. I was pleased with my decision and prided myself on being proactive, taking control of my life, doing what I believed was the right action. And I must admit, for the first six months, I felt great. I was additionally happy not to have to lay out that monthly chunk of money.

HIV, however, is tenacious. It's greedy. It has no sympathy, no understanding and no appreciation for the fruits of reciprocity. It doesn't give a damn. It doesn't care that if I die, it dies.

After nine months of being off my meds, the virus reclaimed its status. My viral load soared. I began to exhibit uncomfortable skin problems. I scheduled an appointment to see my doctor. When I told him what I'd done, he didn't say, "Galen, you're an idiot." He might have thought it. He merely shook his head, then strongly suggested I resume treatment. "Let's do a new blood work-up," he advised. "We need to see where you are with your CD4 and especially your viral load count."

Two weeks later, the results came back. I was disappointed, of course, when I discovered my CD4 count was back down to where it'd been eight years earlier, perilously low, and my viral load was soaring.

"Stupid. Stupid. Stupid." became my theme song for several months.

And yes, I know, I'd promised myself that if it didn't work, so be it. I've lived plenty long enough. But now, being so damned cavalier didn't sit right. I wasn't ready after all. I've too much yet to do and, of course, there's always Ida's "You gotta make do with what you have. Sell the monkey," rolling around in my head like rocks in a hubcap.

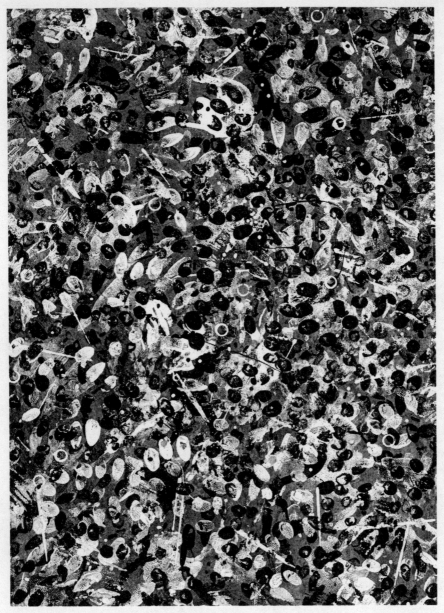

'Battle' oil on paper on panel, 43" x 31" 2016

I resumed taking the meds.

Every evening, at 9:45 p.m., give or take a few minutes on either side, I swallow my tablet, unsheathe my sword, and lie in bed, waiting for battle. My *Oneroi* swoop down and carry me dreaming into their world, leaving my body below, sleeping with my brother's killer, coursing through my blood like a horde of Vikings plundering a dark sea.

Hypnos comforts me.

But I'm all too aware that his brother, *Thanatos*, is close by, standing just beyond the door, whistling, and waiting.

THE FISHERMAN

He sat on the rocks, by the river,
his robes hiked high, legs
paddling the water,
his tired feet dancing in the current
among the fish and gray-blue stones.

"Make no mistake," he said, "I'm no messiah,
not at all, and no cause
for celebration. I am not a god.
Don't be stupid. I'm the same as you,
amply mortal, a pod
full of shit, and seeds, and stardust.
Yet even so, more sacred than myth.

All at once he rolled back upon a boulder,
his bare azimuthal knees fluttering like a butterfly
in the wind. Trapped
in his remarkably prehensile feet,
twisted a magnificent carp.

"Let's eat," said the Master.
"Let's eat."

Galen Garwood
2007

Chapter Twenty-Seven **THE HEART'S SONATA**

Can anyone adequately define art? Do we know? One has only to sift through a surfeit of quotes about what it is, what it is isn't, and what it should be or could be, from philosophers, painters, dancers, musicians, the man on the street, children, the ancients, the futurists, and more than a few scientists, to understand how pervasive yet elusive art is. We call it a jealous mistress, a muse, a spirit. Braque thought it should disturb us and Degas believed it a vice. Some say it's madness while some believe it is a discovery of the elementals of nature. Others embrace it as aesthetic expression.

Many years ago, when I was participating in the Washington State Artists-in-Schools Program, a fourth-grade student raised his hand, stood, then asked, "Mr. Garwood, where do you art at?"

His question struck me like an arrow, dead center on target.

Art is a verb, a doing. Thou art here, a 'coming into being.'

While I can't define art—I don't think anyone can and maybe there's a reason we can't—I know it has a purpose. It matters.

I'll soon be seventy-four. There's no particular comfort in knowing I've slightly exceeded today's average life expectancy, though, sure, I'm grateful, even pleased, to be here still. I have no definitive answers to any questions about art and why it's made, about my art and why I've made it, and still do, and for whom. Is there some pathological angst pushing against parts of my brain? No doubt, there is, but it's nothing I want to change, mind you.

I've long been fascinated with cave art, especially the Chauvet-Pont-d'Arc cave paintings in Southern France. Early humans created many of these over thirty millennia ago. The gallery of horses and lions is stunning. To me, the only thing primitive about these drawings and paintings are the tools that were used to make them. I question even that. What intentions, what hopes, did our ancestors have in mind when they created such powerful images of animals, objects, and patterns? Our brains evolved so slowly, we can only speculate, but by the Paleolithic Era, we seemed to have begun transferring ideas into graphic symbols on stone. We don't know the duration of time this took nor, in fact, do we have any idea of our concept of time that far back.

Do these images on the walls of caves represent our earliest aesthetic expressions? Or did they come from something more essentially urgent? Could they be transformational symbols of things necessary for survival—water, food, and warmth—recreating a ritualized 'self' within human consciousness?

Evidence suggests that Paleolithic cave painting (20,000-40,000 BC), disappeared before the Neolithic Period, (5000-12,000 BC), when more functional, ornamental art evolved with the first stirrings of written language, principally as numbers and symbols.

If I'd been born in Paleolithic times and didn't die in infancy from disease, snakebite, starvation, by accident, or as prey, and if I'd been lucky enough to survive until my fifteenth year, I might have lived on into my third decade. I might even have become an elder, possibly a cave painter.

Memory and imagination have been lovers for a long time...I stand in the dark recesses of the cave, my back to the shadows made by flickering light—small fires burning in shallow bowls carved into the stony earth. In my left hand, I hold a stick of wood, burnt and sharpened on one end. I move it deftly back and forth across the rough stone. *Animal* emerges as an idea of fullness. I spit on my thumb and smudge the black carbon across the stone surface: volume moves outward, toward me. I pick up a torch, hold it close and study the image. I step back, looking from a distance. I want more. I need *Animal* to live, to die, to feed my family. I bend to the ground and grab a shard of broken tortoise shell. I dig deeper into the outline of *Animal*, setting it free, scraping through the charcoal, down into the hard layers of ancient stromatolite, into the rock itself, exposing a white line of limestone and quartz...until...there it is, separate and breathing, leaping into the light of the fire.

I'm mostly a practical man, though I do ruminate a lot, and, clearly, much of it fanciful. I've been somewhat seminomadic, often solitary and the older I get, the more sacred becomes my solitude. I inhabit a body of wrinkled skin, brittle bones, and thinning meniscus. My joints are disappearing, and my earlobes are growing. My two testicles still work fine but fall like ripe fruit further and further toward the earth. None of these conditions, however, alter my imperturbable curiosity. It remains the same as when I found my first breath in 1944, and it'll be the same tomorrow as I ponder what'll happen when I lay that Prussian blue against this Venetian red.

This plot of land on which I live is not large by human standards—80 feet by 110 feet. I sit in the middle of it, in the shadows of bamboo with my eyes closed and listen to the sound of the small river that borders one side, only a few meters from my garden.

I live with a variety of creatures, different but similar to those of my childhood habitat. Mice and mosquitoes, rats, snakes, lizards, the persistent gecko, and its noisy cousin, the considerably larger tokay lizard, which, I might add, sounds an awful lot like someone with a mouthful of bread yelling 'Fuck you, fuck you, fuck you. They all manage to share some part of my open-air studio. Dragonflies and beetles, swoops of birds, scorpions and freshwater crabs thrive in nearby grasses. The villagers, tending their paddies of rice, and other crops, come and go without a great deal of hurry, as they have for centuries.

The monsoon season brings much-needed rain. The river that flows between my house and the rice paddies almost disappeared during April and May, but now it's full again. The farmers and fish are happy. Birds, frogs, and insects express themselves in a sound-sluice of delight.

Thailand's insects and arthropods arrive in every shape, color, size, and song. Among them is 'Pretty Red Bug,' *Probergrothius nigricornis*, marching out, newly hatched, from beneath the leaves of the forest, crowding into my garden, sometimes crawling through the crack beneath my front door.

Pretty Red Bug has evolved a colorful survival suit—a large, often ominous face, painted by necessity over its entire back with complimentary colors of blues and greens, along with black dots that look like eyes. Even its pericarp has been shaped to suggest contours of a mouth ready to open and snap if necessary. If you're a hungry bird, the face might appear rather intimidating. If you decline the meal, looking back over your wing as you fly onward, you'll see the mask upside down, appearing now as a grateful smile.

A large adult, perhaps a female, about three-quarters of an inch long, appears on the wooden shelf above my kitchen sink. The insect moseys along the surface, turning left and right and back again, her tiny antennae reading the air's vibrations. Then she stops as if she's waiting for me to do something. I do. I gently place my finger in front of her. She inspects it, crawls up and perches on the tip. I bring her close to my eyes and study her, amazed at her meticulous camouflaging. I want to photograph her, but I doubt she'd stay still. "Do you ever sleep? How long will you live?" She gives me no answers. I'd like to capture her image before she dies; before her colors disappear; before she's carried off by the giant huntsman spider hiding in the shadows of the room.

I lay my finger down on the shelf, and she steps off, crawls a few inches then stops. She's in no hurry.

The next morning, filling my coffee pot with water, I notice she's gone. No, there she is, moved to another part of the shelf. She remains here during

'Three Songs,' 2018

most of the day, while I zigzag like a bee, from one clump of 'busyness' to another, in and out of the house, into town and back, forgetting this, fudging that, crashing through the world, as we do. And unlike the bee, without much precision.

This evening, just before I go to sleep, I find Pretty Red Bug hiking the perimeter of the kitchen floor. Is she merely having a stroll? Perhaps she's hungry, searching for food. Or does she need a better place to die? I don't know. I reach down, and she crawls into my palm, scurrying up my arm to my right shoulder. When I slip into bed, she moves down to my chest. Can she feel the beating of my heart? I'm sure she can.

I pick her up, place her on the nearby curtain, then hold my reading light a few inches from her body. She appears to be using it as a musical instrument, alternately crossing one middle leg over her back legs in gentle stroking, as if her middle leg was a fiddle bow she draws delicately across the finely tuned filaments of her back legs. Is she playing music for me? A sonata, perhaps? Surely a sound is made, but my hearing is inadequate to discern it.

Still, I have my imagination, and it unfolds like ten thousand lotus petals.

In 2003, at eighty-six, my father died. For the most part, his life had been a quiet, alcohol-free passage. A quiet man, a good father, and husband, Sam spent his last days reading, watching TV, tending his garden, or his grandchildren, always patiently abiding the firm but tender directions laid out by his beloved wife, Ruby, who would die eight years later. I wasn't able to return to the United States for their funeral.

I was in Alaska in 1970 when my grandfather died and couldn't get back to his funeral, nor MaUdi's when she died in 1984. I'd not seen her in a long while, and I was sad not to have been with her in her dying nor to celebrate her remarkable life with the rest of my family. Whatever it is, whatever you call that curiosity for creating something out of nothing, and to whatever degree it blesses me, it comes mostly, I believe, from my grandmother.

In 1982, MaUdi visited me in Seattle. By then, she was eighty, her energy waning. We spent a morning in my studio, talking about one thing then another. She seemed pleased that I'd become an artist; she was proud of me, even though she understood not an inkling of what strange abstract images I painted, or why.

Still, she was keenly aware we shared something durable.

It'd been a long while since I had spent time with her. Her southern accent was as thick as ever, quicker than I could catch, even though I once sounded the same. Mine is now mostly gone.

From behind her thick glasses, her dark eyes seemed twice as large, confused and sad, as if trying to understand how her family had gotten so far from her. My grandmother grew up and struggled through times of such impenetrable hatred and racism. She wasn't immune to it, yet she'd tried her best to move beyond it, to make something beautiful outside of it.

Several months after her death, I took a break from the studio and drove across the mountains to spend a quiet few days at Galax. There was no cabin, no electricity, no plumbing, and no neighbors. The creek crossed the land then fell steeply to the valley below. The wooden deck I'd built from fallen timber, and the stone fire pit on the edge of the platform became my universe. Japanese paper lanterns, illuminated with candlelight, floated like moons in the trees that leaned over the deck.

That afternoon, I hiked across the property to the far side where I'd built the hot tub. I soaked for an hour, reading, occasionally looking out across the Yakima Valley, toward Ellensburg, while there was still enough light from the sky. I finished my bath then headed back to the main deck.

Halfway across the ten acres, on a knoll overlooking my campsite, I stopped and sat on a pine stump, soaking in the beauty of the land around me. Galax was far inside the Kittitas National Forest. My only neighbor lived a half a mile away, and she wasn't there that week. The isolation was profound. I looked across the hillside at my camp, my cooking area, the chair on the deck, the lanterns I'd soon be lighting. My wild imagination began to gallop, and I stumbled upon a curious question. What would I do if I saw myself moving about on the deck? Would I approach me? Would I stay sitting on the stump, waiting for one of us to disappear, or would I turn and flee? What I did, of course, was laugh at the ramblings of such unfettered thoughts—too many days alone. My rumbling stomach and cooling skin ended my curious reverie; I hiked on back to the campsite, started the evening fire, and made dinner.

After my meal, I read awhile, sat and watched the sky darken, waiting for the first stars to appear. The silence was palpable, occasionally broken by gusts of wind sweeping up the mountain and the yipping of coyotes, circling somewhere out in the night.

In this solitude, with no television or radio to distract me, and because reading by candlelight quickly fatigued my eyes, I retired early. I crawled into my sleeping bag on the deck above the creek, the mountain's water rushing below me. My mind was grateful for a shutdown.

I don't know how long I'd been asleep but, suddenly, I was catapulted awake by an explosive whispering of my name: "Galen!"

In a nanosecond, I was wide awake, sitting up, the Milky Way cradling my entire field of vision. I'd never seen stars so incredibly illuminated or felt such breathtaking blackness. Immediately, I knew it was my grandmother who'd called me. She was there—we were there—among the stars. Where else can any of us ever be?

Yes, of course, my grandmother might merely have been lodged in the shoals of my memory, my love for her calling out to me, just as Pretty Red Bug might only have been scratching an itch, removing unwanted creatures smaller than she is. Does it matter, though? Does it, if we can't know with certainty that death ends all? When we die, are we truly gone? Do we do live on in a multiplicity of universes that are born then die like minnows in a pond, over and over again with infinite expressions?

I stood on the diving board sixty-seven years ago, ready to jump. The blueness of the sky fell into one part of my brain; the sweet smell of oleander blossoms climbed into another. Wind against my skin, the song of the ocean, children's laughter. Each sensation—sound and smell, fear of height, human touch, love, sense of falling, of knowing myself—found a place inside me, each memory a dance of neurons exploding across the universe. I marvel at the journey, its texture, symmetry, architecture, and possibility. It is a world within me.

It is my world, awake and ever-present. I am more than happy to give my heart's sonata for gravity's last dance.

I was eleven when I was sent away to live with my father who took me away from the ocean and beaches that had been my life. I missed the sea, and the marshes, the crabbing, my lazy summers, and my green bicycle. I missed the live oak trees with their limbs bending to the earth like sad, old women weeping for someone long lost.

Twelve years later, I was about as far away from the coast of Georgia as one can be and still live in the United States, working and studying in the panhandle of Alaska.

One evening, in 1967, I went to a small café with a few friends for dinner. It was mid-winter, dark and cold, about twenty below outside. My waitperson came to the table and handed me a menu. All at once, I was back on the warm beach at St. Simons. I was dumbstruck; my brain scrambled to understand. I looked at the woman and clumsily asked, "What are you wearing?"

"What?" she asked, pretending to be indignant, though I could see she was more amused than upset.

"I'm sorry. I mean, what's the name of your perfume?"

At first, she seemed hesitant to answer such an intimate question from a strange young man. She finally said, "Shalimar. Why?"

"Um...hard to explain. Thanks."

I turned back to my friends.

Several days later, I drove out to visit my mother at her cabin in Ester. She was standing in the kitchen, stirring a thick stew. She'd already sliced up a loaf of sourdough bread she'd made earlier. Somewhere she'd gotten hold of an old wood-fired cook stove and oven, which stood in the center of the main room. She loved using it.

"Go make yourself a drink," she said, "The bourbon's in the cupboard. You know where it is."

I made us both one, and after a few minutes of village gossip, I shifted the conversation, "I'm curious, Mama. When we lived on St. Simons, back in the early fifties, did you have a favorite perfume? One that you wore a lot?"

'*Tree and Sky,*' *photograph, Savannah, Georgia, 2005*

She stopped stirring, put the big spoon down on the kitchen counter, and turned to me. "Where on earth did this come from?" she asked.

"Just wondering."

"Yeah, I did. It was Shalimar. That's all I ever wore. I just loved it."

Shalimar. There it was. My childhood held sacred in a fragrance, an endless, unwinding mystery, smelling of rose, and jasmine, and a delicate touch of gardenia.

Shalimar: An 'abode of light' drifting across a Persian desert.

I felt like an infant discovering its hands for the first time.

I told my mother why I'd asked. She laughed.

"Fix us another drink," she said, "then we'll eat."

GALEN GARWOOD was born in 1944, and spent most of his young life growing up on St. Simons Island, Georgia, and in Charleston, South Carolina. In 1966, after one year of art at University of Georgia, he moved to Fairbanks, Alaska, where he majored in Art and Music with a minor in English. He moved to Seattle, Washington, in 1971 and began showing his paintings at Foster/White Gallery in 1974. He has exhibited his work in the United States, Europe, and Asia, and his creative contributions express themselves in photography, writing, multimedia, and film.

In 1976, he won First Place in Painting at the Pacific Northwest Annual Exhibition and in 1979 he received the Hassam, Speicher Award at the Academy of Arts and Letters, New York, New York. In 1995, his multimedia piece 'Adagio' won the Bronze Award at the International Multimedia Film Festival in Philadelphia, and in 1996, 'Adagio' was included in the Venice Biennale's 'Xenograhia, Nomadic Wall' and again at 'Art Affair' in New York. His film 'Cadmium Red Light' received First Place for Narrative/Documentary at the Port Townsend International Film Festival in 2007, and his film 'Ed and Ed' received First Place Award for Short Documentary at DeReel Film Festival in Australia in 2008. Along with poems by Sam Hamill, he created *Passport*, paintings and poems, publshed by Broken Moon Press, 1987, and *Mandala, an Homage to Morris Graves*, Milkweed Editions, 1989.

In 2011, he collaborated with the poet Peter Weltner on *The One-Winged Body*, Marrowstone Press, and again with Peter Weltner, *Where Everything Is Water As Far As He Can See*, Marrowstone Press, 2012. In 2014, he produced and published *Maenam, Of Water, Of Light*, a series of photographs with poems by William O'Daly, Marvin Bell, Sam Hamill, James Broughton, Peter Weltner, Linda Gregg, Emily Warn, Jeanne More, and a foreword by Kathleen Moles, Marrowstone Press. A selection from a new series of photographs, 'The Dream Sea,' is featured in The *Road to Isla Negra*, poems by William O'Daly, published by Folded Word Press in 2015. Other images from 'The Dream Sea' are published in collaboration with poet Peter Weltner, in *Water's Eye*, Brick House Books, 2015.

Galen Garwood lives in Northern Thailand and is currently working on a new series of paintings and photographs.

www.galengarwood.com

271

CPSIA information can be obtained
at www.ICGtesting.com
Printed in the USA
FFOW02n1552160618
47155756-49757FF